Myth, History, and the Resurrection in German Protestant Theology

Myth, History, and the Resurrection in German Protestant Theology

Brent A. R. Hege

PICKWICK *Publications* · Eugene, Oregon

MYTH, HISTORY, AND THE RESURRECTION IN GERMAN PROTESTANT
THEOLOGY

Pickwick Publications
An Imprint of Wipf and Stock Publishers
199 W. 8th Ave., Suite 3
Eugene, OR 97401

www.wipfandstock.com

PAPERBACK ISBN: 978-1-5326-1753-9
HARDCOVER ISBN: 978-1-4982-4227-1
EBOOK ISBN: 978-1-4982-4226-4

Cataloguing-in-Publication data:

Names: Hege, Brent A. R.

Title: Myth, history, and the resurrection in German Protestant theology / Brent
A. R. Hege.

Description: Eugene, OR: Pickwick Publications, 2017 | Includes bibliographical
references and indexes.

Identifiers: ISBN 978-1-5326-1753-9 (paperback) | ISBN 978-1-4982-4227-1 (hard-
cover) | ISBN 978-1-4982-4226-4 (ebook)

Subjects: LCSH: Bultmann, Rudolf, 1884–1976. | Jesus Christ—Resurrection. |
Protestant churches—Germany—Doctrines—History—20th century.

Classification: LCC BT30.G3 H3 2017 (print) | LCC BT30.G3 (ebook)

Manufactured in the U.S.A.   10/04/17

You can never be too dead for resurrection.

—Graffito in Glasgow[1]

---

1. Quoted in Dalferth, "Volles Grab, leerer Glaube?"

Contents

Preface

My work on this book began back in the summer of 2000, when I was a student at the Goethe Institut in Dresden, Germany. I was fortunate to receive a scholarship jointly funded by the Evangelical Lutheran Church in America and the Evangelische Kirche in Deutschland allowing one student from each of the ELCA's eight seminaries to spend a summer studying German in Germany. One result of that immensely enjoyable and transformative summer was my decision to write my master's thesis on Rudolf Bultmann. One year later I submitted and defended the thesis at the Lutheran Theological Seminary at Gettysburg, Pennsylvania. That thesis forms the core of this book.

I continued on to doctoral work at Union Theological Seminary in Richmond, Virginia, where I wrote my dissertation on Georg Wobbermin, a frequent sparring partner of Bultmann's and Karl Barth's but considerably less familiar to English-speaking audiences. One of the themes of my dissertation was the significance and usefulness of the distinction in German between *Geschichte* and *Historie* (the two German words for "history"), which Wobbermin made a central principle of his theological program. Readers familiar with German Protestant theology in the nineteenth and twentieth centuries will no doubt be familiar with that distinction and its significance in Bultmann's work as well. I published my work on Wobbermin as *Faith at the Intersection of History and Experience: The Theology of Georg Wobbermin* and the book was selected for the 2010 John Templeton Award for Theological Promise by the Forschungszentrum Internationale und Interdisziplinäre Theologie at the University of Heidelberg. The formal colloquia and informal conversations with fellow laureates and judges in Heidelberg that summer reignited my interest in Bultmann and the interpretation of the resurrection in the German Protestant tradition.

When I moved to Butler University in Indianapolis in 2008 I found myself teaching religion, although my training was in theology. Familiarizing myself with the literature and methodologies of religious studies consumed most of my time in those first years, though I continued to publish work based on my dissertation, mostly in Weimar-era Protestant theology. But Bultmann and the question of the resurrection were never far from my mind. The topic kept presenting itself to me in surprising and uncanny ways, through conversations with colleagues and friends, discussions with students in my courses, work with Butler's Lutheran-Episcopal campus ministry, and in my own worship and Christian formation at Bethlehem Lutheran Church in Indianapolis. When in 2015 David Congdon published his massive, magisterial study of Bultmann, *The Mission of Demythologizing: Rudolf Bultmann's Dialectical Theology*, and when I noticed that he had cited with approval my book on Wobbermin, the pieces fell into place and I returned to the work I began seventeen years ago.

Returning to this project has felt like reuniting with an old friend. In some places I have been struck by how much has changed between us in the intervening years, but in other places I have appreciated the deep continuity between my former and current selves. The questions I wrestled with as a seminarian are questions I still wrestle with today, because, I believe, these are among the questions that will continue to determine the power, promise, and relevance of the Christian faith.

The Christian life, as Luther wrote in the Smalcald Articles, is one of "mutual conversation and consolation" among the brothers and sisters. It has been my great joy to have learned so much from conversations with cherished friends and colleagues and to have given and received consolation along life's way. There are too many conversation partners to thank each of them individually, and I beg forgiveness of anyone who may feel slighted by their absence. Know that my gratitude to each of you surpasses my ability to give you adequate thanks.

Eric Crump, my mentor at LTSG, first suggested I write on Bultmann and guided me with his characteristic intensity. More often than not, I would arrive at my desk in Wentz Library to find another book or article he had placed there for me to read, and our conversations on myriad topics (theological and otherwise) were a constant source of inspiration and joy. My thesis was far better thanks to his guidance, and I hope this book will meet with his approval. Brooks Schramm and J. Paul Balas, members of my thesis committee, each offered their encouragement and advice as I made finishing touches. The *"Alte Gettysburger Stammtisch,"* Friday-afternoon regulars at the (sadly now defunct) Gettysburg Brewing Company, are some of the most delightful and dedicated servants of the church I have had the privilege to know: Ryan Fischer, Karl Runser, Dan Smail, David Byerly, B. J. Collins, Debra Avery, Eric Crump, Brooks Schramm, and many others. As the saying goes, beer is a sure sign that God loves us and wants us to be happy. While she was not directly involved in the work on this book, I would be remiss if I did not thank my *Doktormutter*, Dawn DeVries, for her enthusiastic support and encouragement of my doctoral work on Wobbermin. I am a far better theologian, and human being, thanks to her tutelage. Finally, Mandy Gingerich was a partner and friend through these years and will always be family to me.

My colleagues at Butler deserve special recognition for their collegiality, friendship, and support. Chad Bauman, James McGrath, and Paul Valliere in Religion, Chris Bungard and Lynne Kvapil in Classics, Katharina Dulckeit, Stuart Glennan, Tiberiu Popa, and Harry van der Linden in Philosophy, Charles Allen at Grace Unlimited, Brynnar Swenson, Kristin Swenson, Travis Ryan, Terri Carney, Allison Harthcock, Chris Hess, Bill Watts, Mary Proffitt, and Claudia Johnson each in their own way contributed to my thinking and writing on this and many other projects.

To the "Indy Lutherans" group: Robert and Kristin Saler, Derek and Kelly Nelson, Matt and Libby Manning, Wade and Heather Apel, and Chris and Jessicah Krey Duckworth. The conversations shared over hearty food and drink have sustained and nurtured me as a Christian and as a scholar. Likewise, the people of Bethlehem Lutheran Church in Indianapolis, particularly my fellow choristers, have been a model for me of Christian community.

I am grateful to colleagues who have read and provided much-appreciated feedback on this manuscript, especially Robert Saler and Brynnar Swenson in the manuscript's current form and Dirk von der Horst in an earlier form. Whatever of merit is to be found in these pages is due in large part to their careful reading and constructive critiques. Responsibility for any errors, oversights, or shortcomings is entirely mine.

Kate Boyd, companion and friend on this adventure we have undertaken together, has challenged me with her fierce intelligence and sharp wit, occasionally lit fires under me, modeled discipline and dedication to a craft, helped me with my rusty German, dragged me away from my work for lovely hikes, bike rides, and walks with the dog (and delicious Indiana craft beer afterwards), and reminded me to enjoy every sandwich.

My mother, Debra Reeder, true to her vows at my baptism, brought me to the services of God's house, taught me the Lord's Prayer, the Creeds, and the Ten Commandments, placed in my hands the Holy Scriptures, and provided for my instruction in the Christian faith. For that and for so much more, I am forever grateful. To her and the rest of my family in Perry County and elsewhere in southcentral Pennsylvania, this book is lovingly dedicated.

A Note on Texts and Translations

THE VAST MAJORITY OF texts consulted in this book were originally published in German. In the second and third parts of the book I have relied on the original German publications almost exclusively because of the technical precision of theological language in German, among other reasons. Where they are available, I have also listed the English translations of the texts in the footnotes (preceded by "ET"), following the citation to the original German text. Throughout the book, where there are citations to the original German text the associated translations are my own. Where there is only a citation to the English text the translations are taken from those texts.

Following academic convention, I have abbreviated journal titles according to the guidelines established by the *Theologische Realenzyklopädie Abkürzungsverzeichnis*, 2nd ed., comp. Siegfried M. Schwertner (Berlin: de Gruyter, 1994).

CHAPTER ONE

Some Introductory Remarks

THE CHRISTIAN FAITH STANDS or falls with the confession that Jesus is risen. Christianity traces its origin to the proclamation of the first disciples that God raised the crucified Jesus from the dead, and Christians throughout the history of the church have confessed the decisive significance of this act of God. And yet for at least the last several centuries, many people both inside and outside the church have wrestled with this claim that God raised the crucified Jesus from the dead. The fundamental confession of the Christian church is characterized by this apparent paradox: the crucified and dead Jesus is now the exalted, living Lord. The twentieth-century German New Testament theologian Willi Marxsen, writing in the 1960s, a period of intense controversy in the German Protestant churches concerning just this question, succinctly summarizes the issues that will occupy us in the following pages:

> Jesus is risen.
>
> At this point there is complete agreement. There is no Christian who would not be able to give his [sic] assent to this statement. Nor is there any theologian—irrespective of the camp or school to which he belongs—who would not agree with it. This is a point perhaps worth noting in our present situation, and this fact alone would recommend the sentence as a starting point.
>
> The unity which may be found here is not to be underestimated, even though we must immediately add that it does not take us very far. Why not?
>
> We could answer quickly enough by pointing out that there is a distinction between what we say and what we mean by what we say . . . [W]e are easily inclined to read our ideas into words, and to think that ours is the only correct way in which the words can be used. But it is important to realize that other people express other

ideas in exactly the same words. This means that our language is not unambiguous . . . When two people say the same thing it by no means follows that they must therefore mean the same thing; and so the same expression can sometimes actually cover up a dissension. This very thing can in fact be illustrated by our example. Our generally accepted statement "Jesus is risen" is necessarily followed by the question "what does this mean?" We must go on to define, to explain what the various concepts signify. And then the disagreement quickly shows itself.[1]

The confession that Jesus is risen raises a number of questions. What is resurrection? Is it the return of a corpse to normal physical life? Is it a transformation into a new body? Is it a bodily event at all? What sources or evidence do we have for the resurrection of Jesus? How reliable are those sources? Is the resurrection a historical event? Or is it something else? Is it something that happened once upon a time in the distant and receding past? Or is it a present reality? Or is it both? It is the task of Christian theology to determine just what this claim means; the history of theology bears witness to a number of disagreements about the *meaning* of the confession that Jesus is risen, disagreements that have erupted in a number of controversies resulting from theologians' efforts to name, interpret, confess, and respond faithfully to the resurrection of Jesus.

The resurrection of Jesus from the dead has been a focal point of a number of controversies within theology, especially after the Enlightenment. In the eighteenth century, with the concurrent emergence of rationalism and secularism, the debate over the resurrection moved beyond the confines of an intramural Christian discussion to include a more diverse number of conversation partners, so that during this period the debate was fueled by developments in the academic study of history, myth, literature, and science, alongside internal theological developments.

The debate over the resurrection of Jesus assumed the form it took in the twentieth century largely due to the introduction of critical reflection on history and myth in the nineteenth century. During this century theologians applied the newly developed historical-critical method to the texts of the Bible, while historians of religions compared Christianity with other religious traditions. The conclusions drawn from these investigations placed Christianity in the context of a pluralistic religious environment, while the critical spirit of the age allowed scholars to question what had

---

1. Marxsen, *Resurrection of Jesus of Nazareth*, 14–15.

typically been accepted as incontrovertible fact for centuries before. The results of these inquiries occupied a range from reaffirmation of the church's ancient teachings, on the one hand, all the way to complete rejection on the other. These investigations forced many Christian theologians to recognize that simply handing on uncritically what had always been believed, despite the introduction of new tools for scholarship and new cultural and intellectual assumptions, was no longer possible. In light of this realization, many Christian theologians assumed the task of reinterpreting the doctrines and suppositions of Christianity in an effort to make them intelligible in new and often challenging contexts.

In the twentieth century, as Christians came to terms with the death of "Christendom" and a rapidly changing North Atlantic world, theologians renewed their efforts at making the message of the New Testament intelligible and meaningful to contemporary women and men. One of these theologians, Rudolf Bultmann, developed a program of demythologizing in recognition that the message of the New Testament is expressed in the mythical world-picture of the first century and thus is no longer immediately intelligible to modern people who assume a predominately scientific world-picture. Bultmann believed that there is a truth in the message of the New Testament that is expressed in this mythical world-picture, but that the message has to be demythologized in order to reveal its deeper meaning, expressing something profoundly true and meaningful about human existence.

As anyone familiar with this period of theology already knows, Bultmann's efforts did not meet with universal approval. More conservative theologians decried him as a heretic who had taken away their Lord, protesting that he had sacrificed the message of the New Testament on the altar of secular philosophy.[2] Other, more progressive theologians argued

---

2. For example, the bishops of the United Evangelical Lutheran Church of Germany (VELKD) released a public statement to be read from the pulpit in each of their parishes on the Sunday before Advent, 1953. While not mentioning Bultmann by name, he is clearly the primary target of this statement. It reads, in part, "In recent years a new anxiety has arisen within the church, and with good reason. Some theologians in our universities, eager to find new ways to commend the message of the gospel to the modern world, have intended to 'demythologize' the New Testament, as they call it. In doing so, they are in danger of limiting parts of the New Testament or even of abandoning it altogether. They rightly perceive that the New Testament is couched in the language and thought forms of the age in which it was written. But we are bound to ask whether this movement is not leading to a denial of the facts to which scripture bears witness." The statement goes on to defend the "purity of doctrine" expressed in the Apostles' Creed,

SOME INTRODUCTORY REMARKS

that Bultmann did not go far enough, believing that he failed to follow his own method to its logical conclusion and insisted on attributing the resurrection of Jesus to an act of God, which, they suggested, also belonged to the mythical world-picture of the ancient world.[3] Regardless of their conclusions, both sides of the debate recognized that Bultmann had exposed a sensitive nerve in Christian theology and acknowledged that his questions would not soon disappear.

Bultmann's methods and conclusions are certainly debatable, but Bultmann is most significant perhaps not in his conclusions but in the questions that he raised. A good question never disappears, and Bultmann raised probing and challenging questions. He sought to clarify the relationship between faith and history and he emphasized the importance of an existential encounter with the word of the gospel. He also recognized that there had been a fundamental and irreversible change in the operative world-pictures between the first and twentieth centuries (at least in the West), and he asked how something formulated within one conceptual framework of reality can be intelligible to people who share a completely different conceptual framework. Bultmann also recognized that, above all, theology is discourse about salvation by the God of Jesus Christ, and his theology exhibits this theocentric concern in both a christocentric and soteriological key. Therefore one of Bultmann's most significant contributions was his insistence on the centrality of the word of the gospel, a word that confronts and addresses each person in their own situation and offers them the possibility of authentic existence.

Generations have passed since Bultmann wrestled with these questions, and yet theology continues to bear the mark of his influence. Theologians and biblical scholars have continued to wrestle with his program of demythologizing as questions of the relevance and power of the Christian gospel in our own time continue to confront us with their irresistible urgency. The resurrection of Jesus remains a burning question, as the continuing attention of biblical scholars, historians, theologians, as well as the sometimes contentious, sometimes fruitful dialogue between theology and science, remind us. Bultmann's specter haunts the work of theology

which will "strengthen and encourage us to live our lives amidst toil and tribulation." Qtd. in Bartsch, *Der gegenwärtige Stand der Entmythologisierungsdebatte*, 1–2. ET: "Present State of the Debate."

3. Schubert Ogden, an American student of Bultmann and one of the leading translators and interpreters of Bultmann's work, offers just such a critique in his own work. See, for example, *Christ without Myth*.

such that new generations will continue to wrestle with his questions and struggle with his conclusions.

The question remains for theology even today: what does it mean to speak theologically about the resurrection of Jesus? More specifically, how do the concepts of myth and history inform Christian understandings of the resurrection of Jesus?

This book is divided into three parts according to the chronological development of German Protestant engagement with these and related questions. The first part begins with a brief summary of the emergence of historical consciousness and history as an academic discipline (*Wissenschaft*) in the nineteenth century and beyond. Our guide in this section is Ernst Troeltsch, one of the most significant figures in the history of religions school in liberal theology at the turn of the twentieth century. The remainder of the first chapter considers two important rationalist and liberal critics of traditional modes of theologizing about the resurrection of Jesus. Hermann Samuel Reimarus and David Friedrich Strauss, each in their own way renowned and vilified for their work on these questions, will focus our attention on the topics of myth, history, and the resurrection, topics that also occupied Bultmann and his colleagues in the middle of the twentieth century.

The second part forms the heart of this study and features the work of Rudolf Bultmann on myth, history, and the resurrection of Jesus. The first chapter is a summary and analysis of Bultmann's own constructive work and his framing of the questions and responses that would serve as the grist for succeeding generations of theologians and biblical scholars to work out their own approaches to the resurrection of Jesus, most often in dialogue with Bultmann and his legacy. The second chapter engages the debate between Bultmann and Karl Barth under the sign of "the whale and the elephant." With the help of private correspondence between these two giants of twentieth-century theology, in addition to relevant publications by each, their debates on theological method and hermeneutics help to shed light on two divergent approaches to these enduring questions concerning the resurrection of Jesus.

The third and final section picks up the threads of these debates and follows them through the work of three important contemporary German Protestant theologians: Wolfhart Pannenberg, Eberhard Jüngel, and Ingolf Ulrich Dalferth. While Pannenberg has been well-known and generally highly regarded by at least two generations of American theologians,

Jüngel and Dalferth are still not as familiar to American audiences as they rightly deserve to be. All three, in their own register, continue Bultmann's work on the resurrection, but each brings unique questions and insights to bear on the topic, often leading to dramatically different conclusions that in significant ways mirror the differences between Bultmann and Barth, but in other, equally significant ways signal new trajectories that continue to this day.

Part I

Precursors to Bultmann

CHAPTER TWO

History, Myth, and the Resurrection in Rationalist and Liberal Theology

I. History

THE FORMAL STUDY OF history as an academic discipline is a relatively recent development in the history of thought. The Greeks and Romans wrote histories of military campaigns, political events, and famous figures, but this attempt at historiography is only distantly related to the academic study of history as it developed in modernity. Ancient histories were written to record names and deeds, often ascribing ultimate causality to the deities, so that there was no fully developed historiography or philosophy of history in the ancient world. The relationship between cause and effect was largely unexamined, and it was not until the revolutionary development of a new scientific method in the eighteenth century that the investigation of the relationship between cause and effect was appropriated by historians. The new scientific method, developed especially by Francis Bacon in the early modern period, permeated other academic disciplines, including history, philosophy, and theology, and in its wake the critical study of history developed as an academic discipline.

A number of concurrent and complementary cultural-historical forces contributed to the emergence of the new historical consciousness. Gregory Dawes, in the introduction to his survey of some significant figures in historical Jesus research, identifies five of these forces that together signaled the slow transition from the late medieval period to modernity:

1. A new sense of the past birthed in Renaissance humanism
2. The effect of religious controversy, particularly the wars of religion in the seventeenth century and the emergence of Deism

3. The new astronomy and its challenge to biblical authority and medieval Aristotelian cosmological orthodoxy

4. The voyages of discovery and Christianity's encounter with non-Abrahamic religious traditions

5. The limits of reliable knowledge, exposed by the new scientific method and the philosophical revolutions of Descartes and Spinoza[1]

Within this broader context of profound and epoch-making cultural and intellectual shifts, the new historical methodology gained acceptance as a legitimate way of making sense of the past and the present. Political events and military campaigns, for example, came to be interpreted in light of this methodology, dependent on analysis of primary sources colored by philosophical assumptions regarding human agency and subjectivity, resulting in a way of thinking about history that privileged the power of the human being to act responsibly or irresponsibly with historic implications. Other disciplines soon were subjected to historical criticism as well. Theology, so long the queen of the sciences, bore the scrutiny of the new historical method with mixed results. Not only history, but science also engaged theology in the critical process. Advances in the sciences effectively destroyed the cosmology of the Bible and historical criticism built on scientific discoveries to reevaluate the authenticity of biblical history. As Dawes remarks,

> No longer did the biblical narrative offer the taken-for-granted starting point of human knowledge. Rather than beginning with the Bible and fitting everything else into its picture of the world, an increasing number of scholars were beginning with the data of the natural sciences and of history. They were starting to understand the Bible within the framework provided by these secular disciplines.[2]

Theology responded to this critical onslaught in a variety of ways and with varying degrees of success. Despite some attempts either to ignore this new critique or to repristinate the biblical world-picture and worldview, historical criticism forever altered the landscape of Western Christian theology.[3]

---

1. Dawes, *Historical Jesus Question*, 1–33.

2. Ibid., 34.

3. See, for example, Stuhlmacher, *Historical Criticism*; McKenzie and Haynes, *To Each Its Own Meaning*; Barton, *Nature of Biblical Criticism*; and Collins, *Bible after Babel*.

Ernst Troeltsch

Ernst Troeltsch (1865–1923) in many ways represents the high water mark of the marriage of historical and theological sensibilities in pre-war German Protestant theology. Troeltsch embraced the historical-critical method because he recognized the possibilities of historical criticism and the contributions it could make to theology in the new century.[4] Above all, Troeltsch did his work in constant awareness of the pervasive influence of the new historical worldview, which he defined as "the fundamental historicizing of all our thinking about human beings, their culture and their values."[5] In an essay on historiography published in English in 1914,[6] Troeltsch assesses the development of historiography and its scientific character, the nature of historical causality, and finally the relation of historiography to the philosophy of history. This brief essay reflects on the evolution of the emergence of the historical consciousness that so profoundly shaped modernity and also outlines the course of the discussion for the next several generations, as the discussion of the nature of history and its relation to theology would occupy and shape the theological enterprise well into the twentieth century.

Troeltsch traces the development of historical consciousness and the rise of a science of history from the earliest civilizations in the Fertile Crescent and its environs, through the Classical Mediterranean, the European Renaissance, and into the modern period. The earliest beginnings of history are found in religious narratives, which take the form of myths and legends. The Greeks, due to their passion for philosophy, laid the foundations for modern historiography by explaining events by reference to material or psychological causes. The advent of Christianity heralded a remythologizing of history and historiography and focused its attention on supernatural causality and intervention. As Troeltsch notes, "interest was once more concentrated upon the inexplicable and the desire to explain came to be regarded as the mark of a profane mind."[7] There arose in the Christian schema of history three ages: the supernatural age of miracle and prophecy, which served to prepare the way for Jesus the Christ; the age of Jesus the Christ who lived on earth and established the church as a divine

---

4. While only a brief sketch of Troeltsch's philosophy of history and its role in theology is included here, a far broader and more descriptive exploration of Troeltsch is Chapman, *Ernst Troeltsch and Liberal Theology*.

5. Troeltsch, *Der Historismus und seine Probleme*, 102.

6. Troeltsch, "Historiography," 716–23.

7. Ibid., 717.

institution; and the longest age of secular history, where miracles are rare, where Satan and his demons rule, but where God occasionally intervenes. In this system, according to Troeltsch, the mythology of redemption takes the place of historical reflection.[8]

This three-age schema dominated the historiography of the early church and the medieval period until the rediscovery of classical texts in the later medieval period and the Renaissance. The histories of Herodotus, Thucydides, and Tacitus were read anew and classical historical composition found new expression. The "emancipation of scholarship" of the late Renaissance and early modern period effectively freed scholars from the limitations of the medieval schema of history, and Troeltsch credits such intellectuals as Voltaire, Hume, and Gibbon with the creation of modern historiography.[9] History and historical criticism were now free to examine the course of human history and institutions, and with the development of philology and the natural sciences in the nineteenth century, history became what Van Harvey has called a "field-encompassing field."[10] Humanity came to be understood as one part of a much larger whole, as one part of a larger interrelated and interdependent system. Historians contemplated human existence as part of the vast array of complex systems at work in the universe, firmly establishing the vital importance of causality and contingency in the historical enterprise. This is the essence of modern historical reflection for Troeltsch: causal explanation, understanding human life in its relations, interpreting events in their interaction, and placing humanity within the greater system of endless change and evolution. This modern historical reflection is, in Troeltsch's estimation, at all points an "absolute contrast to the biblical and theological views of antiquity."[11]

It is an inescapable reality that historical judgments are necessarily judgments from a specific perspective. The historian is never able to remain divorced from history, and so the historian can never fully understand history in its entirety. Every historical judgment, therefore, involves a value judgment on the part of the historian. As Troeltsch acknowledges, "the knowledge of what should be often serves as a heuristic principle for the

---

8. Ibid.

9. Ibid.

10. Harvey, *Historian and the Believer*, 55.

11. Troeltsch, "Historiography," 718.

understanding of forces actually at work."[12] In other words, historical work is always interpretation and thus an exercise in hermeneutics.

Because the writing of history takes its cue from the examination of the past, it is necessarily dependent upon sources. The historian requires sources—texts, traditions, artifacts, eyewitness accounts, etc.—in order to reconstruct the causes and effects upon which history depends. There is a risk inherent in the use of sources, however, as sources must be interpreted if they are to be understood. These sources do not reconstitute completely the object of inquiry, which means there is always an element of uncertainty in historical investigation. Because this method ought to be self-critical and self-correcting, every generation must continue the work of historical investigation. The work of the historian is never complete, because each new moment requires a new interpretation of the past if it is to speak to the present. This is so because the purpose of historiography is never simply to understand the past for its own sake; rather, history is always written at least in part to address a present concern. The modern person is one who thinks historically and constructs the future by means of this historical self-knowledge.[13] Complete knowledge of the meaning and purpose of history is impossible so long as the historian remains within history, so it is only at the end of history that it is possible to know history's full meaning.[14]

In an earlier essay, "Historical and Dogmatic Method in Theology," published in 1898, Troeltsch highlights three key principles of the historical method: criticism, analogy, and correlation.[15] The historical method is a *critical* method because it is primarily concerned with the evaluation, interpretation, and analysis of sources. The only access historians have to the events and figures they study are the sources left behind; very often, these sources will be fragmentary or corrupted, will privilege one perspective over others, and will always be only part of the larger picture. This means, then, that any judgments made on the basis of these sources can only ever demand provisional assent and can never rise above the level of probability. This awareness of the limitations of historical sources and the need for critical analysis revolutionized the reading, interpretation, and use of scripture

12. Ibid., 719.

13. Ibid., 721.

14. As we will see below, Bultmann makes this insight a central principle of his theological analysis of history.

15. Troeltsch, "Über historische und dogmatische Methode in Theologie." ET: "Historical and Dogmatic Method."

and gave birth to a host of methods and approaches to the Bible, with far-reaching consequences for Christian theology.

The historical method operates using the principle of *analogy* as its interpretive lens. Because the past is past and closed to our direct experiencing of it, in order to say anything meaningful at all about the past the historian must assume a certain constancy and consistency of experience. For example, the historian must assume that human beings share some essential qualities across time and space and that the physical laws of nature are likewise consistent and immutable. Historians assume, then, that it is possible to judge the past by the standards of the present, at least in terms of physical laws and human nature.[16] But the principle of analogy also means that historians must acknowledge and account for the limitations, flaws, and biases inherent in human nature, such that any interpretation of historical sources must consider that the events they describe could be distorted—intentionally or unintentionally—by their recorders. Here Troeltsch remarks that in the nineteenth-century use of the historical method to investigate the life of Jesus this principle of analogy was often granted two significant exceptions: the moral character of Jesus and the resurrection. Impartiality and consistency in applying the method are required, but often neglected, especially when the results could have potentially devastating doctrinal consequences.

Finally, the historical method must be *correlational*, meaning that events and figures must be situated within their broader historical, political, cultural, social, economic, and geographical contexts rather than abstracted from their constitutive relationships. While earlier generations of documentarians and biographers might have elevated the subjects of their studies above the vicissitudes of daily life and the web of relations in which they existed, doing so only serves to obscure the myriad causes and effects without which these figures, events, and institutions cannot exist in the first place. For Christian theologians, this insight begs the challenging questions of the unique status of Jesus, the church, and the entire Christian tradition, now that even these must be understood as originating in at least some sense within history rather than outside of it, dropped, as it were, on a silver platter from on high.[17]

16. Wolfhart Pannenberg strenuously objects to the assumption that genuine novelty is a priori excluded from historical reasoning, as we will see below.

17. Troeltsch, "Über historische und dogmatische Methode in Theologie."

Troeltsch's work is saturated with his reflections on the significance of the historical method for the method of theology, specifically in light of the pervasive influence of historicism on modern consciousness. Given the historical foundations of the Christian faith, what sense is the theologian to make of those foundations, now viewed through the prism of historical consciousness? How might the results of historical research force a reinterpretation or perhaps even a rejection of Christian doctrines? How ought theologians to go about their task, armed with this new method? For Troeltsch, these are questions that cut directly to the heart of the possibility of an authentic Christian faith and therefore ought not to be debated solely within the confines of the academy. As he puts it in an essay on the historical Jesus,

> It is impossible to want to withdraw historical facts in general and in principle from scientific criticism. There does remain in this respect ... a dependence upon the general feeling of historical reliability produced by the impression of scientific research.
>
> This should not be matter for complaint. It is not a difficulty that is limited to the historical problems of faith. In a scientifically educated world faith has never been independent of the effects of learning ... It is an illusion to suppose that faith can avoid debate, accommodation and opposition to the views on offer as the scientific knowledge of the day. It cannot withdraw into itself while absorbing all positions which bring it into opposition ... To escape by abandoning all those elements which science lays claim to means to renounce content, definiteness, power and the formation of a community.[18]

The nineteenth century was thoroughly steeped in and profoundly influenced by this historical consciousness, as evidenced by the proliferation of historical studies in religion and theology, studies that took these questions with utter seriousness and sparked fierce debates inside and outside the church. The renewed interest in the historical Jesus in light of this historicizing wave fed a desire in many theologians and lay Christians to secure some firm and certain historical foundation for faith.[19] At the same time, other theologians and lay Christians began to question the wisdom or even

---

18. Troeltsch, "Significance of the Historical Jesus for Faith," 198–99.

19. For example, Martin Kähler memorably sought an "invulnerable area" (*ein sturmfreies Gebiet*) for Christian faith that would be insulated from the instability and insecurity of historical investigation. Kähler, *Der sogenannte historische Jesus und der geschichtliche*. ET: *So-called Historical Jesus*.

the possibility of finding such a foundation.[20] Despite profound disagreements about the usefulness and possibility of historical support for the Christian faith, it was virtually impossible to find a Protestant theologian in the nineteenth century who was not pervasively shaped by the historical consciousness of the era. This embrace, or at least acceptance, of historicism would forever alter the trajectory of Western Christian thought, perhaps nowhere more so than in Germany, where the historical-critical method revolutionized biblical studies and theology.[21]

The nineteenth century witnessed diverse attempts to appropriate historiography and apply it to Christian theology, especially, but by no means exclusively, by those theologians who, according to Troeltsch, "accept[ed] the whole-hearted historical criticism of and research into the gospel narratives, and at the same time wish[ed] to preserve Christianity as redemption through faith's constantly renewed personal knowledge of God." In other words, these questions "apply only for those who recognize modern thought and at the same time see in Christianity religious powers which should not be given up."[22] Ground zero for these concerns in the nineteenth century was the life of Jesus, and dozens of books on the historical Jesus were published by theologians who sought to reconstruct his life with the help of the historical-critical method.[23]

This project, initiated toward the end of the eighteenth century with the anonymous publication of the *Wolfenbüttel Fragments*, occupied a privileged position in nineteenth-century theology and New Testament studies, with works being published by such notable theologians as Friedrich Schleiermacher and David Friedrich Strauss.[24] These Lives of Jesus used the historical-critical method to examine the biblical witness of the birth, life,

20. Wilhelm Bousset is an interesting example of an early twentieth-century theologian who is perfectly content to allow full rein to historical research into the life of Jesus because, for him, the power of Jesus to awaken faith lies in his poetic symbolism rather than his historical life and work. See Hege, "Jesus Christ as Poetic Symbol."

21. The dominance of German theological faculties in the pursuit of historical-critical research into the New Testament is clearly demonstrated in Baird's *History of New Testament Research*, vol. 1, *From Deism to Tübingen*, which, once moving on from Deism to consider historical criticism, deals exclusively with German Protestant thinkers.

22. Troeltsch, "Significance of the Historical Existence of Jesus for Faith," 191.

23. For a summary and critique of these nineteenth-century lives of Jesus, the landmark study remains Schweitzer's *Von Reimarus zu Wrede*. ET: *Quest of the Historical Jesus.*

24. Selections from several significant contributors to the quest for the historical Jesus are included in Dawes, *Historical Jesus Quest.*

death, and resurrection of Jesus. The very integrity and dignity of the theological enterprise itself seemingly hung in the balance of these discussions, and this alone warrants continued study of these texts. But what was truly at stake in the nineteenth-century Life-of-Jesus controversy? What compelled them to embark on these projects, often at great risk to their reputations and their careers?

The application of the historical-critical method to the biblical texts exposed undeniable inconsistencies between these texts. Implications of the findings of the historical-critical method revealed similar inconsistencies in the theological systems that were based on these texts. Once these inconsistencies were discovered, they could not be ignored. Several questions arose as a result of these critical investigations. What is the nature of the divine inspiration of the Bible? What can be known and asserted as "true" in the biblical texts? If these texts are myths, how can anything contained in them be true? And finally, if these texts are not true, and if Jesus might not be who the church has claimed he was (and is), then is faith an illusion?[25] The nineteenth-century Lives of Jesus embraced these questions and sought to find some secure foundation for the Christian faith in the life of the historical Jesus of Nazareth. But long before the first Life of Jesus was written, the publication of critical fragments by an anonymous German author shook the foundations of the Protestant churches in Germany and beyond. In these fragments, the author systematically turned his critical historical attention to the gospel texts and found little within them to believe.

Hermann Samuel Reimarus

The godfather of the Life-of-Jesus research was Hermann Samuel Reimarus (1694–1768). His lasting legacy, the so-called *Wolfenbüttel Fragments*,

---

25. The simmering controversy occasionally boiled over into full-fledged crises, first with the posthumous publication of Hermann Samuel Reimarus's *Wolfenbüttel Fragments* in the eighteenth century (see below) and again in the early twentieth century with the appearance of Drews's *Die Christusmythe*, ET: *Christ Myth*. In both cases, these salvos across the church's bow prompted a flurry of responses, many of which proved to be significant and highly influential contributions to the church's thinking about Jesus. In response to Drews, see especially Troeltsch, *Die Bedeutung der Geschichtlichkeit Jesu für den Glauben*, ET: "Significance of the Historical Existence of Jesus" and Gerrish, "Jesus, Myth, and History."

were published anonymously after his death by Gotthold Ephraim Lessing.[26] While the public Reimarus apologetically labored to show the harmony that existed between natural religion and Christianity, the private Reimarus remained intensely critical of the experiential religion of pietism and favored the rationalism of Christian Wolff and of English Deism.[27] It is the private Reimarus whom we regard in the *Fragments*, and it is this Reimarus who lives on in theology's memory. Albert Schweitzer offers the following estimation of Reimarus's work:

> To say that the fragment on "The Aims of Jesus and His Disciples" is a magnificent piece of work is barely to do it justice. This essay is not only one of the greatest events in the history of criticism, it is also a masterpiece of world literature . . . At times . . . it rises to heights of passionate feeling, and then it is as though the fires of a volcano were painting lurid pictures upon dark clouds. Seldom has there been a hate so eloquent, a scorn so lofty; but then it is seldom that a work has been written in the just consciousness of so absolute a superiority to contemporary opinion. And throughout there is dignity and serious purpose; Reimarus' work is no pamphlet.[28]

Reimarus approaches the life of Jesus as recorded in the canonical gospels as a skeptic shaped by the cultural and intellectual milieu of the Enlightenment. His primary motivation in examining the texts of the gospels is to determine what can be accepted as true and what must be rejected as false, and he remains resolutely materialist in his historical investigation of the texts, reading them as literal accounts of events that will either stand up to rigorous scrutiny or be revealed as fabrications and deceptions. He pays no attention to the narrative structure of the texts, nor does he even seem to be aware of the symbolic nature of mythical language because, ultimately, he regards myths as fictions that cannot be true precisely because they are fictions.[29]

Reimarus begins his investigation of the resurrection by examining the account in the gospel of Matthew, where the Pharisees and chief priests

26. Reimarus, *Fragmente des Wolftenbüttelschen Ungenannten*. ET: *Fragments*.

27. Talbert's introduction to Reimarus, *Fragments*, 11.

28. Schweitzer, *Quest*, 15–16.

29. In this sense, Reimarus can be considered the forefather of the contemporary "New Atheists," who read the biblical texts with similarly restricted assumptions about their purpose and meaning. See, for example, Dawkins, *God Delusion*; and Hitchens, *God is not Great*.

urge Pontius Pilate to post guards by the tomb so that the body might not be stolen (Matt 27:62–66). Reimarus critiques this passage by arguing that, were this a historically accurate account, the disciples certainly would have defended themselves and their assertion that Jesus had been raised by referring to Pilate's order to post guards at the tomb. From the absence of any such reference in later literature, Reimarus concludes that the account cannot be truthful.[30] Later, when vigorously attacked and persecuted for their testimony, the disciples would have had several options before them: they could have asked for a copy of Pilate's written order, they could have summoned those on the Sanhedrin who witnessed the events described, or they could have located the guards who were posted at the tomb. This evidence certainly would have cleared them of the accusation that they stole the body of Jesus from the tomb and hid it in an unknown location. And yet there is no reference to these facts anywhere else in the New Testament: Matthew stands utterly alone.[31]

In his investigation of the possibility of theft, Reimarus again focuses on the contradictions of the gospel narratives themselves. The disciples knew the location of the tomb, and the tomb's owner, Joseph of Arimathea, was a secret disciple of Jesus. Having demonstrated the inaccuracy of Matthew's account of Pilate's order to place guards at the tomb, Reimarus concludes that the disciples could have stolen the body with relative ease.[32] The gospel narratives contain several predictions of Jesus' resurrection, and yet when it supposedly occurred, it occurred at night and before the predicted full three days had elapsed. If the disciples had truly foreknown the exact day of Jesus' resurrection (three days after his death), then why would they not invite all those who doubted, so that they could also witness the event themselves? Jesus' resurrection occurs in the middle of the night, in total isolation, with no witnesses, and the account of his appearances likewise have Jesus appearing only in seclusion, and only to those who already believed in him.[33] Reimarus concludes from his investigation of Matthew that the entire account of Pilate posting guards at the tomb was contrived by the evangelist to divert suspicion of fraud from the disciples.[34]

---

30. Reimarus, *Fragments*, 153–64.
31. Ibid., 158–61.
32. Ibid., 161–62.
33. Ibid., 163.
34. Ibid., 172.

Reimarus criticizes the unity of the four gospels and their accounts of the resurrection based on an analogy of a modern legal trial. The accounts of the four gospels are so inconsistent and contradictory, in his opinion, that their validity would not be recognized in any secular court, and no judge would ever be convinced of their trustworthiness.[35] How then, Reimarus wonders, can anyone want the whole world to base their faith and their hope—indeed, an entire religion—on such an inconsistent and contradictory testimony? For Reimarus "it is foolishness to sigh and complain about mankind's disbelief if one cannot furnish men with the persuasive evidence that the matter demands, based on healthy reason."[36] Recourse to miracles as proof of events provides no viable alternative in Reimarus's estimation because miracles cannot establish articles of faith; besides, if the articles of faith upon which Christianity is based guarantee their own credibility, what need is there of miracles, and who would dare require them? Furthermore, no miracle can amend the fact that the truth of these events is based partly on contradictory evidence, partly on events that never took place, and partly on doctrines that themselves contain contradictions. As he concludes, "It is always a sign that a doctrine or a history possesses no depth of authenticity when one is obliged to resort to miracles in order to prove its truth."[37]

Reimarus concludes his work with an investigation into the "real intention" of the disciples. Based on the biblical witness, Reimarus assumes that the disciples, before their encounters with Jesus, had been men of low class, with little or no education. When they encountered Jesus they abandoned their livelihoods and followed him. Reimarus finds a motive for their discipleship in Jesus' preaching of the coming kingdom of God. The disciples, in his assessment, hoped to achieve great political stature and wealth in this new political reign, but when their hopes were dashed at the moment of Jesus' death, they concocted a new doctrine in an attempt to win power and wealth in spite of their failed dreams. Their motives in following Jesus did not change; only the means by which they hoped to accomplish their goals changed as a result of their master's untimely death.[38]

35. Ibid., 176.

36. Ibid., 200.

37. Ibid., 234. In this judgment he would have the enthusiastic support of David Hume, who drew the same conclusion in his essay "Of Miracles," in Hume, *An Enquiry concerning Human Understanding*, first published in 1748.

38. Reimarus, *Fragments*, 240–43.

After the death of Jesus, the disciples hid together for fear of punishment. They could not return to the poverty and social disgrace of their former occupations, and so they were forced to reevaluate their situation. They remembered the public fame preaching had brought their master, and they remembered that they never lacked shelter or food when they traveled with him. They had learned that with preaching came not only provision, but honor, power, and glory. They remembered Jesus' prophecy of his return, which would surely elevate them to positions of great power and wealth, but this could not be accomplished with Jesus' body still in the tomb. If they could steal and hide the body, they could proclaim Jesus risen and ascended, and their words would then bear divine favor. They plotted to wait forty days before they revealed this information, so that they might recount episodes of eating and speaking with the risen Lord during the forty days between his resurrection and ascension.

The proof of resurrection was not difficult to provide. The body of Jesus had been hidden away, and in forty days it surely would have decayed beyond recognition.[39] The precedent for resurrection had already been established in the Hebrew Scriptures and in Pharisaic theology, and in the courts truth consisted in the evidence of only two or three witnesses. With eleven men unanimously attesting to the resurrection of Jesus, the people were forced to allow the possibility of it actually occurring. Having succeeded in establishing the "fact" of Jesus' resurrection, the disciples gathered several hundred followers of Jesus in Jerusalem at Pentecost to inaugurate their movement. With one final sequence of miracles (Acts 2), the disciples accomplished their original goal of recapturing the former honor and glory of their time with Jesus.[40] By then enough time had passed so that their tales of encountering the risen Jesus would be met with awe and wonder rather than doubt and disbelief, and the story they told was rehearsed so well that it sparked a revolution in religious thought, giving birth to Christianity.

To summarize, Reimarus attributes the rise of Christianity to a band of lower-class social outcasts who, deluded with dreams of power, mistook Jesus' eschatological proclamation of the kingdom of God to be a promise of political victory and worldly glory. When their hopes and dreams were shattered by Jesus' untimely death, they schemed to concoct a fantastic story

39. Reimarus bases his entire discussion on his assumption of the validity of the empty tomb tradition.

40. Ibid., 248–68.

of resurrection and ascension, which they then preached to the world. For Reimarus, the entire Christian religion is based on this deceit. This does not necessarily mean that faith itself is lost, but for Reimarus the only legitimate conclusion to be drawn is that the entire Christian religion is inherently and perhaps fatally flawed.

David Friedrich Strauss, in an essay on Reimarus, offers a bleak assessment of the "Wolfenbüttel Fragmentist." For Strauss, Reimarus is hopelessly enmeshed in the "either-or" spirit of the eighteenth century. Either the resurrection occurred as recounted in the gospels, or it did not; either the disciples were telling the truth, or they were lying. There was no third alternative. The eighteenth century, according to Strauss, was in a unique position regarding the Christian religion, because it was the first century to sense the slightest cracks in the façade of Christendom. The development of modern science and historical criticism allowed the eighteenth-century theologians to approach Christianity in a way previous generations could not. For eighteenth-century criticism, however, the law of agreement and contradiction occupied a position of superiority in critical investigations. Therefore Reimarus was unable to conceive of a third possibility to his "either-or" interpretation of the resurrection. He was unable, according to Strauss, to suggest that perhaps the disciples truly believed that Jesus had risen from the dead. He was unable to admit that there could be a subjective truth in the disciples' claims despite their objective falsity. For Reimarus, finally, Christianity remained a false and reprehensible deception.

Nevertheless, this is no cause to dismiss Reimarus completely, because, as Strauss believes, Reimarus's "no" to Christianity remains a firm "no." It is the task of later theologians to produce a better "yes." Strauss laments the current theological trend simply to respond to negative criticism with even more fantastic positive assertions. He criticizes nineteenth-century theology's attempts at interpreting the resurrection as a supernatural event, for which a typical argument is made that, because no proof can be given for the abduction of Jesus' corpse, theologians are then free by default to proclaim the resurrection as a supernatural event that reliably took place. Reimarus presents a challenge to nineteenth-century theology and Strauss concludes that it is the task of theology in the new century to embrace the work of the eighteenth-century critics, to continue and complete it.[41] To do so, Strauss himself undertook a fearless analysis of the gospels to determine

41. Strauss, "Hermann Samuel Reimarus and his Apology," 44–57.

what could be known with certainty as historical fact, and what must be discarded as myth.

II. Myth

Myth is among the most ancient and enduring creations of the human spirit.[42] In the ancient world, myth assumed many forms, including myths of creation, myths of national or ethnic origins, and myths of nature, among many others, but all myths seek to provide narrative structure and access to modes of experience or wisdom that would otherwise elude our grasp.[43] In the case of myths of creation or of nature, myth could also function as pre-scientific reflection on natural phenomena. These myths very often have religious origins, as early cultures attempted to explain their surroundings and events by referring to various deities. Mythology, then, was also an early attempt at theology.

In the modern period, as history and the natural sciences developed as critical methods of inquiry, myth, in the sense of "pre-scientific" explanations of natural phenomena, no longer appeared to be capable of serving its purpose of explaining the inexplicable. Myths of cosmic battles and of the creation of the world faded in favor of scientific explanations, and myths of national or ethnic origins faded in favor of critical historical reflection on the political, social, and geographic causes of migration, settlement, and social organization. With the Enlightenment privileging of reason, myth came to be understood as a pre-rational, primitive stage of human knowledge that should and eventually would be displaced by reason.[44] Historians, philologists, archaeologists, and anthropologists all examined classical texts and artifacts saturated with myth in an attempt to separate the "facts" from the myths, believing, along with many early theorists of religion, that myth belonged to the benighted realms of magic and religion that would fast dis-

---

42. For a general introduction to myth, see Segal, *Myth*.

43. On this unique, indeed necessary function of myth, especially as it functions in concert with metaphor and symbol within Christian theology, see two early works by McFague, *Metaphorical Theology* and *Models of God*; Ricoeur, "Biblical Hermeneutics"; and Tillich, *Dynamics of Faith*, esp. 47–83. For a broader discussion of the religious functions of myth, see Eliade, *Myth and Reality*.

44. This modern assumption about the linear progression from myth to reason is summarized with particular attention to the ancient Greek world by Nestle, *Vom Mythos zum Logos*. As we will see below, the assumption of a linear progression from myth to reason is itself a myth of the Enlightenment.

appear as the light of reason and science grew brighter.[45] This assumption, it turns out, rested on an ideologically-motivated rejection of myth in favor of a privileging of reason as the sole source of knowledge, as well as a purely materialist notion of truth, an assumption that was challenged beginning in the middle of the twentieth century, as we will see in subsequent chapters, but which profoundly influenced theological controversies from the seventeenth to the nineteenth century and, in some instances, far beyond.[46]

Meanwhile, theologians and historians practicing the new "higher criticism" uncovered the complex origins of the Jewish and Christian scriptures, sparking an obsession with understanding the "strange new world" of the Bible. Among other discoveries, historians and biblical scholars encountered the presence of myth in the Bible. This discovery created a disturbance in the church, as the question of truth in relation to the mythical character of the biblical witness required sustained, critical theological attention.[47] Divine inspiration of the Bible became a tenuous doctrine, as theologians struggled to determine what in the scriptures could be salvaged after the critics had done their work. Biblical criticism was therefore decried by some within the church as the greatest threat to Christianity in centuries,[48] while it was welcomed as a much-needed breath of fresh air by others, especially within mainline Protestantism, so that the search for truth within the myths occupied mainline Protestant theology for much of the nineteenth century and well into the twentieth century.

It is worth nothing that for much of the nineteenth century it was simply assumed that myth and truth were diametrically opposed to one another, so that the critical task was to separate the kernel of truth from its

45. Such was the assumption of James Frazer and E. B. Tylor, among many others.

46. One example of the continuing relevance of these questions is the persistence of Creationism, particularly in the United States, which recalls many of the same debates of the eighteenth and nineteenth century concerning the relationship between myth and history. See, for example, Hege, "Contesting Faith, Truth, and Religious Language."

47. Two important commenters on the theological meaning of myth who would influence many of the theologians discussed later in this book were Johannes Weiss (a teacher of Bultmann's at Marburg and an early proponent of form criticism) and William Wrede (famous for coining the phrase "Messianic Secret" to describe the portrayal of Jesus in the Gospel of Mark as well as famously declaring Paul to be the second founder of Christianity).

48. In the United States the growing influence of the higher criticism, first imported into American seminaries and universities from Germany, was a primary motivation for the publication of *The Fundamentals*, marking the origins of modern Christian fundamentalism. Dixon and Torrey, *Fundamentals*.

mythical shell. One particularly urgent question, then, was the reliability of narratives about salvation history, narratives that, until quite recently, were assumed to have been reliable historical reports that could be accepted as self-evidently true. If critics were to demonstrate conclusively that some or all of these narratives were in fact myths and not historical accounts, the destabilizing effects of those discoveries could prove disastrous for Christian faith.[49]

Not coincidentally, then, increased attention to the person of Jesus of Nazareth in light of these concerns about myth and history resulted in a quest for the historical Jesus in the nineteenth century. This critical investigation had its roots in the German Enlightenment, so that the vast majority of works on the historical Jesus were written by German theologians in the nineteenth century. The so-called "first quest for the historical Jesus" was not motivated by purely historical interest, however, but was in many cases an explicit effort to free the historical Jesus from dogmatic portraits of him, so to liberate the "real" Jesus from the stranglehold of an ossified orthodoxy.[50]

In Albert Schweitzer's estimation, the greatest works on the life of Jesus in the eighteenth and nineteenth centuries were written by dissenters with a hatred that sharpened their critical insight. Despite the sometimes hostile motivations for their work, these authors of the modern Lives of Jesus made a lasting contribution to the history of Christian thought that has continued to resonate down to our own time. Above all, they sought to penetrate the "supernatural nimbus" that obscured the human Jesus and to unveil the "real Jesus" for the modern age.[51] In so doing, they revealed as much—and in some cases far more—about themselves, their era, and their concerns, than they did about their subject.[52]

---

49. As Dawes points out, it was in the nineteenth century when the burden of proof shifted from those who denied the legitimacy and revelatory status of the Bible to those who assumed it. Dawes, *Historical Jesus Quest*, 34.

50. Schweitzer, *Quest*, 5.

51. Ibid., 6.

52. As the Irish Jesuit theologian George Tyrrell famously remarked of Adolf von Harnack, the Jesus discovered in the quest for the historical Jesus "is only the reflection of a Liberal Protestant face, seen at the bottom of a deep well." Tyrrell, *Christianity at the Crossroads*, 14.

David Friedrich Strauss

Perhaps the most tragic figure in nineteenth-century theology, David Friedrich Strauss (1808–1874)[53] approached the historical study of the life of Jesus with critical tenacity and devastating honesty, and the publication of his *Life of Jesus Critically Examined* in 1835 effectively destroyed his career and permanently sullied his reputation.[54] His was not the first historical work on the life of Jesus, nor was it the first attempt to apply the concept of myth to the Bible. Nonetheless, Strauss's work evoked unparalleled scorn, but the questions he raised still demand a response. The defining character of Strauss's work was, in Albert Schweitzer's appraisal, that although Strauss's predecessors wondered anxiously how much of the historical Jesus would remain as the foundation for religion after systematically and unreservedly applying the concept of myth, for Strauss "this question had no terrors."[55] Strauss was not willing to sacrifice his method for the sake of dogma, for his very task was to unmask dogmatic representations of the Christ of faith by revealing the Jesus of history.

Begun by Hermann Samuel Reimarus with the posthumous publication of his *Wolfenbüttel Fragments* and brought into the mainstream by Friedrich Schleiermacher's lectures on the life of Jesus,[56] Life-of-Jesus research occupied a distinctive niche in nineteenth-century German protestant theology. Biblical scholars and theologians engaged the biblical accounts of the life of Jesus with critical acumen and tenacity, and through their work they inaugurated the development of modern biblical criticism. Strauss's two-volume *Life of Jesus Critically Examined* exploded onto the

---

53. Schweitzer cites an autobiographical section in Strauss's *Conversations of Ulrich von Hutten* in which Strauss reflects on the negative and positive results of his *Life of Jesus*: "I might well bear a grudge against my book, for it has done me much evil ('And rightly so!' the pious will exclaim). It has excluded me from public teaching in which I took pleasure and for which I had perhaps some talent; it has torn me from natural relationships and driven me into unnatural ones; it has made my life a lonely one. And yet when I consider what it would have meant if I had refused to utter the word which lay upon my soul, if I had suppressed the doubts which were at work in my mind—then I bless the book which has doubtless done me grievous harm outwardly, but which preserved the inward health of my mind and heart, and, I doubt not, has done the same for many others also." Strauss, quoted in Schweitzer, *Quest*, 6. Karl Barth does not agree that Strauss should be regarded as a tragic figure; we surely can sympathize with him, but we may not regard him as a tragic figure. Barth, *Protestant Theology*, 528.

54. Schweitzer, *Quest*, 68.

55. Ibid., 75.

56. Schleiermacher, *Das Leben Jesu*. ET: *Life of Jesus*.

German theological scene in 1835.[57] Strauss attempts to determine with certainty what can be accepted as historically true about the life of Jesus by analyzing the mythical character of the gospel narratives and by then extracting the historical from the mythical. His program begins with an analysis of mythology and an interpretation of the various types of myths found in the Bible, after which he applies the results of his interpretation to the accounts of the life of Jesus contained in the four gospels. He concludes with an attempt to salvage whatever dogma might remain after his analysis.[58] Of chief concern for us here is Strauss's analysis of the various types of myth found in the Bible.[59]

Strauss begins his analysis of the biblical thought world with an analysis of myth as found in the Old Testament. He borrows the terminology of Christoph Friedrich von Ammon in his distinction between three types of biblical myths:

1. *Historical Myths* are narratives of historical events that conflate the divine and human, or the supernatural and the natural.

2. *Philosophical Myths* are primitive thoughts, ideas, or concepts that are related in the guise of historical narratives.

3. *Poetical Myths* are a mixture of historical and philosophical myths in which the original fact is obscured by the literary artistry of the author.

Historical myths are mythicizations of historical events, while philosophical myths are myths where it is clear that the purpose of the narrative is to symbolize a true idea under the guise of historical events. Poetical

---

57. Strauss, *Das Leben Jesu kritisch bearbeitet*. ET: *Life of Jesus, Critically Examined*.

58. The Strauss of the *Life of Jesus* hoped that this was possible, but by the end of his life he had abandoned even this modest hope. See Strauss, *Der alte und der neue Glaube*. ET: *Old Faith and the New*.

59. It must first be clarified that Strauss operates with a specific understanding of the relationship between myth and history. For Strauss, there is a very clear distinction between form and substance within a narrative. If the form is mythical but the substance is determined to be historical, then the myth may be discarded and the historical salvaged. However, if both form and substance are mythical, then for Strauss the historical is forever lost. It is the task of the exegete to determine what is mythical and what is historical, and to proceed according to this determination. For a discussion of Strauss's "radical-mythical" view of the life of Jesus and Strauss's place in the history of the development of the concept of myth in modern biblical studies, see Hartlich and Sachs, *Der Ursprung des Mythosbegriffes in der modernen Bibelwissenschaft*. See especially their fifth chapter "D. F. Strauß' radikal-mythische Ansicht des Leben Jesu und ihre hermeneutischen Grundlagen," 121–47.

myths are the most difficult to distinguish, as these myths are distinguished only when the narrative appears to be so fanciful as to make its facticity impossible.[60] There are obvious difficulties inherent in distinguishing between the three types of myth, as it requires the interpreter to determine the literary style and possible motivation of the author, as well as the possibility of the narrated events actually occurring in history. The interpreter must assume these risks when analyzing biblical myths.

Strauss detects a fundamental difficulty and inconsistency in the transfer of the mythical model from the Old Testament to the New. He maintains that myths in the Old Testament pose no difficulty for interpreters, because the mythical world-picture was universally accepted at the time the Old Testament was composed, edited, and collated into the canon we recognize today. However, the same cannot be asserted in reference to the New Testament thought world. Development of a primitive philosophy of history among the Greeks and increased literacy signaled the beginning of the end of the mythical age. Nevertheless, Strauss notes that it might be appropriate to extend the use of the term "myth" to those narratives that were orally transmitted, or to allow for the origin of certain myths within the New Testament itself.[61]

In terms of the New Testament accounts of Jesus, Strauss makes a further distinction between myth and legend. In the case of the life of Jesus, if this history is mythical (insofar as it records the original idea the early church had of Jesus), then, though unhistorical in form, this history is a faithful representation of the idea of the Christ. If, however, this history is legendary (that is, if the facts themselves are distorted, are represented falsely, or represent a false idea), then this particular historical datum about the life of Jesus is forever lost.[62] Legends in the gospels are those stories that have no real internal connection, that display signs of mutation or confusion as a result of oral transmission, or are distinguished by imaginative and pictorial representations. Besides myth and legend, the interpreter must also distinguish that material which does not fit the description of either myth or legend, and must therefore be interpreted as a creative addition of the author.

---

60. Strauss, *Life of Jesus*, 53.

61. Ibid., 57.

62. Ibid., 62.

Strauss recognizes particular forms of myth in the gospel narratives, which he places within the category of evangelical myth.[63] Evangelical myth is a narrative relating directly or indirectly to Jesus, which must be understood as an expression, not of fact, but of an idea of the early Christians. This myth can be expressed either as the historical narrative itself, or alongside a narrative of historical fact. Evangelical myth can be distilled into two forms: pure myth and historical myth.

1. *Pure Myth* has two sources: a.) the messianic idea already existing in Judaism before Jesus, which was then applied to him; and b.) a particular impression left by Jesus on his followers, which was then attached to the messianic idea. (This type of evangelical myth corresponds to the category of philosophical myth described above.)

2. *Historical Myth* is based in historical fact, which is then appropriated by Jesus' followers and transformed into mythical expressions based on the messianic idea. Certain nature miracles contained in the gospels might be historical myths as well, as they could be based on an actual natural occurrence and later transformed into a mythical expression of supernatural intervention.[64]

Having delineated the function of myth in the gospel narrative, Strauss turns to the criteria by which the interpreter can determine what is unhistorical in the narrative. Myth, for Strauss, can be determined by two criteria, one negative and one positive. First, the content of the narrative is not historical, and second, it is fictional. The first criterion provides the interpreter with a negative means by which to recognize myth. The negative criterion determines that an account is not historical and that the event described could not have occurred in the manner described. A narrative is unhistorical first when it is irreconcilable with the universal laws that govern the course of events, and second when it is internally inconsistent or when it contradicts other historical accounts.

63. Ibid., 86.

64. Ibid., 87. A classic example of the use of this type of myth is found in Rationalist interpretations of the account of Jesus walking on water (Mark 6, Matt 14, John 6), which has been interpreted by various authors as relating something that really happened, but in a way that embellishes the natural event with supernatural, miraculous overtones. For example, perhaps Jesus was actually walking on shore but appeared to the disciples to be walking on water due to high winds and darkness, or perhaps Jesus was walking on a sandbar and only appeared to walk on top of the water. In relating this story the evangelists exaggerated the event that took place to present it as a miracle.

The second criterion is the positive determination that the myth is fiction. The fictional character of the gospel narratives can be recognized either in the form or in the content of the narrative. The narrative is fictional if its form is a literary device, as when people converse in poetry. But even if the literary style of the narrative appears to be relating historical events, it does not always follow that the narrative is therefore historical. For narratives of this type, the clue lies in the content of the narrative. If the content of a narrative strikingly resonates with prevailing ideas from within the story's community of origin, then it is possible that the narrative is mythical. If the content of the narrative reveals knowledge of events that had yet to have occurred (e.g., the prediction of the destruction of the Temple), then the narrative can likewise be characterized as mythical.

The necessary question that arises from this discussion is the question of the boundary between the historical and the unhistorical, which is the question Strauss perceives as "the most difficult question in the whole province of criticism."[65] This boundary line is never static but remains in perpetual flux. Not only the form and content of the narrative itself but also the perspective, motives, and "pre-understanding"[66] of the interpreter must be considered as this boundary is approached. What appears to be historical to one interpreter with particular motives in a particular context might appear to be unhistorical to another interpreter with different motives in a different context.

When he applies this complex set of criteria to the resurrection of Jesus, Strauss opens with a thorough investigation of the gospel narratives. He specifically exploits the contradictions in the accounts of the first witnesses at the tomb and the striking contradiction between Matthew and Luke in terms of the location of Jesus' post-resurrection appearances. Matthew records a series of appearances in Galilee (Matt 28), while Luke records a series of appearances in Jerusalem (Luke 24). This contradiction is irreconcilable for Strauss and it raises crucial questions concerning the historicity of Jesus' appearances.[67] Because of the questions raised by the inconsistencies of the appearance traditions, Strauss is especially concerned with the quality of the bodily life of Jesus after the resurrection. Here the four gospels contain a variety of inconsistencies. On the morning of the

65. Strauss, *Life of Jesus*, 90.

66. For more on pre-understanding, see Bultmann, "Ist voraussetzungslose Exegese möglich?" ET: "Is Exegesis without Presuppositions Possible?"

67. Strauss, *Life of Jesus*, 718–28.

resurrection, Matthew has the women at the tomb embracing Jesus' feet, and he has Jesus speaking to them (Matt 28:9). In Luke Jesus joins two disciples on the road to Emmaus, but the disciples do not recognize him. Jesus converses with them and breaks bread with them, and only then do the two men recognize him. At that moment Jesus disappears from them and immediately (in the narrative) appears to the other disciples who are gathered in another location, where he offers his body to be touched and where he eats a piece of broiled fish (Luke 24:13–31, 36–43).

John's gospel presents the most complicated scenario. First, Jesus appears to Mary Magdalene, but she mistakes him for the gardener. Only when he speaks to her does she recognize him, but he forbids her to touch him (John 20:14–17). Jesus later appears among his disciples in a closed room and presents them with his pierced hands and feet. When Thomas, who was absent, demands proof, Jesus again offers his pierced hands, feet, and side (John 20:19–29). Finally, Jesus appears by the Sea of Galilee and eats bread and fish with his disciples (John 21:4–14).

These various accounts present two general ideas: either Jesus lived a completely natural human life after his resurrection, in which case his body would be subject to natural, physical, and organic laws, or his life was of a higher, supernatural quality and his body was already transfigured. The accounts of Jesus eating, speaking, and being touched favor the assumption that his life and body after the resurrection were contiguous with his life and body before his death, but the accounts of Jesus suddenly appearing and vanishing, materializing in a room with locked doors, remaining unrecognizable to his friends, and forbidding himself to be touched favor the alternative assumption that his life and body after the resurrection were in some way supernatural and thus radically different than his life and body before his death.

The fundamental claim of the evangelists is that a dead man has returned to life. This claim presents significant problems for Strauss, because if Jesus really returned to life then he was not really dead, or, conversely, if he was really dead then it is difficult to believe that he really returned to life. Whenever one attempts to maintain the former position, the latter threatens to disappear, and vice versa. For Strauss there can only be one solution: either Jesus was not really dead, or he was not really risen.[68] Rationalist interpretations of the eighteenth and early nineteenth centuries favored the former conclusion that Jesus was not really dead. Called a

68. Ibid., 736.

Scheintod in German (an "appearance of death"), these theories often proposed elaborate situations in which Jesus would only appear to have been dead, leading to a belief that he had been raised. One particularly popular interpretation along these lines suggested that Jesus, dehydrated and suffering massive blood loss due to his having been beaten and scourged and then nailed to the cross with a crown of thorns thrust onto his head, passed out or possibly even entered into a coma until he was placed in the cool, damp tomb, which eventually revived him. Strauss (to his credit) is totally unconvinced by these theories.

If Jesus really did die on the cross, the only option remaining is that he was not really raised from the dead. In order for the resurrection to be taken as a historical fact, evidence from impartial witnesses would be required. Such impartial evidence is not to be found in the Bible, for the evangelists record Jesus' appearances to believers only. Precisely because the gospels contain so many contradictions in their accounts of the resurrection, they cannot be taken as compelling evidence. Even Paul, who is usually precise and consistent, speaks generally and vaguely about the resurrection of Jesus. The gospel narratives, although more detailed in their accounts, do not provide a coherent historical account but merely a series of visions in a fragmentary compilation.[69]

Strauss is inclined to doubt the reality of Jesus' resurrection based on these texts. Earlier theologians attributed tales of the resurrection to the deluded visions of the disciples, or others (such as Reimarus) concluded that the disciples stole the body of Jesus and concocted a fantastic story of his resurrection. Some of Strauss's contemporaries argued that the progression from the deep depression of the disciples after the death of Jesus to their confident preaching of Jesus' resurrection at Pentecost would have been impossible had not something extraordinary have occurred in the interim. This progression from depression to joy, however, by no means proves a real appearance of Jesus or the reality of the external event at all. Thus the possibility remains that even though Jesus might not have been raised from the dead, the disciples nevertheless might have sincerely *believed* that this actually happened.[70]

69. Ibid., 739.

70. Strauss, in his essay on Reimarus's *Apology*, highlights this third possibility: "The disciples would have lied only if they had known that Jesus really had not risen; who is to prove that they must have known that or that they cannot have really believed that he arose? If, however, they proclaimed what they themselves believed, then they were guilty of self-deception at most, not of lying, if it was not so; thus they can have spoken

Strauss investigates the possible origins and motives of the disciples' faith in Jesus' resurrection, beginning with their messianic idea. The disciples spent several years following Jesus, during which time they became convinced that he was the promised Messiah. His death rendered this belief untenable, and in their shock they were unable to process what had happened. After this initial shock subsided, they reevaluated their expectations and beliefs and they struggled to resolve the contradictions caused by Jesus' death. They solved this dilemma by adopting elements of Hebrew prophecy (most significantly the concept of the suffering and dying of a righteous servant of God) into their messianic idea. Having reconciled the seemingly incongruous concept of the suffering and death of their master with their messianic idea, they interpreted Jesus' death as his entry into messianic glory, in which he was eternally present with them.

It remained for the disciples to reconcile their new conviction with the fact that Jesus' body remained buried in Jerusalem.[71] Strauss believes they accomplished this by returning home to Galilee, where they would be at some distance from the location of Jesus' corpse and not be subjected to accusations of fraud and deceit. In Galilee, removed from the stress and danger of Jerusalem, their new faith in Jesus as the Christ was free to develop unhindered. Here, far removed from Jesus' body and hostile authorities, they could safely work out their idea of the resurrection of Jesus. The disciples slowly grew in courage and confidence, eventually venturing out into public to proclaim their convictions. Their proclamation naturally evolved into the more embellished tales recorded in the gospel narratives, as the disciples searched the scriptures for additional support. The accounts of the resurrection of Jesus as found in the gospel narratives are the culmination of years of diligent searching, development, and codification of the disciples' Easter faith.[72] To summarize, Strauss concludes that the resurrection of Jesus was nothing other than a product of the disciples' faith in Jesus as the Christ.

Having critically examined the New Testament accounts of the resurrection and having systematically applied the categories of myth to the gospel narratives of Jesus' life, Strauss finds himself standing amidst the ruins

---

and acted as honest men. The unbearable contradiction that a deliberate lie would have to make of their enthusiasm and its effectiveness thus disappears." Strauss, "Hermann Samuel Reimarus," 51.

71. In contrast to Reimarus, Strauss denies the validity of the empty tomb tradition.

72. Strauss, *Life of Jesus*, 742–44.

of the tradition he has so vigorously critiqued. In an attempt to salvage whatever dogma might be retained at the conclusion of his critical project, Strauss writes a final "concluding dissertation" on the dogmatic importance of the life of Jesus. He begins this dissertation with the following realization:

> The results of the inquiry which we have now brought to a close, have apparently annihilated the greatest and most valuable part of that which the Christian has been wont to believe concerning his Saviour Jesus, have uprooted all the animating motives which he has gathered from his faith, and withered all his consolations. The boundless store of truth and life which for eighteen centuries has been the aliment of humanity, seems irretrievably dissipated; his dignity, and the tie between heaven and earth broken. Piety turns away with horror from so fearful an act of desecration, and strong in the impregnable self-evidence of its faith, pronounces that, let an audacious criticism attempt what it will, all which the Scriptures declare, and the Church believes of Christ, will still subsist as eternal truth, nor needs one iota of it to be renounced. Thus at the conclusion of the criticism of the history of Jesus, there presents itself this problem: to re-establish dogmatically that which has been destroyed critically.[73]

There does not appear to be an immediate crisis for Strauss, for the Christian's faith need not be subverted by criticism, and the critic should likewise be able to withstand the results of their own labor.[74] The essential problem, for Strauss, is that faith and criticism are not so easily separated. Faith by its very nature must include some doubt, and just as importantly, every critic has some commitment to the subject of their criticism, else they would not bother with the effort of engaging in the critique. Just as the honest believer is intrinsically a critic, so the honest critic is intrinsically a believer.

Strauss consistently and without prejudice applied his concept of myth to the gospel narratives, and only after determining the mythical could he proceed to the conclusion that what is contained in the gospel narratives (what he terms the "data of Christianity") is not historical in form, but rather dogmatic.[75] The natural result of this conclusion is to proceed with

73. Ibid., 757.

74. Perhaps Strauss is trying to convince himself that this is in fact the case.

75. Van Harvey attributes Strauss's success in applying the concept of myth to these texts to his Hegelian understanding of history. Because Strauss was able to think historically, he also was able to operate within the category of myth. Without the tools of historical criticism, the interpreter is unable to distinguish fact from fiction or the historical from the unhistorical. If one proceeds with the method of historical criticism in biblical

a critical investigation of dogma, and for Strauss the key to dogma is to be found in Christology. The intention of Christology, for Strauss, is to relate an idea of the union of the finite and the infinite. But rather than locate this union in one man, as in orthodox Christology, Strauss locates it in the entire human race. Humanity itself, then, and not Jesus alone, comprises this hypostatic union of the divine and human natures. Humanity as a whole dies, rises, and ascends to heaven, and by faith in the death and resurrection of Christ humanity is justified by God; that is, by nurturing in their own person the idea of humanity as a whole, the individual participates in the apotheosis of the entire human race.[76] This universal sense is realized most fully in the individual person of Jesus Christ, as it necessarily must take historical form.[77]

Due to these admittedly heterodox conclusions, Strauss recognizes the difficulty of the critical, speculative theologian feeling at home in the church. The church presumes that Christology refers to an individual man who lived in a particular historical moment, while the Straussian speculative theologian proposes that Christology instead refers to an idea that exists in the "totality of individuals." The church regards the gospel narratives as history, while the critical theologian regards most of them as myths. There are thus four options available to such theologians who wish to remain within the church:

1. They may attempt to elevate the church to their own perspective by resolving the historical into the ideal. This attempt will surely fail, because the church lacks the premises upon which theologians must build.

2. They may attempt to adopt the perspective of the church in order to better educate the people. This attempt is also difficult, because the people will view such theologians as hypocrites for preaching something they suspect or know that the theologians do not personally accept as true. For example, theologians may wish to preach on the resurrection. The church cannot conceive of faith in the dogmatic

interpretation, this inability is corrected and one is then able to apply other concepts to those texts that have been determined to be either fact or fiction, historical or unhistorical. Thus, it is only because of Strauss's use of the historical-critical method that he is then able to use the concept of myth. Harvey, "D. F. Strauss' *Life of Jesus* Revisited," 192.

76. See Harvey, "D. F. Strauss' *Life of Jesus* Revisited" for a discussion of Strauss's Hegelian influences.

77. Strauss, *Life of Jesus*, 780.

truth of the resurrection apart from its historical reality. The theologians, who may not agree, may nevertheless find great significance and truth in the resurrection, but the church surely will regard them as hypocrites.

3. They may ultimately appear to themselves to be hypocrites and may leave the ministerial office. This provides no viable alternative, however, for anyone who has found truth in their theological studies will be unable simply to abandon a career in theology.

4. Finally, they may adhere to the forms of popular discourse in preaching, while seizing the opportunity at every possible moment to exhibit the deeper significance of the material. For example, preachers on Easter Sunday may begin with the bodily resurrection of Jesus but will dwell on the greater significance of the resurrection for faith.[78]

It is understood in this fourth option that merely recounting the gospel narratives is not sufficient; the interpreter, preacher, and theologian must make a transition from the historical to the dogmatic. History, for Strauss, does not contain the whole truth. Truth must be brought from the past to the present, the external must be internalized, and the dead must be made alive if the truth is to be made meaningful in the lives of contemporary people.

Strauss remains a complicated figure in modern theology. Friedrich Nietzsche, perhaps rather surprisingly, lambasts him as a "cultural Philistine" and a "parasitic worm" whose only delight is destruction and whose only worship is digestion.[79] Karl Barth admits him into the ranks of the most significant theologians of the nineteenth century because of the problems he uncovered, but at the same time Barth commends Strauss more for the questions he raised than for the credibility of his responses to his own questions. Nevertheless, Barth admits a grudging respect for Strauss: "One must love the question Strauss raised, in order to understand it. It has been loved only by a few; most people have feared it."[80] Albert Schweitzer hails him as a "prophet of the coming advance in knowledge,"[81] while Van Harvey accuses him of being a bad interpreter because he failed to make the past genuinely

78. Ibid., 782–83.

79. See Nietzsche, "David Strauss."

80. Barth, *Protestant Theology*, 554.

81. Schweitzer, *Quest*, 90.

intelligible to the present.[82] Harvey finds Strauss's ultimate failure in his use of myth and in his misunderstanding of the historian's task, which is to make the past intelligible to the present through interpretation. Strauss completely separates these two concepts so that reconstruction of the past has no real connection to making the past intelligible to the present.

This is most evident in Strauss's twofold understanding of the purpose of myth. First, he uses myth as a historical-critical device with which to separate fact from fiction. Under Hegel's influence, he also regards myth as a philosophical tool to be used in extrapolating eternal ideas (corresponding to Hegel's *Darstellung*) from their naïve, mythical form (corresponding to Hegel's *Vorstellung*). Harvey understands the dual character of the concept of myth as contributing to Strauss's misconception of the historian's task of reconstructing and interpreting the past. Strauss does not recognize the ability of myths to communicate meaning in themselves, and he is largely unconcerned with the events myths were used to interpret. He fails to ask the most important question of the texts he sought to interpret, namely, why these texts were believed and are still believed to provide answers to fundamental human questions.[83]

Nevertheless, Strauss continues to haunt modern theology precisely because of the fearless questions he raised. Horton Harris summarizes the lasting impact of Strauss's work and its existential challenge to Christianity:

> Strauss's *Life of Jesus* was the most intellectually reasoned attack which has ever been mounted against Christianity . . . Strauss confronted theology with an either/or: either show that the Christian faith is historically and intellectually credible, or admit that it is based on myth and delusion. That was the alternative. Nothing less was at stake than the whole historical and intellectual basis of Christianity. If Strauss cannot be convincingly answered, then it would appear that Christianity must slowly but surely collapse.[84]

Although many dismiss Strauss's work as an antiquated relic of a collapsed philosophical worldview, his questions endure in their importance for modern and contemporary theology. Strauss investigated the nature of myth and theological interpretation of the New Testament, the eschatological character of Jesus' preaching, the relationship between John and the Synoptic gospels, the application of historical criticism to the New

82. Harvey, "D. F. Strauss' *Life of Jesus* Revisited," 208.

83. Ibid., 205–6, 208.

84. Harris, *David Friedrich Strauss and His Theology*, 282.

Testament, the significance of the historical Jesus for faith, and, perhaps most significantly, the possibility of an intellectually defensible Christian faith. Despite his failure to propose satisfying answers to all of the questions he himself had raised, his work cast a long shadow over the landscape of modern theology, which took up the gauntlet Strauss threw down and set itself the task of responding to Strauss's challenge.

PART II

Bultmann

CHAPTER THREE

Rudolf Bultmann on Myth, History, and the Resurrection

RUDOLF BULTMANN (1884–1976) WAS one of the most significant and controversial New Testament theologians of the twentieth century. Praised as a genius who opens a new future for theology or vilified as a heretic who threatens to destroy the Christian faith, Bultmann cannot be ignored.[1] His contributions to New Testament exegesis (especially form criticism), theological hermeneutics,[2] the relationship between theology and history, theological engagement with philosophy, and, most significantly for our purposes, his program of demythologizing the New Testament, have provided generations of theologians and biblical scholars with invaluable tools for interpretation. Bultmann is also perhaps one of the most consistently misunderstood and misinterpreted theologians of the twentieth century.[3] Critics vehemently decry his work without always understanding it, and even those sympathetic to his project vary widely in their interpretations.

Bultmann was primarily a New Testament scholar. His texts *Jesus*[4] and *Theologie des Neuen Testaments*[5] are considered classics in New Testament

1. Indeed, there has been something of a resurgence of interest in Bultmann in the last decade, thanks in part to the appearance of recently unpublished letters and other documents from Bultmann's *Nachlass* as well as a new biography of Bultmann: Hammann, *Rudolf Bultmann*. For a new introduction in English, see Congdon, *Rudolf Bultmann*. For a collection of essays on the lingering legacy of Bultmann in contemporary New Testament studies, see Longnecker and Parsons, *Beyond Bultmann*.

2. For an especially cogent discussion of Bultmann's program of demythologizing as it relates to theological hermeneutics, see Ricoeur, "Preface to Bultmann."

3. David Congdon is particularly concerned to rehabilitate Bultmann after generations of criticisms and frequent misunderstandings.

4. Bultmann, *Jesus*. ET: *Jesus and the Word*.

5. Bultmann, *Theologie des Neuen Testaments*. ET: *Theology of the New Testament*.

studies. More specifically, he was especially interested in the Johannine corpus and the letters of Paul. His treatments of the gospel of John and Paul's letters to the Corinthians reveal a masterful understanding of these traditions. As a New Testament scholar, however, Bultmann's work extended into other fields, such as theological hermeneutics, systematic and philosophical theology, and the philosophy of history.[6] His work is influenced by Martin Heidegger's existential philosophy[7] and this influence finds its most powerful manifestation in Bultmann's program of demythologizing.[8]

Bultmann on Myth

The question of myth in the New Testament pervades Bultmann's work. For Bultmann the world-picture of the New Testament is fundamentally a mythical world-picture. The universe is perceived as a three-tiered structure, with God in heaven "above," hell "below," and this world as the battlefield of good and evil supernatural forces. History does not proceed according to immutable laws, but is constantly manipulated by supernatural intervention. For Bultmann the fundamental question concerning myth in the New Testament is whether the New Testament kerygma contains a truth that is in some way independent of the mythical world-picture of the New Testament.[9] If the New Testament kerygma is inseparable from the mythical world-picture of the New Testament, then its truth is lost to modern generations who can no longer accept this mythical world-picture. If the truth of the New Testament kerygma *can* be discerned apart from the mythical world-picture in which it is expressed, then it is the task of the theologian to demythologize the New Testament to understand the kerygma in its significance for faith.

6. Barth, *Rudolf Bultmann*, 4. ET: "Rudolf Bultmann: An Attempt to Understand Him." Barth understands the boundary between New Testament exegesis and systematic theology to have been abolished in Bultmann's own work.

7. In discussion with Kuhlmann (see Kuhlmann, "Zum theologischen Problem der Existenz") Bultmann elaborates on the relationship between his theological interpretation of existence and human being, on the one hand, and Heidegger's philosophical interpretation of existence and human being, on the other. See Bultmann, "Die Geschichtlichkeit des Daseins und der Glaube."

8. For a contemporaneous summary of Bultmann's program of demythologizing and its impact on continental theology, see Tillich, "European Discussion of the Problem."

9. Bultmann, "Neues Testament und Mythologie," 16. ET: "New Testament and Mythology."

Bultmann recognizes the impossibility of simply repristinating the mythical world-picture of the New Testament because the modern scientific age has no room within it for recourse to the spirit world of the New Testament. To accept this world-picture blindly is to perform a *sacrificium intellectus* and to make acceptance of it a demand of faith is to reduce faith to a work.[10] Modern women and men are pervasively informed and influenced by modern science, and, for Bultmann,

> People cannot use electric lights and radios and, in the case of illness, take advantage of modern medical and clinical means, and at the same time believe in the spirit and wonder world of the New Testament. And whoever intends to do so must be aware that they can profess this as the attitude of Christian faith only by making the Christian proclamation unintelligible and impossible for the present.[11]

If the Christian kerygma has a universal truth, then it must be possible to express it independently of its first-century mythical form, especially if the kerygma is to speak a powerful word to those who no longer inhabit such a world-picture. If this is not possible, then the power and relevance of the Christian proclamation has faded along with the cultural forms of the first century. If it is to be salvific, the kerygma must be communicable to every time and every place, without demanding that hearers accept the mythical world-picture of the New Testament in which it was originally expressed. This does not mean, however, that the kerygma is simply "accommodated" to modern culture, as many critics charge (against Bultmann and, perhaps with more justification, against his liberal forebears); rather, Bultmann's program seeks to clarify first what the Christian kerygma is, and only then to make it relevant to modern people[12] (something akin to Paul Tillich's method of correlation).

David Congdon has proposed the conceptual framework of "constantinianism" and "translationism" to describe Bultmann's theological project

10. For this notion of forced acceptance of an alien world-picture as a *sacrificium intellectus* and a reduction of faith to a work Bultmann is drawing on the work of Herrmann in *Der Verkehr des Christen mit Gott im Anschluss an Luther dargestellt*. ET: *Communion of the Christian*.

11. Bultmann, "Neues Testament und Mythologie," 18.

12. Congdon, *Mission of Demythologizing*, xxvi. Congdon goes on to suggest that Bultmann's theological program is best understood as "missionary" theology, insofar as "clarifying the faith for people in a particular cultural situation is the very definition of the missionary enterprise." Ibid.

of demythologizing. Specifically, Congdon describes "constantinianism" as a "nondialectical-nonmissionary theology that confuses the kerygma with a cultural worldview" and "translationism" as a "dialectical-missionary theology that differentiates the kerygma from every culture on the basis of God's transcendent extraneity." He goes on to give a more precise synopsis of Bultmann's project:

> [Bultmann's] missionary hermeneutic therefore entails (a) the criticism of constantinianism and (b) the recontextualization [i.e. translation] of the kerygma. Specifically, the latter involves (1) the appropriating work of situating the kerygma within the present cultural-historical situation and (2) the transpropriating work of freeing the kerygma for new cultural-historical situations in the future . . . A missionary theology must therefore take intercultural and crosscultural translation as its starting point and mode of operation . . . If a hermeneutic is going to be unreservedly missionary, it cannot shrink from recognizing that the very conceptualities with which both past biblical writers and present interpreters articulate the kerygma are themselves elements of particular cultures that the kerygma crosses in its missionary movement through history. This is one of the key insights provided by Bultmann's theology.[13]

In terms of Bultmann's method, this raises three important questions: What is the New Testament kerygma? What is myth? And what is demythologizing?

First, it is necessary to understand what the New Testament kerygma is before asking about the possibility and promise of demythologizing it.[14] The New Testament kerygma, simply put, is the proclamation of God's saving act in Jesus the Christ. This is proclaimed in the word of address, but the proclamation itself is paradoxical: God's eschatological act takes place in human history, in a historical person, but precisely because it is historical it cannot be proved to be eschatological. The proclamation presents itself as a scandal and faith in this proclamation is a risk precisely because the act of God cannot be verified by historical research.[15] The kerygma as presented in the New Testament assumes mythological forms (e.g., the pre-existent Son of God emptying himself and becoming flesh), but the essence of the

---

13. Ibid., 572–73.

14. Bultmann finds attempts at demythologizing already at work in the New Testament itself (e.g., the Gospel of John in relation to the Synoptic gospels).

15. Bultmann, "Neues Testament und Mythologie," 48.

kerygma, that God has acted in Jesus the Christ *pro me*, if this is to make a claim on modern people, must be demythologized.

Before the New Testament kerygma can be demythologized, it is first necessary to define myth. In Bultmann's estimation myth accomplishes two goals. First, myth expresses the transcendent in worldly, objectifying terms.[16] Early cultures used mythical expressions to communicate their understanding of the strange, the surprising, or the mysterious.[17] Myth expresses the basic understanding that the human is not master of the universe but exists in a world full of mystery that is beyond human control.[18] Second, the true intention of myth is not to provide an objective picture of the world, but rather to express how human beings understand themselves in relation to their world. This is the difficulty of myth: the form of myth attempts to give worldly objectivity to the unworldly,[19] but the substance of myth must be interpreted, not in cosmological but rather in anthropological (i.e. existential) terms.[20]

For example, Christian mythology speaks of the transcendence of God in spatial terms. Rather than speak philosophically about the nature of transcendence, the New Testament prefers to imagine this transcendence in terms of spatial distance: God reigns "above" in heaven. Evil is likewise described in spatial terms and is personified in the form of demons who dwell "below" in hell. In order to overcome evil, a battle must ensue in which the champion of good defeats the forces of evil. What is expressed in these myths is the understanding that the world (and humanity's place within it) does not find its end in itself, but depends upon powers at work beyond human control. Thus mythology should not be interrogated in terms of the content of its objectifying representations, but in terms of the understanding of human existence expressed by these myths.[21] For Bultmann the issue at hand is the truth expressed by the myth, and faith in this truth—if it is to be meaningful today—cannot be bound to or limited by the mythical world-picture of the New Testament.

16. Bultmann, "Zum Problem der Entmythologisierung" (1952), 182. ET: "On the Problem of Demythologizing" (1952).

17. Ibid., 180–81.

18. Bultmann, *Jesus Christ and Mythology*, 19.

19. As Bultmann himself puts it, "*Der Mythos objektiviert das Jenseitige zum Diesseitigen.*" "Neues Testament und Mythologie," 48.

20. Ibid., 22.

21. Ibid., 23.

An additional question regarding myth in the New Testament concerns the method of demythologizing the New Testament witness in order to make it relevant to modern people. The term "demythologizing" (*Entmythologisierung*)[22] is, by Bultmann's own admission, problematic.[23] This term implies the elimination of myth, as if myth were a disposable husk containing a kernel of truth, which is how myth was often understood in the nineteenth century. For Bultmann myths are to be interpreted but not eliminated, because the form cannot be eliminated without also endangering the content. Instead, the kerygma is always contained and expressed in a particular cultural form, but the kerygma itself can and must be translated into the cultural forms of those to whom it is addressed.[24] For the New Testament writers, that cultural form was the mythical world-picture of the first century. For modern people a very different cultural form is operative, which is why the New Testament kerygma must be demythologized, or translated, from an alien cultural form into a familiar cultural form.

It is vitally important to understand Bultmann on this point because this is a frequent cause of misunderstanding. Bultmann is not suggesting that there is a linear progression from myth, through demythologizing, to a "pure kerygma" stripped of any mythical form. That would presume that myth is something belonging solely to the past, while we more enlightened contemporary people have transcended myth.[25] This is by no means the

22. With Congdon, I have chosen to translate the term *Entmythologisierung* with the gerund "demythologizing" rather than the more common "demythologization" to accent Bultmann's insistence that this is a continual process and not one step in a method that is finished before moving on to the next step.

23. Despite the near-universal identification of demythologizing with Bultmann and his theology, Bultmann did not coin the term. It was first used in a 1914 review of Herrmann's *Ethik* by Hermann Strathmann, but Bultmann most likely borrowed it from Hans Jonas's study of Augustine published in 1930. For more on the history of the term, see Congdon, *Mission of Demythologizing*, 693.

24. It would be a mistake to assume that Bultmann believes it possible to eliminate the mythical husk of the kerygma by translating it into "nonmythical" scientific language because, for Bultmann, the modern scientific world-picture is just as mythical in its own way as the New Testament mythical world-picture; it just happens to be "our" myth. As Congdon points out, "Science has not replaced myth because science is itself mythical, in that both myth and science perpetuate a false understanding of God, the world, and ourselves—myth unreflectively and science reflectively." Ibid., 608.

25. This is precisely how earlier historians and theologians (such as Strauss) understood myth. Ingolf Ulrich Dalferth (see below) turns this conception on its head and critiques the myth of logos in order to move beyond a facile opposition between these two concepts.

case, however, because every age has its myths precisely because every age has its unique cultural form and world-picture. Demythologizing, therefore, is not one stage in a progression from a mythologized kerygma to a demythologized, naked, "pure" kerygma. The kerygma will always be expressed in a particular cultural form, with its particular myths. The purpose is to translate the kerygma from an alien world-picture into a familiar one, which means that the task of demythologizing must continue as long as the Christian faith endures. The point is not to eliminate myth; rather, the point is to recognize myth as myth so to create space for the kerygma to makes its claim on our lives here and now.[26] Demythologizing, then, is always a task in hermeneutics: it is an act of interpretation.[27]

In order to understand Bultmann's method of demythologizing, it is first necessary to understand his conception of history and existential interpretation. Bultmann understands history as the "field of human decisions."[28] Even the interpretation of history (perceiving a historical process) is itself a historical act. What separates human beings from other creatures is that human beings are aware of themselves standing at least partially outside the causal nexus of natural and historical processes; they have been given the freedom of choice.[29] The human being is given the opportunity to choose between authentic and inauthentic existence.[30] Authentic human existence is existence in which individuals become responsible for their own life, and this includes opening themselves to the future. Thus human historical life is never complete, but stretches into the future of limitless opportunities for choice.[31]

For Bultmann this reality is understood in light of the dual possibility of authentic and inauthentic existence. In inauthentic existence, individuals regard themselves solely in terms of the past and present, whereas in authentic existence, individuals understand themselves primarily in terms

26. See Congdon, *Mission of Demythologizing*, 825n329.

27. Bultmann, *Jesus Christ and Mythology*, 18.

28. Bultmann, "Zum Problem der Entmythologisierung" (1961), 130. ET: "On the Problem of Demythologizing" (1961).

29. This is reminiscent of Schleiermacher's discussion of relative freedom, relative dependence, and absolute dependence in the *Glaubenslehre*, where he proposes that the human being is relatively free and relatively dependent within the causal nexus of human and natural relations and processes, but is absolutely dependent on God.

30. Bultmann, "Zum Problem der Entmythologisierung" (1961), 130. For more on this aspect of Bultmann's thought, see Harrisville, "Bultmann's Concept."

31. Bultmann, "Zum Problem der Entmythologisierung" (1961), 130.

of the future.[32] Myth, according to Bultmann, intends to speak of human existence, and thus he sees the need for an existential interpretation of myth, or what Congdon calls a "missionary translationism" in which "a participatory mode of God-talk takes the hermeneutical form of intercultural translation."[33] Demythologizing seeks to determine the intention of myth to address authentic human existence here and now, not its theoretical description of the world.[34]

The task of demythologizing cannot begin without first justifying its use. Is demythologizing a necessary theological endeavor? In other words, can Christian faith dispense with the mythical world-picture in which it was first expressed? Bultmann insists that this task is both possible and necessary, because the "mythological" in the New Testament transmits a meaning and an understanding of human existence itself. The key, for Bultmann, is to translate this meaning from its original expression in a first-century mythical world-picture.[35] To do otherwise is simply to remythologize the kerygma in such a way that it says nothing to modern people in their own situation.[36]

The concept of "world-picture" (*Weltbild*) plays a central role in Bultmann's theology and must be defined precisely in order to understand what Bultmann is proposing in his demythologizing program. According to Congdon,

> The category of *Weltbild*, as Bultmann uses it, thus refers to the general cultural framework—that is, the matrix of social relations constituted by shared implicit norms, assumptions, practices, customs, and concepts—that people presuppose in their everyday lives. It is the condition for the possibility of one's sociohistorical existence. Culture names that plastic and hybrid nexus of normative institutions and ideas that people in a particular historical situation take for granted ... No *Weltbild*, whether mythical or scientific, ancient or modern, western or nonwestern, is ever final or secure. As Bultmann puts it, everyone "knows that all the results of science are relative and that any world-picture worked out yesterday, today, or tomorrow can never be definitive."[37]

32. Ibid., 131.

33. Congdon, *Mission of Demythologizing*, 688.

34. Ibid., 449.

35. Bultmann, "Zum Problem der Entmythologisierung" (1952), 184.

36. Bultmann, "Zum Problem der Entmythologisierung" (1961), 134–35.

37. Congdon, *Mission of Demythologizing*, 654–55. Quoting Bultmann, "Zum

Demythologizing essentially is recognition of the objectifying nature of the mythical world-picture of the New Testament, which, Congdon suggests, "uncritically confuses its divine subject matter (revelation) with a particular sociocultural matrix of presuppositions, precisely because the lack of differentiation between divine and human was an implicit norm of the ancient *Weltbild*."[38] Just such a critical distance is needed to avoid conflating the kerygma with its particular cultural form, which Congdon describes as "a constantinian distortion of the gospel kerygma into a piece of cultural propaganda."[39] Based on this awareness, demythologizing interprets this mythical presentation in order to translate the New Testament kerygma in terms of our own cultural forms and our own world-picture. The critic does not make a modern scientific world-picture the standard for interpreting the biblical texts, because this is simply to impose a foreign world-picture onto the New Testament. Rather, the critic seeks to determine the deeper intention of the biblical writings within their own mythical form and then to translate that deeper intention into other cultural frameworks.[40]

Bultmann is not the first theologian to apply the method of demythologizing to the New Testament. But these earlier attempts (Strauss,[41] Schleiermacher, von Harnack, etc.) failed in Bultmann's estimation because these theologians did not fully comprehend the task and intent of demythologizing. They sought only to eliminate the myth, but more often than not they eliminated the kerygma along with it. In the case of von Harnack and other liberal theologians, they thought they could eliminate myth in order to uncover the essential kernel of a supposedly timeless religious and moral truth. The kerygma was reduced to a moral idea or a religious ethic, and the kerygma *qua* kerygma (the message of God's eschatological act of salvation in Jesus the Christ) was lost.[42] What remained was a supposedly "timeless" religious and ethical truth that was in fact fully synonymous with the culturally-conditioned world-picture of liberal Protestantism. The goal of demythologizing in Bultmann's estimation is not to eliminate the myth

Problem der Entmythologisierung" (1951), 181.

38. Congdon, *Mission of Demythologizing*, 659.

39. Ibid.

40. Bultmann, "Zum Problem der Entmythologisierung" (1952), 184. This is the process Congdon describes as the critique of "constantinianism."

41. See Backhaus, *Kerygma und Mythos*.

42. Bultmann, "Neues Testament und Mythologie," 24–25.

but to disclose the truth of the kerygma *qua* kerygma for people who do not inhabit a first-century mythological world-picture.[43]

Bultmann on History

The formal study of history was firmly established in university curricula after the First World War, at which point historical criticism became an invaluable tool for theologians and biblical scholars who availed themselves of this methodology to facilitate the development of form, redaction, and source criticism in the interwar period. Theology developed an enduring relationship to history and the full weight of historical criticism was brought to bear on the biblical texts and the traditions of the early church. This generation of historical critics distinguished itself from the nineteenth-century theologians interested in the historical Jesus by applying their method not only to the life of Jesus and the early church, but to the sources that contain these traditions as well. This hermeneutical move allowed the interwar theologians to critique the texts themselves to determine what traditions within the texts are authentic accounts, and to interpret those texts in light of the present situation. Most significant for Bultmann's project, the continuing development of existential philosophy led theology in new and potentially fruitful directions.[44] Bultmann, one of the leading advocates of an existential interpretation of biblical texts, also developed a philosophy of history, which he first presented in his text *Jesus* in 1926 and later outlined in his Gifford Lectures of 1955 on the topic of history and eschatology.[45]

Bultmann understands the primitive philosophy of history in ancient cultures as proceeding from pre-critical mythical thinking. Before ancient cultures wrote history, they referred to the past in terms of myths.[46] He locates the origin of historiography proper in peoples who became a nation. Only when a self-conscious political identity is achieved can a culture produce genuine history. These historical narratives may be infused

---

43. Ibid., 26.

44. Theological engagements (especially by Bultmann) with existential philosophy are based largely on the early work of Martin Heidegger (1889–1976), particularly his landmark text *Sein und Zeit* (1927), ET: *Being and Time*. Bultmann was also in correspondence and debate with another German existential philosopher, Karl Jaspers, whose thought is well summarized in his 1937 lectures in English as *Philosophy of Existence*.

45. Bultmann, *History and Eschatology*.

46. Ibid., 12.

with remnants of pre-critical mythology, but the shared experience of a political society creates the opportunity and luxury of historical reflection on the past. At this stage of historical reflection, as in ancient Greece, history is concerned exclusively with the past and does not intend to make judgments on the present or the future in light of historical knowledge. In other words, historiography has not yet concerned itself with determining meaning in history.

Historiography in ancient Israel developed in different directions. Here the experiences and deeds of the people of Israel, not the politics of a state, were the center of historical reflection. The community and its history developed in terms of their relationship to God, and thus supernatural intervention was accepted as part of history. God's intervention in the life of the people and the conduct of the people in light of their relation to God served as examples for the present, and thus ancient Israel developed an understanding of historiography as serving to inform the present life of the community.[47]

By the time of the writing of the New Testament, historical understanding among the Greeks had developed into a specific learned discipline. The development in Judaism of an eschatological view of history and the more "secular" Greek understanding of history clashed in the New Testament. By the time of the New Testament, according to Bultmann, history had been "swallowed up" by eschatology.[48] The early Christians understood themselves and the church not as historical, but eschatological phenomena. The Christian community believed that it lived not in the present world, but in the new age that is already breaking into the world but is not yet fully realized. This eschatological radicalizing of history created new problems for the early church. The delay of the Parousia forced a reevaluation of previous assumptions and expectations, resulting in a "re-historicizing" of eschatology in Pauline and Johannine literature.[49] The Christian movement became an institution; the eschatological community became a historical phenomenon. As the early twentieth-century French Roman Catholic theologian Alfred Loisy quipped, "Jesus came preaching the kingdom, but what arrived was the church."[50]

---

47. Ibid., 19.
48. Ibid., 37.
49. Ibid., 38.
50. Loisy, *L'Évangile et l'Église*. ET: *Gospel and the Church*.

Bultmann interprets Paul in light of his eschatology and anthropology.[51] For Paul, according to Bultmann, history is understood in light of eschatology; Paul's apocalyptic understanding of history is grounded firmly in his anthropology.[52] Paul recognizes meaning in history, but this meaning is not fully known and realized in history itself. Meaning in history is given by God, who gives grace to sinners. Thus history for Paul becomes the history of the individual *coram deo* and not primarily the history of the nation or community. Each human being has a personal history, and each person's history is determined by a series of decisions in every new situation. Each new decision is informed by prior decisions, or by each person's past. In order to enter into each new moment freely, each person must become free from the past. The problem, for Paul, is that the human being does not wish or will to be free from the past. This is the essence of sin. The Christian, however, lives in freedom—the freedom to decide—such that each situation is a call to decision and a call to freedom. This freedom is given by the grace of God, which appeared most fully in Jesus the Christ.

To be justified by faith, in Bultmann's reading of Paul, is to be set free from the past, to enter into a historical life of free decisions.[53] Thus faith, for Bultmann, is characterized by a radical openness to the future. This faith is a risk because the future remains unknown to us. Faith involves free openness to the future and grants freedom from anxiety in the face of nothingness. This freedom is not a decision of the will, but is given in faith itself through grace.[54] Thus, for Bultmann, eschatology, faith, and history are inexorably linked. Only by understanding and thereby being separated from the past can one be open to the future, but the fact that one will always remain uncertain about the future is the risk of faith.

In terms of historical method, there are two primary issues for Bultmann: the problem of hermeneutics and the question of the objectivity of

51. Bultmann treats the concept of history, anthropology, and eschatology of Paul in several essays, most notably "Geschichte und Eschatologie im Neuen Testament," ET: "History and Eschatology in the New Testament"; "Römer 7 und die Anthropologie des Paulus," ET: "Romans 7 and the Anthropology of Paul"; and in *Theologie des Neuen Testaments*, the first sub-section, "Die anthropologischen Begriffe," of the first section, "Die Theologie des Paulus," of the second part, "Die Theologie des Paulus und des Johannes," 193–226.

52. Bultmann, *History and Eschatology*, 41. For an excellent discussion of Paul's anthropology and the "inner human being," see Betz, "Concept of the 'Inner Human Being.'"

53. Bultmann, *History and Eschatology*, 41–47.

54. Bultmann, *Jesus Christ and Mythology*, 77–78.

historical knowledge.[55] First, there is always a problem of hermeneutics in doing history. Because history is based on sources and tradition, every work of historical investigation is also a work of interpretation. Historical documents must be understood if they are to be used to reconstruct the historical past. As the discipline of history developed, historians gained a deeper appreciation of the problem of hermeneutics in relation to historical knowledge. First, philology was used to interpret the literary structures of texts, and later psychology was employed to understand the personal situation of the author of a text. For Bultmann there is a third means to historical knowledge, and that is the "pre-understanding" of the historians themselves.[56] There are several questions a historian must pose before working with a text: What is my interest in interpreting these sources? Which questions direct me to approach these texts? For what purpose will I deploy my interpretation?[57] These questions aid the historian in discovering the motives for historical investigation. And so for the historian there must first be a relation in life (*Lebensverhältnis*) to the material if there is to be a genuine understanding of it.[58] This is possible because interpreter and subject live in the same historical world. These motives for historical inquiry and this "relation in life" to the subject matter inevitably lead to Bultmann's second question, namely whether it is possible to have objective knowledge of history.

Here the distinction between the facts and the meaning of history becomes crucial and it is important to mention here the distinction the German language can make between two senses of history. There are two words in German for what we in English simply call "history": *Geschichte* and *Historie*. In everyday usage these terms can be and often are used interchangeably, but in technical usage their meanings are strictly distinguished. *Geschichte* (related to the verb *geschehen*, meaning "to occur") can be used to refer to what has happened in the past, but in its more technical use it refers to the effects and the significance of the past, the past as it continues to exert its influence in and on history. *Historie* (ultimately

55. Bultmann, *History and Eschatology*, 110ff.

56. Ibid., 113.

57. Bultmann insists not only that historians approach history as historical beings with specific questions and demands of history, but also that history itself makes demands on historians. Only when historians are prepared to hear the demands of history, to listen to history as an authority, are they prepared to understand history. See Bultmann, *Jesus*, 7–8.

58. Bultmann, *History and Eschatology*, 113.

derived from the Latin word *historia*, which is cognate with the English word "history" but in later Latin takes on the more precise meaning of knowledge of the past gained through investigation), when distinguished from *Geschichte*, means the past as it actually happened, specifically as it is accessible to historical research; *Historie* also refers to the results of historical research. *Historie*, when used as a technical term, by its very nature is always accessible to historical research and can be described as "facts"; *Geschichte* might be accessible to historical research or it might not, just as it might be a fact or it might not.

A few examples will help to clarify this distinction in its various permutations. It is possible for the historian to have objective knowledge of certain historical (*historisch*) facts, e.g., my order of an Indiana IPA at my local bar last evening, which is a historical (*historisch*) fact but *not* a historic (*geschichtlich*) event because it will in all likelihood have no deeper meaning or enduring significance for anyone. It is also possible for the historian to have objective knowledge of certain historical (*historisch*) facts, e.g., the assassination of Abraham Lincoln on April 14th, 1865, or the attacks on the Pentagon and the World Trade Center on September 11th, 2001, both of which are, at the same time, historic (*geschichtlich*) events because of their deeper meaning and enduring significance. Here, though, it is impossible for the historian to have truly *objective* knowledge of the historic (*geschichtlich*) significance of these events for at least two reasons: first, the meaning and significance of these events is still unfolding in complex and unforeseen ways and will very likely continue to do so long into the future; and second, historians are themselves caught up in the effects of the events they are investigating and their involvement will necessarily color their interpretation of those events. Finally, it is also possible for something to have profound historic (*geschichtlich*) meaning and significance but remain unverifiable as a historical (*historisch*) fact: e.g., the resurrection of Jesus. The distinction becomes especially critical in terms of the death and resurrection of Jesus, because the two terms overlap in this case. The crucifixion and death of Jesus are both historical (*historisch*)—they actually happened in history and can be verified by historical research—and historic (*geschichtlich*)—they have lasting significance and meaning for history. The resurrection of Jesus, however, is not a historical (*historisch*) event—it cannot be verified by historical research, and thus cannot be proven to have actually occurred in history—but it is a historic (*geschichtlich*) event—it has lasting effects and significance for history.[59]

History is a process that is more than single, isolated events, because these events are connected by the chain of cause and effect. How these events relate to one another and influence one another is not within the realm of purely objective knowledge. The meaning of history is only gained by subjective interpretation of history, and because there are a multitude of possible perspectives in historical inquiry, there will also be a multitude of interpretations of history. This subjective character of historical inquiry is inevitable in the interpretation of history, because the historian is always also a historical being with a historical life and with concrete concerns, which means the interpretation of history will not be complete until the end of history itself.

For Bultmann, the inherent subjectivity of the historian's perspective involves an existential encounter with history.[60] History is meaningful to the historian only when the historian stands within history, and historical experiences are only objectively known because the historian also lives these experiences as a subject. Thus historical phenomena only have significance "in relation to the future for which they have importance."[61]

---

59. For an analysis of the importance of this distinction specifically in Bultmann's theology, see Perrin, *The Promise of Bultmann*, 33–56. For a detailed analysis of the history of these terms and their use in theological discussions in the nineteenth and twentieth centuries, see Hege, *Faith at the Intersection of History and Experience: The Theology of Georg Wobbermin*, chap. 2, "*Geschichte und Historie*: The Problem of Faith and History," 15–77. Making even finer distinctions than is possible with *Historie* and *Geschichte*, Herberg suggests that in the theology of the nineteenth and twentieth centuries there are in fact five meanings of the word "history": 1. History as past facts; 2. History in opposition to the timeless or the eternal; 3. History as it influences the future course of events (i.e. *Geschichte*); 4. History as constitutive of the essence of the human being (its key sense in Reinhold Niebuhr's work); and 5. History as existentially self-constituting the human being in face of an open future (its key sense in Bultmann's work). Herberg, "Five Meanings of the Word 'Historical.'" Despite some hesitation to insist on a strict distinction between *Historie* and *Geschichte* when translating Bultmann's work (especially in the translations of Roy Harrisville and Schubert Ogden), a practice also affirmed by David Congdon, I believe that the distinction is worth retaining because of the greater opportunity for clarity and nuance. Thus for the remainder of these chapters I will use the English "historic" to translate *geschichtlich* and "historical" to translate *historisch*. Because English does not distinguish between the two terms in their nominal or adverbial forms, I will indicate the German in parentheses if the meaning would otherwise be unclear.

60. Bultmann, *Jesus*, 7–8.

61. Bultmann, *History and Eschatology*, 120.

Now that we have inquired into Bultmann's conceptions of myth and history, a further question presents itself: what is the relationship between myth, history, and faith in the theological analysis of the resurrection of Jesus of Nazareth?

Bultmann on the Resurrection

As we have already noted, use of the term "demythologizing" is, by Bultmann's own admission, problematic. The term inaccurately implies the elimination of myth, though Bultmann's own intention is not to eliminate but rather to interpret the myths of the New Testament. Bultmann operates with a precise definition of myth, so that an accurate understanding of this definition is essential if one is to understand Bultmann.[62] He understands "myth" to be a specific historical phenomenon and "mythology" to be a specific mode of thinking. "Myth" is a report of an event in which superhuman, supernatural forces or persons are at work. "Mythology" as a worldview refers certain events or phenomena to supernatural powers. Thus mythical thinking, in which the world and events in the world are "open" to the intervention of otherworldly powers, is directly opposed to scientific thinking, in which the world and events within the world are "closed" within the causal nexus, i.e., the law of cause and effect.[63]

This opposition can be expressed in terms of the individual human being as well. In mythical thinking, human beings are open to supernatural intervention, whereas in scientific thinking human beings understand their existence to be a closed unity of decisions in terms of feeling, thinking, willing, responding, and acting.[64] Myth objectifies the transcendent in an

62. The crucial problem in mythology is that mythology seeks to objectify that which is either otherworldly or non-objectifiable. This tendency in mythology obscures the deeper intention of the myths, which is to express something meaningful about human existence. When these myths speak about God in objectifying terms, a new problem arises, because for Bultmann any attempt to speak *about* God inevitably leads to sin because to speak *about* God requires both the objectification of God and also my detachment or distance from the claim of God on me and my life, as the reality determining my existence. Thus, to speak *about* God is atheism and sin; faith, rather, speaks *of* God as the reality that determines my life, as that reality in which I live, move, and have my being (Acts 17:28). See Bultmann, "Welchen Sinn hat es, von Gott zu reden?" ET: "What Does It Mean to Speak of God?"

63. See Congdon, *Mission of Demythologizing*, 666ff, for a helpful excursus on the significance of Bultmann's views on science and demythologizing.

64. Bultmann, "Zum Problem der Entmythologisierung" (1952), 180–82.

attempt to express the conviction that human beings are grounded in a reality that is beyond their control.[65] But at the same time, myth intends to talk about a reality that lies beyond the limits of objectification. The question is whether myths intend simply to talk about the observable world or whether myths intend to say something about our reality as human beings, and thus of our existence.[66]

Bultmann asserts that the true intention of myths is to say something fundamental about human existence, and because this is so they cannot simply be eliminated. There is a tension inherent in myths, for myths simultaneously objectify the transcendent and express an understanding of human existence. The problem posed by myth is that modern people no longer think within the framework of a first-century mythical world-picture. Scientific thinking has rendered the mythology of the New Testament completely unintelligible to us. Christians, however, are presented with the word of God in the New Testament kerygma. Because the mythical world-picture of the New Testament is meaningless to modern people, it must be demythologized and interpreted for the present.[67]

Bultmann is often criticized for forcing a modern scientific world-picture onto the New Testament, thus elevating science over scripture. This is a misunderstanding of Bultmann's position, however, because for Bultmann the kerygma is above all an *eschatological* event, not a historical relic. If the kerygma truly is God's address to human beings in their own situation and not just to first-century people in the Mediterranean basin, then it should, in theory, be possible to demythologize the New Testament mythology and translate it into the world-picture of any time and any culture, not just our own. As Congdon suggests, "As long as an existential encounter with the eschatological event of Christ remains an ongoing possibility, any cultural context may be the occasion for the genuine proclamation of the kerygma."[68]

---

65. Bultmann, *Jesus Christ and Mythology*, 19.

66. Bultmann, "Zum Problem der Entmythologisierung" (1961), 134.

67. Bultmann here does not take into account the persistence of fundamentalism and biblical literalism among substantial portions of modern Christianity; instead, he simply assumes that all modern Christians have been shaped by Enlightenment rationalism and disenchantment. Presumably, fundamentalist Christians and biblical literalists would have no problem whatsoever inhabiting a first-century mythical world-picture while still using electricity, computers, and modern medicine. One suspects Bultmann would accuse them of inconsistency, but the fact remains that there are many Christians who do inhabit both worlds simultaneously. My thanks to Robert Saler for raising this issue.

68. Congdon, *Mission of Demythologizing*, 669.

But what, specifically, is the New Testament kerygma?[69] According to Bultmann, it is the proclamation of God's liberating act in the cross of Jesus the Christ; it is the proclamation of salvation to a fallen humanity in terms of the possibility for authentic human existence. Above all, the kerygma is the event of God's personal address to sinners. Because the kerygma is above all an event of address here and now, it cannot simply be equated with any concrete instantiation of it in any one theology, creed, or world-picture, not even in that of the New Testament itself. Bultmann expresses this insight in a letter to Martin Heidegger from 1932:

> It is becoming increasingly apparent to me that the central problem of New Testament theology is to say what the Christian kerygma actually is. It is never present simply as something given, but is always formulated out of a particular believing understanding. Moreover, the New Testament, almost without exception, does not directly contain the kerygma, but rather certain statements (such as the Pauline doctrine of justification), in which the believing understanding of Christian being is developed, are based on the kerygma and refer back to it. What the kerygma is can never be said conclusively, but must constantly be found anew, because it is only actually the kerygma in the carrying out of the proclamation.[70]

This kerygma, the proclamation of the eschatological liberating act of God, is presented mythologically in the New Testament, and so it must be interpreted. In the New Testament expression of the kerygma, the pre-existent Son of God takes on human flesh, dies on the cross as a vicarious sacrifice for sin, and is raised on the third day, destroying the power of death. This is the essence of the salvific Christ-event. But what can this mean for modern people who no longer think in terms of this mythology? What is the meaning for us of the Christ-event and of the kerygma that proclaims it? Because this event constitutes the kerygma, it is most important that it be carefully interpreted.

69. The word "kerygma" (κηρυγμα) in Greek originally referred to the proclamation of a herald. For a helpful study of the use of the term "kerygma" in modern theology, see the section "Zum Gebrauch des Wortes 'Kerygma' in der neueren Theologie," in Ebeling, *Theologie und Verkündigung*, 109–14. Also see the chapter "Kerygma und historischer Jesus," 19–82. ET: *Theology and Proclamation*.

70. Bultmann and Heidegger, *Briefwechsel*, 186, quoted in Congdon, *Rudolf Bultmann*, 71. Here Bultmann's line of thinking is consistent with Luther's own insistence on a distinction between the Word (Jesus Christ) and the Bible, which contains and points to the Word. As Luther puts it in a memorable image, the Bible is "the swaddling clothes and the manger in which Christ lies." Luther, "Prefaces to the Old Testament," 236.

The New Testament represents the Christ-event as a mythical event, and as such it must be demythologized. It is indeed a unique myth, because the object of the myth (Jesus the Christ) is simultaneously a historical person and a mythical representation, and his destiny is at once historically and mythically represented. Throughout the history of modern New Testament interpretation there have been continuous attempts to uncover the life of the historical Jesus of Nazareth that lies behind the gospel narratives. The nineteenth-century Lives of Jesus hoped to discover eternal truth and moral significance in the life of the man and to uncover what is authentic and historically (*historisch*) true about the accounts of Jesus' life in order to establish a secure foundation for faith.

Bultmann, however, insists that the quest for the historical Jesus is theologically unnecessary and ultimately impossible.[71] What is most important for faith is not the "how" or the "what" of Jesus' life, but only the "that." Faith should not be interested primarily in the historical details of Jesus' life and ministry, whether he really said a particular word or performed a particular deed. Rather, what is most important is the simple fact of Jesus' existence. It is "the *that*, the here and now, the facticity of the person [of the earthly Jesus] that constitutes the revelation."[72] Here Bultmann counts both Paul and John as forefathers, as neither New Testament author was nearly as concerned with the life of Jesus as they were with the *event* of Jesus the Christ.[73] And so the kerygma is grounded in the historical Jesus only insofar as the historical Jesus is the site of God's revelation as an event. The emphasis here, for Bultmann, should be on the event of God's revelation in

---

71. Bultmann, *Jesus*, 12ff. Some of Bultmann's own students criticized their teacher for creating a seemingly unbridgeable gap between the Jesus of history and the Christ of faith. See especially Käsemann, "Das Problem des historischen Jesus." ET: "Problem of the Historical Jesus."

72. Bultmann, "Die Bedeutung des geschichtlichen Jesus für die Theologie des Paulus," 208. ET: "Significance of the Historical Jesus." See also Bultmann, "Der Begriff der Offenbarung im Neuen Testament" for his discussion of the concept of revelation in the New Testament. ET: "Concept of Revelation in the New Testament." For a discussion of Bultmann's concentration on the "that" of Jesus' life, see Ebeling's essay "Das bloße 'Daß' und die Lehre von der Anhypostasie," in Ebeling, *Theologie und Verkündigung*, 115–16.

73. Despite the fact that Bultmann himself questioned the theological usefulness of the historic creeds, in this instance the creeds do corroborate Bultmann's suggestion that the "how" and "what" of Jesus' life are insignificant for faith, as the creeds move directly from Jesus' birth to his passion, death, resurrection, ascension, and second coming, glossing over the entirety of his teachings and deeds.

the person of Jesus the Christ, not on the historical-biographical details of Jesus of Nazareth.[74]

Bultmann was, of course, aware of the controversy such a dismissive attitude toward the significance of the historical Jesus would generate, but he was unfazed. His response to his critics in a 1927 essay on Christology captures something important about Bultmann the theologian:

> They want to know how I rescue myself from the situation created by my critical radicalism, how much I can save from the fire . . . I have never yet felt uncomfortable with my critical radicalism; on the contrary, I have been entirely comfortable. But I often have the impression that my conservative New Testament colleagues feel very uncomfortable, for I see them perpetually engaged in salvage operations. I calmly let the fire burn, for I see that what is consumed is only the fantasies of Life-of-Jesus theology, and that means nothing other than Χριστος κατα σαρξα [Christ after the flesh].[75]

The salvation event that occurred in Jesus the Christ has meaning only insofar as it can be comprehended in its significance, and the kerygma is only valid if it is addressed to individuals in their own situation. If this is to be meaningful today, it must be comprehensible and meaningful beyond mere *Historie*; otherwise genuine faith would be impossible without a personal relationship with the earthly, historical (*historisch*) Jesus, which we do not have. The salvation event, if it is truly salvific, must be available as a present

---

74. This does raise some significant questions about the possibility of having any accessibility to God's revelation apart from *some* knowledge of the historical Jesus, which is a thread taken up in earnest by Bultmann's students, especially Ernst Käsemann.

75. Bultmann, "Zur Frage der Christologie," 100–101. ET: "On the Question of Christology." Berger notes with interest that Bultmann *the Christian theologian* seems perfectly content to allow Bultmann *the historian* to demolish the historical foundations of Christian faith. Berger, *Questions of Faith*, 60. However, Berger is creating a false dichotomy here between the task of the historian and that of the theologian. Bultmann is content both as a theologian and as a historian (and as a Christian) to let these fires burn; there is no inherent contradiction or conflict for him. However, this is not the case for everyone who engages in historical study of the Bible. One prominent example of historical study leading a Christian theologian to abandon their Christian faith is Gerd Lüdemann, who declared that he had lost his faith as a result of his work as a New Testament scholar and was subsequently almost fired from his position at the University of Göttingen because of pressure from some church bodies. Instead, the university changed the name of Lüdemann's position from "New Testament" to "History and Literature of Early Christianity." See Lüdemann, *Resurrection of Christ*; and Lüdemann, *Great Deception*.

reality, not just as a historical relic. But what is the salvation event, and what is its significance for contemporary people?

Before addressing the issue of the salvation event proper, it is important to understand Bultmann's understanding of sin, for which salvation is the remedy. The Bible presents the picture of a humanity that is not what it ought to be, represented as fallenness, as sin. Sin for Bultmann means inauthentic existence: human beings exist inauthentically, that is, we insist on clinging to the past, desperately working to guarantee our own existence through the false security of our own efforts. Human beings refuse to be open to the future and we refuse to submit ourselves to the God who calls to us from the future. The New Testament kerygma addresses us in our sinfulness and exposes our inauthentic existence. Sin is rebellion against God because it is ingratitude for God's gift of grace. The grace of God is the love that encounters human beings in their fallenness, a love that accepts us in spite of what Bultmann calls our "radical highhandedness" (*radikale Eigenmächtigkeit*).[76]

The grace of God offers us the future: it offers us freedom from our fallen, backward-looking selves to be our authentic selves. Thus God's gracious gift of faith is the condition for the possibility of authentic human freedom. Faith is possible only in light of God's gift of freedom for the future. Faith is trust in the God who offers us authentic existence in the future, and thus faith is our decision for, our wholehearted "yes" to, this authentic existence.[77] Thus forgiveness of sin is not the forswearing of punishment, but it is the gift of freedom from self-incurred bondage to ourselves, from our past. It is freedom for obedience to the God who calls us to freedom. But this freedom, this forgiveness of sin, is possible only in light of the salvation event of the cross.

Before discussing the meaning of the Christ-event, Bultmann believes it is first necessary to demythologize the New Testament account. The question for Bultmann is whether this is possible. The Christ-event as recorded in the New Testament differs from Hellenic cultic myths, for example, in that the New Testament myth takes as its object a historical person. The divine pre-existent Logos is also the historical Jesus of Nazareth, and his destiny is not only mythical but is also a human life that ends with his death

76. Bultmann, "Neues Testament und Mythologie," 38.

77. Ibid. This grace is offered from God as *totaliter aliter* (totally other) because the word of God is addressed to us externally, from God the wholly other. It is because of this external character of the word that we encounter God always as God encounters us in our own situation. See Bultmann, "Welchen Sinn hat es, von Gott zu reden?," 29ff.

on the cross. The cross is a historical event that is at the same time presented as a mythical event, alongside the mythical event of the resurrection that is also presented as a historical event. This intertwining of the historical and mythical creates particular difficulties for the interpreter who wishes to distinguish the historical from the mythical. The question is whether these narratives intend to express something that happened to the historical Jesus or whether their true intention is to express something else. For Bultmann the significance of the historical Jesus lies not in the facts and events of his life, but in what God says to humanity through this particular person.[78] This intention becomes especially clear in the question of the significance of the cross and resurrection of Jesus.

Jesus' death on the cross is a historically verifiable event. Through historical research, historians can verify that a Jewish man named Jesus was crucified by the Romans in the vicinity of Jerusalem in the first third of the first century CE. But the Christian conviction that this cross is *Christ's* cross, that it is the event of God's salvific act, cannot be verified as a historical event. The meaning and significance of the cross can only be comprehended with the eyes of faith (*Glaubensaugen*).[79] In the New Testament the event of the cross is also represented as a mythical event. The Son of God is lifted up on the cross as a sacrifice of atonement, and the death of a sinless God-man placates God's wrath as a vicarious sacrifice for the sins of the world.[80] But can the cross be understood in its significance apart from the mythical representation of it in the New Testament? It is theology's task to interpret the historical event of the cross in its historic significance for faith. If this is not possible, then Christian faith has lost its foundation.

To believe in the cross of Christ is not to believe in the mythical process that takes place entirely outside of us, nor is it to believe in a historical event that occurred two thousand years ago. For Bultmann, to believe in the cross is to believe that it is *Christ's* cross, and that God has acted in the cross *pro nobis* and, more importantly, *pro me*.[81] The cross as the salvation event is not only something that happened to one historical person long ago, but more significantly it is a cosmic event that happens in the eschatological here and now, through the preached word, and thus to participate

---

78. Bultmann, "Neues Testament und Mythologie," 41.

79. Bultmann, "Zum Problem der Entmythologisierung" (1952), 196.

80. Whether this is the only way to understand the atoning power of the cross is certainly debatable. For a summary of atonement theories, see Schmiechen, *Saving Power*.

81. Bultmann, "Neues Testament und Mythologie," 46.

in the cross of Christ is to be willing to be crucified with Christ, to take Christ's cross as one's own cross. The cross is not merely a historical event: it is a historic event with origins in the historical event of the crucifixion of Jesus of Nazareth. It is an event with historic significance because it is the cross of *Christ*, through which God liberates the world. But is it not possible to understand the cross as *Christ's* cross only by first being convinced of the significance of Christ? Would we not have to understand it as the cross of the historical Jesus before we understand it as the cross of Christ? We know about the cross only as a historical event, but the New Testament does not proclaim the cross merely as a historical event, but as a cosmic, historic event. Jesus is proclaimed to be the crucified *and* risen Lord, and thus cross and resurrection belong together as a unity.[82]

The resurrection is presented in the New Testament as a mythical event. The dead man Jesus is returned to bodily life and appears to his followers. After forty days of walking the earth he ascends bodily into heaven. This presentation also must be demythologized if the kerygma it proclaims is to be made intelligible to modern people. What are these mythical elements in the texts attempting to express? What is their meaning for us? The meaning of the resurrection is that death is not the end, that God has acted in the cross to free humanity from the bonds of death. The resurrection is an expression of the meaning of the cross, that the cross is *Christ's* cross. The resurrection is an object of faith for Bultmann, and as such it cannot be a self-authenticating miracle.[83] The believer cannot convince a doubter that the cross is an eschatological event by referring to the resurrection as proof, because the resurrection cannot be established as a historical event. Faith in the resurrection is not faith in a historical event, but it is faith in the cross as the salvation event, and because the cross is the salvation event it is the cross of Christ. Otherwise it is nothing more than the tragic end of a noble man.

But how are we to believe that the cross is the salvation event? Bultmann insists that we believe because it is proclaimed as such. The crucified and risen one encounters each of us in the kerygma, the word of proclamation, and nowhere else.[84] Faith in the resurrection is thus faith in this word of proclamation, that it is God's address and summons to us in our situation. Easter faith is the faith that this kerygma is the legitimate word

82. Ibid., 41–44.
83. Ibid., 45.
84. Ibid., 46.

of God, and this word is itself an eschatological event. In the proclamation of the crucified and risen one, this event occurs in the present: the risen Christ is encountered here and now in the preached word. In other words, Christ has risen into the proclamation of the church.[85] This word proclaims that God's grace has already acted *pro me*. This word is grounded in the death of the historical person of Jesus as the eschatological event, but the significance of this gracious act is comprehended only in God's personal address through the word proclaimed to me here and now. This word is the event in and through which God meets us, offers us forgiveness, and opens the future for our authentic existence.[86]

What does it mean to have faith in the resurrection? Bultmann has already established that faith in the resurrection is not belief in a historical event, but that faith in the resurrection is trusting that God has acted for us and for our salvation in the cross of Christ. But how does this act become available for us in our situation? In other words, what is the significance of the resurrection for faith?

Critics have charged Bultmann with inconsistently applying his method of demythologizing by not fully demythologizing God and God's act in the cross.[87] In a lecture entitled "The Meaning of God as Acting,"[88] Bultmann addresses the issue of the act of God in terms of his program

---

85. While not always rooted in the same theological assumptions, the presence of Christ in the proclamation of the gospel is portrayed quite vividly in many "high church" Christian traditions (e.g., Orthodox, Catholics, Anglicans, Lutherans), many of whom stand for the proclamation of the gospel after the gospel book has been processed with attendant crucifer and torchbearers into the midst of the assembled congregation and in some traditions also censed and blessed by the gospeler.

86. Bultmann, *Jesus*, 199–200. See also Bultmann's essay "Der Begriff des Wortes Gottes im Neuen Testament." ET: "Concept of the Word of God."

87. The most noteworthy of these critics, Karl Barth, outlines these inconsistencies in his essay *Rudolf Bultmann*. Schubert Ogden, in an article on "The Debate on 'Demy-thologizing'," discusses these charges at some length. For a more thorough presentation of Ogden's own criticisms of Bultmann's position, see Ogden, *Christ without Myth*.

88. Bultmann delivered this lecture at Yale University in October of 1951 as one of the Schaeffer lectures, and again at Vanderbilt University in November of the same year as one of the Cole lectures. It is available in Bultmann, *Jesus Christ and Mythology*, 60–85. He also treats this topic in a section on "Die Rede vom Handeln Gottes" in "Zum Problem der Entmythologisierung" (1952), 196–208. For Bultmann's discussion of the distinction between act (*Handeln*) and wonder or miracle (*Wunder*), see Bultmann, "Zur Frage des Wunders." ET: "Question of Wonder."

of demythologizing. The primary question in his discussion is whether all speech of God as acting necessarily must be mythological speech.[89]

In mythological thinking the act of God is understood as an action that intervenes between the natural, historical, or psychological course of events, whereby "the divine causality is inserted as a link in the chain of events which follow one another according to the causal nexus."[90] The act of God can be understood non-mythologically only if it is understood as happening not *between* worldly events, but as happening *within* them. Thus the closed connection of cause and effect remains intact to the observer.[91] The act of God remains hidden and it can be perceived as God's act only with the eyes of faith. God's act remains hidden within the natural course of events to the believer and the non-believer alike, but insofar as believers see the event in its significance, as something happening to them here and now in light of God's word, then they can and must accept it as God's act.[92] God's acts cannot be empirically detected and observed *as God's acts* because God's acts cannot be objectified. They remain hidden to the observer, but the Christian believes that God is working here and now within these events. Faith "nevertheless" (*dennoch*) understands as God's act an event that is completely intelligible in the natural and historical nexus of cause and effect, without remainder. This "nevertheless" is therefore inseparable from faith.[93]

89. Bultmann argues that it is possible to speak non-mythologically about God. His contemporary, Paul Tillich, disagrees and insists that religious language is always necessarily symbolic and mythical language precisely because religious language speaks of the infinite, unconditioned divine reality that, by its very nature, is inexpressible by anything other than symbol and myth. The key, for Tillich, is not to eliminate the myth but to recognize the myth *as myth* (what he calls "broken myth") so that the myth is not taken literally, thereby becoming idolatrous. See Tillich, *Dynamics of Faith*, 47–62. This approach is taken up in different registers by Reinhold Niebuhr and Sallie McFague, among others. See Dorrien, *Word as True Myth*, chapters 3 and 5.

90. Bultmann, *Jesus Christ and Mythology*, 61.

91. While Bultmann proposes this distinction in order to keep the causal nexus intact, contemporary American philosopher of religion Richard Grigg insists that here especially theology cannot escape the scientific implications of its claims. He argues that any theological claim for God's action in the world must in principle be accessible to scientific observation if it is to be credible, which means that any assertion of God's action in the world must meet the standards of proof set by science. For Grigg, the only theological position that can meet these standards is pantheism. See Grigg, *Beyond the God Delusion*.

92. Bultmann, *Jesus Christ and Mythology*, 64.

93. Ibid., 65. There are intriguing points of contact between Bultmann's description

The question remains: how are we to speak of God as acting if we are to avoid mythological language? Bultmann argues that speech of God as acting *on me* is to be understood not mythologically, but rather analogically. When we speak of God as blessing, judging, addressing, etc., we speak of God's action as an analogue to interpersonal human actions.[94] There are two important consequences of this distinction. First, only such statements about God are legitimate as express the existential relationship between human beings and God. Second, images used to describe God as acting are only legitimate if they intend to speak of God analogically and not literally as a personal being acting on persons.[95]

Because Bultmann argues for such an analogical understanding, the objection can be raised that God's action becomes a merely subjective, psychological experience. This implies that God exists only in the inner life of the soul and not as a transcendent reality. Bultmann argues that faith cannot defend itself against the charge that it is an illusion, but nevertheless "faith" does not denote a psychologically subjective quality. Faith is hearing and responding to the word of God addressed to me in my concrete, historical situation. The fact that this word is God's word cannot be demonstrated objectively. God's word is hidden in scripture just as God's acts are hidden everywhere. The fact that God cannot be apprehended apart from faith does not mean that God does not exist apart from faith.[96]

Here Bultmann's argument is reminiscent of the classical polarity of *fides qua creditur* and *fides quae creditur*, the subjective and objective poles

of God's acts occurring *within* events and John Caputo's description of God as the name we give to that which is happening within events but which cannot be contained by them. But whereas Bultmann's God remains in some sense an ontological reality outside the event (a theology that Caputo calls "strong" and "ontotheology"), Caputo's God is the name for "we know not what" is happening in the event, leading Caputo to call his own theology "weak" and "hauntology." See Caputo, *Weakness of God*. The French post-Marxist philosopher Alain Badiou also turns to Paul's treatments of the resurrection and grace to theorize the event in *Saint Paul*.

94. See Betz, "Concept of the 'Inner Human Being.'" In a footnote, Betz quotes Bultmann's statement about the anthropology of the New Testament from Bultmann's *Theology of the New Testament*: "Every assertion about God is simultaneously an assertion about man and vice versa. For this reason and in this sense Paul's theology is, at the same time, anthropology.... Thus, every assertion about Christ is also an assertion about man and vice versa; and Paul's Christology is simultaneously soteriology." Bultmann, *Theology of the New Testament*, 1:191, quoted in Betz, "Concept of the 'Inner Human Being,'" 315, n. 1.

95. Bultmann, *Jesus Christ and Mythology*, 69–70.

96. Ibid., 72.

of faith, as well as Luther's exposition of the First Commandment in the Large Catechism where Luther suggests that

> To have a god is nothing other than to trust and believe in that one from the heart . . . the trust and faith of the heart alone make both God and idol. If your faith and trust are right, then your God is the true one, and in turn where your trust is false and wrong, there you do not have the true God. For the two belong together, faith and God. Anything on which your heart relies and depends, I say, that is really your god.[97]

For Bultmann, as for Luther, God's *existence* is not dependent on faith, so that it is my faith that somehow produces God's existence. Rather, God's existence is ontologically prior to my faith, but it remains purely external and indeed meaningless *for me* until I relate to God in trusting faith.

Because God's actions cannot be objectified, because the events of redemption cannot be rationally, empirically, or historically demonstrated,[98] and because it is possible to speak of such things only when individuals are ultimately concerned with their own existence, then faith must be a new understanding of personal existence.[99] In other words, God's act bestows a new understanding of myself. Bultmann addresses a common misunderstanding of this particular position: the self-understanding of personal existence is confused with philosophical analysis of the human being. The existential understanding of the significance and meaning of my own life authentically pursued (*das Existentielle*) is confused with existentialist philosophical analysis (*das Existential*).[100] It is existentialist analysis that clarifies that my existential self-understanding is realized

---

97. Luther, "Large Catechism," 386.

98. As Lessing and Kant famously put it, the historical serves only for illustration, not for demonstration.

99. This new understanding can be expressed in terms of Heidegger's phrase *Dasein-in-der-Welt* ("Being-in-the-World"). For Bultmann, true faith is a matter of the believer's understanding of this "Being-in-the-World." Bultmann maintains a distinctive relationship between *Glauben* and *Verstehen* (faith and understanding), which he discusses in his essay "Theologie als Wissenschaft." ET: "Theology as Science." For a discussion of the relationship and the distinction between *Glauben und Verstehen* in Bultmann's theology, see Jüngel, *Glauben und Verstehen*. Jüngel discusses Bultmann's conception of theology in terms of its characterization as a science (*Wissenschaft*), the proper boundaries of theology (for example, theology must have a specific object—namely, God—if it is to be called "theology": talk about God), faith as understanding of truth, and the truth of the moment, among others.

100. Bultmann borrows this distinction from Heidegger.

only in the here and now.[101] Theologically, Bultmann argues that in faith we continuously understand ourselves anew. This new self-understanding is maintained only as a continual response to God's word, which proclaims God's act in Jesus the Christ.[102]

But this raises a further question: if one speaks of God as acting on the individual in the concrete here and now, how can it be maintained that God has acted once for all in the cross? Bultmann suggests that the idea of the eternal God becomes effectively real in an individual's existence by God's word spoken in the here and now. God's word is eternal, but not timeless. This eternity is conceived as God's eternal presence always actualized in the here and now, i.e., in time.[103] God's word is not a collection of propositions and doctrines demanding intellectual assent, but an event happening in my own concrete situation here and now, addressed to me in time from outside myself. In this sense God's word is truly the *verbum externum*.

God's word is transmitted through human language, through the Bible and the church. This word originated in history, in the historical event of Jesus the Christ. God's act in the cross of Jesus cannot be objectified or proved, and yet the Christian believes that this is an eschatological, salvific event. Jesus the Christ is the eschatological event, and the question for demythologizing is whether this understanding is inseparable from the New Testament conceptions of cosmological eschatology.[104] The key for Bultmann is found in the Gospel of John's unique eschatology.[105] In John, cosmological eschatology is understood as a historical, realized eschatology. To live in faith is to live an eschatological existence, to pass from death to life, *right now*. This eschatological existence is already realized in a new self-understanding in response to the word, and the eschatological event of Jesus the Christ happens here and now as the word is proclaimed. The

---

101. Bultmann, *Jesus Christ and Mythology*, 74.

102. For a discussion of Bultmann's treatment of faith as a new self-understanding, see Jüngel, *Glauben und Verstehen*, 65–67.

103. Bultmann, *Jesus Christ and Mythology*, 79. Tillich also utilizes this distinction in a sermon entitled "The Eternal Now."

104. Bultmann, *Jesus Christ and Mythology*, 81.

105. See Bultmann's *Das Evangelium des Johannes* for his treatment of the Fourth Gospel as a whole. ET: *Gospel of John*. See also his "Die Eschatologie des Johannes-Evangelium" for his specific treatment of John's eschatology. ET: "Eschatology of the Gospel of John."

"once for all" is understood, not as a historical event, but as an eschatological event.[106]

This event is present for me in the preaching of the word. The word does proclaim that God's grace has already acted in the past for me, but not in a way that I can objectively understand through historical research and reconstruction. God's grace is present here and now as the eschatological event, with its origins in the historical event of Jesus the Christ. This event is "once for all" because the word that is preached here and now is the same word that has been preached for two millennia. It is only in light of this proclaimed word that what has happened or what is happening here or there assumes the character of God's act for those who have faith in God.[107]

What does it mean to have faith, for Bultmann?[108] Christian faith in its most basic sense is trust in the promise of God given in the gospel, and this faith opens me to the future. Faith includes the recognition that as a human being I am incapable of saving myself from my own past and am therefore also incapable of existing authentically for the future. Because faith as trust in God is faith that God will make my authentic existence possible, faith is also obedience and submission to the God who judges me and who gives me grace. This faith is *justifying* faith, in that through faith the sinner is made righteous. Faith is also hope, in that it is readiness for and acceptance of the unknown future that God opens up for me.[109] Finally, faith is freedom, for through God's gracious gift of faith I have the freedom to decide for authentic existence. This gift of freedom liberates me from myself and from my past, setting me free for loving openness to the world.[110]

---

106. Congdon goes so far as to suggest that, contrary to typical assumptions that Bultmann's chief concerns are hermeneutics and existential analysis, Bultmann should be understood first and foremost as an eschatological theologian. In fact, the first chapter of Congdon's introduction to Bultmann's thought is devoted to Bultmann's views on eschatology, not myth and demythologizing. See Congdon, *Rudolf Bultmann*, 1–13.

107. Bultmann, *Jesus Christ and Mythology*, 85.

108. For a more systematic treatment of faith, including its three "classical" components (*notitia, assensus, fiducia*—knowledge, assent, and trust), see Bultmann's fifth chapter, "Der Begriff des Glaubens," in *Theologische Enzyklopädie*, 97–170. ET: *What Is Theology?* For his discussion of God as the object of faith (*fides quae creditur*) and of the eschatological act of God as the theme of theology, see Bultmann, "Theologie als Wissenschaft."

109. For a short discussion of the concept of hope in the context of demythologizing, see Bultmann's essay, "Die christliche Hoffnung und das Problem der Entmythologisierung." ET: "Christian Hope and the Problem of Demythologizing."

110. See Bultmann's section on "Das menschliche Sein im Glauben" in "Neues

Faith is grounded in God's revelation in a historical person.[111] But faith is also eschatological, in that God encounters me in the present through the kerygma, through what Bultmann calls the *Christus praesens*.[112] God offers forgiveness and authentic existence in my current situation, and thus faith requires a decision in each new moment. God's gracious act in the cross is the condition for the possibility of faith, so that faith becomes a response both to God's past act and to God's address to me in the present. Because faith is possible only in relation to God's address in the proclamation of the gospel, it follows that faith must be created in each new moment. True faith is only possible when I act, when I am confronted with a summons to respond to the word. Faith in this sense is not intellectual assent to a series of doctrinal propositions, but a free act of trusting, affirmative response to God's saving word addressed to me in my own existence.[113] Faith is the obedient hearing of this word of law and gospel—the word that condemns me as a sinner and offers forgiveness in Christ—and as such faith is inseparable from the word.[114]

The Christian kerygma is the proclamation of God's eschatological act in Jesus the Christ. This is the message of the New Testament: the gospel, the good news. This is the message that meets people in the proclamation of the word, and this is the message that offers each hearer the opportunity for decision. Faith is possible only when this message is proclaimed, as Paul writes, "for faith comes through what is heard, and what is heard comes through the word of Christ" (Rom. 10:17). To hear this word is to hear God's offer of forgiveness and of liberation: it is the "word of reconciliation" (2 Cor. 5:18–19). This word of the cross makes the cross comprehensible as the salvation event by demanding faith. This faith is not mere belief in the historical facticity of Jesus' life and death, but much more than that: it is the individual's wholehearted "yes" to God's word of address. Because the truth of the kerygma

---

Testament und Mythologie," 29–31.

111. Bultmann, "Der Begriff der Offenbarung im Neuen Testament." ET: "Concept of Revelation." See also the ninth paragraph of his third chapter on "Die Erkennbarkeit Gottes in der Existenz durch die Offenbarung," 59–65, and the eleventh paragraph of his fourth chapter on "Die Offenbarung als geschichtliche Ereignis," 88–96, in Bultmann, *Theologische Enzyklopädie*.

112. For more on this feature of Bultmann's thought, see Kay, *Christus Praesens*.

113. Bultmann, "Welchen Sinn hat es, von Gott zu reden?," 36.

114. This twin emphasis on faith and the word is captured in the title of a collection of essays by one of Bultmann's most famous students, Gerhard Ebeling. See Ebeling, *Wort und Glaube*. ET: *Word and Faith*.

cannot be verified by historical research, because the significance of God's eschatological act in the cross cannot be proved, and because the ground and object of faith are the same (namely, God), this faith involves a risk:

> Those who want to have faith in God as their God must know that they hold nothing in hand in which they can believe; that they are, as it were, poised mid-air and can demand no proof of the truth of the word that has been spoken to them. For the ground and the object of faith are identical. Only the one who abandons all security can find security, only the one who—to speak with Luther—is prepared to enter into the inner darkness.[115]

There can be no security in faith, for in faith one abandons security for the sake of radical openness to the future. Faith is a risk precisely because the truth of the kerygma cannot be proved and because the future is unknown to us. To seek for security or proof for faith is to ask God to justify Godself, which is a refusal to let God be God. This is the scandal of the New Testament. The paradox of faith—that the revelation of God occurs in a historical figure, that God is revealed most fully in the humiliating death of a condemned criminal,[116] that the church and its proclamation are historical and yet eschatological phenomena—cannot be overcome by means of scientific explanations or historical investigations, but only in trusting faith. As Bultmann asserts, it is precisely because these things *cannot* be proved that the Christian kerygma is secure against the charge that it is mythology. The transcendence of God is not made immanent in such a way as to negate God's transcendence, as in myth; rather, the paradox of the presence of the transcendent God in history is affirmed: "the word became flesh."[117]

---

115. Bultmann, "Zum Problem der Entmythologisierung" (1952), 207. Here Bultmann makes an interesting connection between his program of radical demythologizing and the Pauline-Lutheran doctrine of justification by faith alone. He understands his own program to be a consistent application of the Lutheran doctrine of justification to epistemology: just as the doctrine of justification cures us of any hope for security through our works, so radical demythologizing cures us of any hope for security through our knowledge.

116. This is the heart of the Lutheran theology of the cross. For more on this aspect of Lutheran thought, see Saler, *Theologia Crucis*.

117. Bultmann, "Neues Testament und Mythologie," 48. David Congdon makes the intriguing argument that Bultmann, finally, should be understood as a theologian of Advent. See Congdon, *Rudolf Bultmann*, which concludes with a chapter on Advent.

CHAPTER FOUR

Der Wal und der Elefant

The Barth-Bultmann Debate on Hermeneutics
and the Resurrection

IN A LETTER TO Rudolf Bultmann dated December 24th, 1952, Karl Barth (1886–1968) imagined the two men as a whale and an elephant meeting "with boundless astonishment on some oceanic shore . . . They do not have a common key to what each would obviously like to say to the other in its own speech and in terms of its own element."[1] These two great theologians debated one another with equal parts tenacity and sincerity for over forty years, and their correspondence reveals both a mutual respect and a fundamental disagreement. For Barth, Bultmann's insistence on engaging existential philosophy made him impossible to understand, and for Bultmann, Barth's refusal to admit to any philosophical influences made it impossible for the two men to agree. These letters, together with Barth's booklet *Rudolf Bultmann: Ein Versuch, ihn zu verstehen*,[2] represent the bulk of their published debates; within these pages Barth and Bultmann engaged in a lively debate on the message of the New Testament, the nature of understanding, the influence of philosophy on theology, and the problems and promises inherent in Bultmann's program of demythologizing.

In his monumental *The Epistle to the Romans*, first published in 1919, Barth outlines his early understanding of the resurrection. For the early Barth, the resurrection is not a historical event.[3] In Jesus two worlds meet: the known human world and the unknown world of God. The point on

---

1. Jaspert and Bromiley, *Karl Barth/Rudolf Bultmann Letters*, 105. A significant portion of Congdon's book, *Mission of Demythologizing*, is dedicated to "demythologizing" this very description of the relationship between Barth and Bultmann.

2. Barth, *Rudolf Bultmann*. ET: "Rudolf Bultmann: An Attempt to Understand Him."

3. Barth, *Epistle to the Romans*, 30.

the line where the other world intersects our world is the historical Jesus of Nazareth. But insofar as our world is touched by the other world in Jesus, it is no longer observable as history. Within human history, Jesus Christ can only be understood as problem or myth, because, as the Christ, Jesus intersects our plane of knowledge from above and beyond.[4] In the resurrection, Jesus is revealed to be the Christ, in whom the other world touches the human world as a tangent touches a circle. The divine world touches the human world on a new frontier, as a new world.[5] As history, the resurrection lies on the frontier of that which is not history; as non-history, the resurrection lies on the frontier of that which is history.[6] The truth and meaning of the resurrection can only be seen in the cross,[7] and grace, the power of the resurrection, demands nothing less than our total and absolute submission and obedience to God.[8]

In 1924, by which time Barth had decisively parted ways with the liberal theological tradition in which he was trained, he published his detailed study of 1 Cor. 15 entitled *Die Auferstehung der Toten.*[9] Barth divides his discussion into four sections: the message of the resurrection as the foundation of the community, the resurrection as the meaning of faith, the resurrection as truth, and the resurrection as reality.

The resurrection of Jesus is the foundation of the Christian church, as Paul expresses this reality in his opening sentences of 1 Cor. 15. If the gospel is not true, then preaching and faith are in vain. Barth attacks theological attempts to move behind Paul's account of the resurrection in an attempt to uncover the very earliest, purest tradition of the resurrection in the early church. Such attempts are meaningless and impossible because the interpreter will stumble immediately upon the "riddle" of the resurrection.[10] Careful attempts at uncovering chronologically precise historical and factual data in Paul's account reveal this attempt's impossibility, for Paul's relation of the tradition that was handed down to him is not to be understood historically. Barth insists that we must read this section in terms of two pillars—*died* and *rose again*—between which are placed ac-

---

4. Ibid.
5. Ibid., 29–30.
6. Ibid., 222.
7. Ibid., 150.
8. Ibid., 429.
9. Barth, *Die Auferstehung der Toten*. ET: *Resurrection of the Dead.*
10. Ibid., 76.

counts of the burial and appearances of Jesus. Only Jesus' burial can be confirmed as a historical fact, but what kind of historical fact? For Barth, the frontier of history looming "before and behind" the real facts[11] is the key to understanding the resurrection of Jesus, for the intersection of the plane of history by this frontier is manifested in the person of Jesus. Barth believes that Paul cites the appearances of the risen Christ, not as historical proof of the resurrection, but to legitimize his own method.[12] In other words, Paul refers to the appearances of Christ to convince the Corinthians that the church itself—and Paul's apostolic authority—is rooted in nothing other than the appearances of the risen Lord.[13]

In his second section on the resurrection as the meaning of faith, Barth shows that Paul is basing Christian faith on the reality of the resurrection. If there be no general resurrection of the dead, then Christ is not raised. If Christ be not raised, then Christian faith is an illusion and a fiction.[14] "The Christian πιστις, faith, does not exist by itself, but rather by its relation to the πιστις του θεου, to the loyalty of God."[15] The implications of a general bodily resurrection are clear: the difficulty and distress of the Christian life are tempered by the "postulate of compensation from beyond."[16] But in the absence of the hope of resurrection, the resurrection of Christ, the kerygma, the forgiveness of sins, and faith in the beyond, Christian existence with its paradox as a whole is rendered a farce, a folly and a lunacy. The meaning of Christianity itself is nonsense without resurrection, if God is not God.[17]

Barth turns to Paul's discussions of the resurrection as truth and as reality in his next sections. Paul conceives the truth of the resurrection in terms of the resurrection of the body. As the seed must die before it

---

11. Ibid., 77.

12. Bultmann published a review of Barth's essay in 1926 in the *Theologische Blätter* entitled "Karl Barth, *Die Auferstehung der Toten*." ET: "Karl Barth, *The Resurrection of the Dead*." Some of his insights in this essay are particularly useful for understanding the larger scope of their debates. Here Bultmann disagrees with Barth, as he believes Paul attempts to make the resurrection of Christ credible as an objective, historical fact. Otherwise, Paul's reference to those witnesses of the resurrection who are still alive (including himself) becomes meaningless. Bultmann, "Karl Barth, *Die Auferstehung der Toten*," 54–55.

13. Barth, *Die Auferstehung der Toten*, 83.

14. Ibid., 90.

15. Ibid., 92–93.

16. Ibid., 95.

17. Ibid., 95–96.

becomes a plant, so must the human body die before it becomes a resurrection body.[18] For Barth it is crucial to recognize Paul's use of analogy. Of the resurrection proper nothing at all can be proved, but the character of the resurrection, if there is a resurrection, is shown purely hypothetically. Barth argues that between the present body and the resurrection body lies an inconceivable "critical point of new creation." It is the creation of a new body that has its roots in the old, the transition from a "psychical body" (σῶμα ψυχικον) to a "spiritual body" (σῶμα πνευματικον), the "new predication" of the body that is the resurrection of the dead.[19]

In his preaching of the resurrection of the body, Paul places the believer in the midst of the struggle of life. All are created between Adam and Christ, and all are in effect *both* Adam *and* Christ, belonging to both. All must journey from Adam to Christ, from death to life, and it is in this struggle that the resurrection is truth. Not in theory but in struggle is the resurrection to be understood as truth, and this is only possible in light of hope.[20] Barth quotes Calvin on hope in the resurrection: "if the hope of the resurrection be removed, the whole edifice of piety would collapse, just as if the foundation were withdrawn from it."[21] Nowhere is the presence of God stronger or more palpably real than in the eternal future, and for Barth everything depends on the victory given through Jesus Christ being and remaining God's gift present in hope.[22]

---

18. Bultmann rejects Barth at this point, for it is precisely at this point that Bultmann sees the disintegration of Barth's argument. The transition from seed to plant is in no sense a dying, because the seed is already essentially the plant. These two forms of the plant (seed and plant), while impossible to coexist simultaneously, in no way contradict each other. Bultmann accuses Barth of anthropomorphizing the plant, so as to draw an analogy to the resurrection of the human body. Barth attempts to conflate Paul's terms "body," "flesh," and "glory" (σῶμα, σαρξ, δοξα) into various forms of the same substance. Bultmann hesitates to use the terms "substance" and "form" as substitutions for σῶμα, and he accuses Barth of misunderstanding Paul's distinction between "terrestrial bodies" and "celestial bodies." Bultmann argues that for Barth to insist that the resurrection of the body is a mere transformation of forms or substances means that Paul's argument is lost. Bultmann agrees with Paul that the body is *transformed* in the resurrection, and he insists that it is the body that determines human existence as such. Because the body determines human existence, because the body is what I am as a human being, the body belongs to God. Bultmann, "Karl Barth, *Die Auferstehung der Toten*," 59–63.

19. Barth, *Die Auferstehung der Toten*, 114–15.

20. Ibid., 122.

21. Qtd. in ibid., 129.

22. Ibid., 128.

In the second part of the third volume of his *Kirchliche Dogmatik*, Barth engages Bultmann and his program of demythologizing, specifically in terms of the resurrection of Jesus. He begins with a discussion of Bultmann's treatment of the resurrection, as found in his essay "Neues Testament und Mythologie." As Barth reads Bultmann, Bultmann demythologizes the Easter event by interpreting it as the emergence of faith in the risen Lord, since it was this faith that produced the apostolic kerygma. For Barth this is unacceptable. Faith in the risen Lord springs from his historical manifestation, not from the faith of the disciples themselves. The resurrection itself, for Bultmann, is not simply an event in time but more significantly an eschatological event *beyond* time. This eschatological event includes the cross, the resurrection (in the sense of the awakening of the disciples' faith), and the preaching of the church. These events are eschatological, in that they occurred within time but also beyond time, with their significance comprehended only by faith. The bodily resurrection of Jesus (understood as the objective historical event of a dead man's restoration to life) is not included in this category of "eschatological event." Accounts of this event in the New Testament are mythical in nature and must therefore be demythologized. The true Easter event is the emergence of the disciples' faith, which was not based on an event in time but on the eschatological act of God.

Barth criticizes Bultmann here for relegating the earthly person of Jesus to a secondary, supporting role in faith. The disciples' recollections of this time are a memory of Jesus only insofar as it was in this time and this historical moment that the disciples became convinced of Jesus' significance. Jesus is at work at this time only in the faith of his followers, and there was no embodied personal encounter between Jesus and his disciples. Barth reads Bultmann to be implying that there was no real difference between "Jesus" and "disciples" in this time. There was no embodied personal encounter, no self-manifestation, and the disciples' faith "had no object distinct from its own reality, no preceding basis through which it could have been grounded as faith."[23] The act of God was identical with their own faith, and the fact that this happened in the disciples' minds is the foundation of the Christian faith. This, for Barth, is simply untenable.

Essentially disavowing his earlier protestations in the *Römerbrief*, the Barth of the *Kirchliche Dogmatik* maintains the direct opposite. Jesus *did* bodily rise again and *did* appear bodily to his disciples. This occurred as

23. Barth, *Kirchliche Dogmatik* III/2:534. ET: *Church Dogmatics* III/2.

such because the New Testament records it as such. This is the foundation of the Christian faith, the "eschatological event" of Easter. The act of God is the risen Lord's appearance as the incarnate Word, revealing himself to his disciples. The disciples' faith was established by God in this objective encounter, and their faith was the reflection of the meaning of Jesus' death only in a secondary sense. Jesus and his disciples were not identical in this event, but were distinctly separate people. Jesus was with them during this time of revelation. Otherwise, for Barth, there is no resurrection, no revelation, and no faith.

Following his outlining of his interpretation of the resurrection, Barth proceeds to offer five "axioms" of Bultmann's thought in terms of his program of demythologizing.

1. Bultmann maintains that a theological statement is valid only when it can be determined to be a genuine element of the Christian understanding of existence. Bultmann rejects the resurrection of Jesus as an event in time and space because it does not fulfill this first requirement. Barth accuses Bultmann of forcing his systematic theology and exegesis into this "anthropological corner," which continues a tradition reaching past Bultmann to Wilhelm Herrmann, Albrecht Ritschl, and Friedrich Schleiermacher.[24] Because Barth believes that this tradition can be exploited equally well in the opposite direction, there remains in this first axiom no genuine case against the resurrection of Jesus.

2. Bultmann insists that an event alleged to have occurred in time can be accepted as historical only if it can be verified as a historical fact (*ein historisches Faktum*). Bultmann rejects the claim that the resurrection of Jesus is a historical event (*ein historisches Ereignis*) because it is impossible for historical research to verify that this event actually occurred in space and time. Barth argues that even though modern historiography may not be able to verify that these events actually happened as recorded, this is no compelling reason to believe that they did not or even could not have happened. Barth rejects the idea that modern historical scholarship should be the final authority in these matters.

3. Barth reads Bultmann as insisting that the assertion of the facticity of an event that is inaccessible to historical verification is nothing more than blind acceptance of mythology, an arbitrary act, a descent from faith

---

24. One is reminded here of Barth's fulminations against liberal theologians, whom Barth accused of confusing anthropology for theology, or, in his memorable phrase, of speaking of God by speaking of humanity in a loud voice. Barth, *Word of God*, 196.

to works, a dishonest *sacrificium intellectus*. Barth disagrees, arguing that the New Testament presents the resurrection as good news that should be believed with a glad and grateful heart. This faith in the resurrection was made possible only by the resurrection itself. Thus there is no reason why this message, which was just as incredible in its own context as it is in our own, should not be believed today. There is no *sacrificium intellectus* involved for Barth.

4. According to Bultmann, modern thought is shaped by modern science, which means that the modern world-picture is incompatible with the mythical world-picture of the ancient world. Barth accuses Bultmann of rejecting the ancient world-picture based on preconceived criteria informed by modern science. Barth wonders if every modern believer is willing to affirm this sentiment. For some, there may be no difficulty in listening to a radio and at the same time affirming that Jesus rose from the dead as recorded in the New Testament.

5. Finally, Barth suspects Bultmann of believing that we are compelled to reject a statement if it is compatible with the mythical world-picture of the past. Barth rejects this claim as being a type of "politics of catastrophe." He doubts whether it is the Christian's position to accept or reject world-pictures, and he suggests that Christianity might be well served to employ remnants of mythical language if it serves the purpose of effectively witnessing to Jesus Christ. Barth is suspicious of any theologian who wishes to abandon entire systems, and thus he accuses Bultmann of substituting a psychological interpretation of the resurrection as the eruption of faith in the disciples for "genuine" faith in the resurrection of Jesus Christ from the dead.

For Barth, these five "Bultmannian axioms" are decisive reasons why, in spite of Bultmann's insistence on demythologizing, Christians must understand the resurrection of Jesus and his appearances to his disciples as genuine history (*Historie*).[25]

In the second part of the fourth volume of his *Kirchliche Dogmatik*, Barth treats the resurrection within his discussion of revelation. The resurrection is really a two-fold revelation: it is both God's revelation in Jesus Christ and also Jesus' own self-revelation as the Christ. The resurrection serves as the moment of revelation to Jesus' followers, as the "unveiling"

---

25. Barth, *Kirchliche Dogmatik* III/2:531–37. Two of Bultmann's students, Hartlich and Sachs, wrote a response to these five axioms in an essay entitled "Kritische Prüfung der Haupteinwände Barths gegen Bultmann."

of the hiddenness of Jesus' true identity as the Son of God. For Barth, the resurrection is an inwardly coherent event that happened within human history, within time and space. This event might not have been "historical" in the modern sense, but the fact that it was experienced and attested by witnesses affirms that the event occurred within time and space. Otherwise, Barth suggests, it could not be an event of revelation. The revelation is not the revelation of a new and different body, but it is the revelation of Jesus Christ as

> One, [who] in his history and existence is indeed the reconcilia-tion of the world with God, the new human, the dawn of the new creation and world. He is this, however, not first through his resur-rection. He became, was, and is this in his life and death. In his resurrection he reveals himself as the one who was, is and will be this One in his life and death.[26]

This revelation is an event in time and space, and as such it is possible for human beings to comprehend it. The resurrection event is the "con-cretely historical event [*geschichtliche Ereignis*] of the self-manifestation of Jesus after his death."[27] It is the event in which Jesus makes it possible for us to recognize the reconciliation of the world to God that takes place in his person. It is the event in which the will and the act of God are no longer hidden but are actualized on earth. The resurrection is the event of the dec-laration and impartation of the act and will of God. The "light of the event" is the light in which true knowledge arises: knowledge of the will and act of God. In terms of the New Testament texts themselves, Barth reads them as a clear and unanimous declaration that Christ is risen. He also understands that these texts imply the assertion that a dead man is alive and that his tomb is empty. But Barth stresses that these texts only *imply* this. If we abstract these implications from the fact that Christ is risen, we may then either accept or deny (or demythologize) them, but for Barth these implica-tions are wholly irrelevant for understanding the primary claim that Christ is risen. When we approach the resurrection as the event of revelation, we must acknowledge its miraculous character, which means acknowledging the inexplicable and inconceivable nature of the event. If we hope to acquire

---

26. Barth, *Kirchliche Dogmatic* IV/2:163. ET: *Church Dogmatics* IV/2.

27. Ibid. Unlike Bultmann, Barth places very little stock in the distinction between *Historie* and *Geschichte* and often uses the two terms interchangeably, as the context of this passage makes clear.

some kind of knowledge of the event itself, this knowledge can only be of our love for the God who first loved us in Jesus Christ.

But can there be genuine "historical" knowledge of this event? Barth offers a two-part response to this question. First, neutral, objective, historical knowledge of this event can only be found by looking at the texts that speak of it. The historical in this event is to be found only in these texts *as historical documents*. It is fruitless to search behind these texts for historical facts. For Barth, to search behind these texts for objective historical facts can only mean leading these texts away into a "Babylonian captivity," in which the texts have no power to speak of the event but are forced to speak to quite different concerns in quite different languages. Second, historical knowledge must really be impartial knowledge. The interpreter must approach the texts on the texts' terms, listening for what the texts themselves have to say. It is pointless and even dangerous for an interpreter to approach the texts with the "alien spectacles" of another world-picture, asking questions that the texts neither ask nor attempt to answer, and setting limits on what the text can and cannot address. Barth does recognize that truly impartial historical knowledge is not possible, because every interpreter brings a unique perspective to the task of interpretation. But it is not permissible, for Barth, to approach the texts with a predetermined "pre-understanding," for this will only lead the interpreter away from the message of the texts.

For Barth, the resurrection and the ascension are two distinct but inseparable moments of the same event. The resurrection is the event's *terminus a quo* (starting point), while the ascension is its *terminus ad quem* (ending point). The unifying factors in this event are the revelation and exaltation of Jesus. Barth insists that these two termini occur in time and space and that the revelation occurs as history in the resurrection and ascension of Jesus Christ, between these two termini. The New Testament records the resurrection and ascension of Jesus in terms of *directions*: Jesus is risen *from* the dead (εκ νεκρων) and he ascended *into* heaven (εις τον ουρανον). This emphasis on direction is quite significant for Barth, as each location expresses something about the person of Jesus Christ. In being raised *from the dead*, Jesus returns from that place where every human being must go. He returns from death, whence no human being has ever returned. Jesus Christ, the "Royal Man," returns from death to life, and in this return he is revealed to be the exalted Son of Man *and* the humiliated Son of God in all his glory. In his ascension *into heaven*, the place that belongs to God and whence only God can come and go, Jesus Christ is revealed as the One who *does* come from and who *does* go to this place. Barth describes this event as "The Homecoming of the Son of Man."[28]

In 1952, Barth published a pamphlet entitled *Rudolf Bultmann: Ein Versuch, ihn zu verstehen*, in which Barth publicly challenges Bultmann's methodological position. Of chief concern to Barth is Bultmann's insistence upon existential philosophy as a valid tool for theology, and with it the necessity of the program of demythologizing.

Barth begins his essay with a brief outline of Bultmann's hermeneutics, which he describes as being primarily concerned with understanding.[29] Barth also understands Bultmann's primary aim to be a presentation of the New Testament as the document of a *message [Botschaft]*. Thus Barth believes that for Bultmann the boundary between exegesis, dogmatics, and preaching is entirely abolished,[30] as all of it is subsumed under the category of hermeneutics. In terms of this message, Barth understands Bultmann's point to be that to understand the New Testament is to believe it, and to exposit the message is to proclaim it.[31] The essence of this message is its contemporaneity in its proclamation. The message originated in history, but it is present everywhere it is proclaimed for everyone who hears it. This message brings the hearer into relation with God and it challenges the hearer to a decision of faith, the choice between obedience and disobedience.[32] Thus the New Testament message is "existential" and its true understanding becomes an event.

Barth disagrees with Bultmann at precisely this point. For Barth, any relationship between faith and self-understanding can only have negative consequences. Upon hearing the message of the New Testament, one is indeed turned inward in self-understanding, but with purely negative results. The existential act can only be a complete renunciation of every understanding and explanation of the self, a complete contradiction of the previous understanding. This is accomplished because the message of the

---

28. Barth, *Kirchliche Dogmatik*, IV/2:156–72.

29. Barth goes so far as to suggest that "the name Rudolf Bultmann and the concept of 'understanding' remain inseparably linked." Barth, *Rudolf Bultmann: Ein Versuch, ihn zu verstehen*, 3.

30. Ibid., 4.

31. Ibid., 5.

32. Although Barth himself does not make this connection in this instance, perhaps here we can see the important differences between the Calvinist Barth and the Lutheran Bultmann, specifically in the latter's emphasis on the elements of decision and obedience in faith.

New Testament requires the hearer to turn away from the self, to look instead where the New Testament points.[33]

Barth emphasizes the relationship between what he calls the "primary" and "secondary" tasks of New Testament interpretation. For Barth, the primary task of interpretation is to listen to what the New Testament has to say on its own terms. The secondary task is to translate this message into language intelligible in and for the present. He accuses Bultmann of too quickly abandoning the primary task by immediately attacking the historical forms of the New Testament texts. Barth accuses Bultmann of misunderstanding the primary object of New Testament interpretation, which, for Barth, is the One who is contained within the New Testament message: Jesus Christ. He is contained in the "cradle of language," the thought-forms of the first century. But what is the object of interpretation? Is it these thought-forms, or is it the One who is expressed within these forms? Barth accuses Bultmann of ignoring the object because of the form in and through which it is expressed. Barth insists that the task of translation is only a secondary concern, and that the primary concern is the task of encountering the New Testament message on its own terms.[34] If interpreters attempt to translate the message before the message itself is understood, then they will present a skewed interpretation of the text, based more on their own pre-conceived expectations than on a faithful reading of the text.

Barth specifically attacks Bultmann's admission of unavoidable "pre-understandings" in the work of exegesis, and it is through this attack that Barth challenges Bultmann's program of demythologizing. Barth cannot follow Bultmann in his emphasis on "pre-understanding."[35] Is it possible, asks Barth, to understand any text (ancient or modern) if the reader approaches it with a set of preconceived notions about the limits to which the

33. Barth, *Rudolf Bultmann: Ein Versuch, ihn zu verstehen*, 6. As David Congdon points out, this is a typical misunderstanding of Bultmann's use of the term "self-understanding." Rather than turning the individual inward, Bultmann intends "self-understanding" to signal a radical disjunction within the self, such that I am shown my true self in relation to the God who graciously frees me from bondage to myself (i.e., sin). As Congdon puts it, "*Self-understanding is the event in which a person encounters the word of God and so discovers herself to be a sinner who has received justification by God's grace, and who has therefore been given a new future, a new life, a new world.* Faith as self-understanding has nothing to do with a solipsistic turning inward upon oneself. It rather means *being placed outside ourselves* and into a new historical existence . . . " Congdon, *Rudolf Bultmann*, 59; emphasis in original.

34. Barth, *Rudolf Bultmann: Ein Versuch, ihn zu verstehen*, 7–8.

35. See Bultmann's essay, "Ist voraussetzungslose Exegese möglich?"

text can be understood?[36] Would it not be more fruitful to approach the text with an open mind, allowing the text to speak on its own terms? How can the reader decide what is true or false in terms of the text's spirit, content, and aim by utilizing an alien criterion? And what if the exegete assumes that this "provisional working hypothesis" is an infallible interpretive tool? Surely the true spirit, content, and aim of the text would be lost. In Barth's opinion, Bultmann is guilty of precisely this error. Barth criticizes Bultmann for making the provisional hypothesis of demythologizing, which is an alien criterion, the infallible tool for his exegesis.[37]

Barth presses this line of attack: why do the mythical elements of the New Testament need interpretation at all? Why do we not allow them to say what they say on their own terms? For Bultmann, this simply is not possible in a modern world, as modern people do not (and cannot) think mythologically. For modern people, the mythological elements of the New Testament kerygma render the content of the message unintelligible. Barth argues that this is not the case. He believes the New Testament intends to say exactly what it *does* say, that God condescended to become incarnate in this world in Jesus Christ. It is the goal of the New Testament to speak of the God who is capable of just such condescension. And it was precisely this condescended God whom the disciples touched, saw, and heard in their own time and space. Barth accuses Bultmann of refusing to allow the kerygma to reveal that which causes faith (namely, for Barth, the revelation of the crucified one in the visible, historical, earthly realm). He accuses Bultmann of denying the internal and intrinsic significance of the Christ-event, and this ultimately leads Barth to accuse Bultmann's demythologized kerygma of a creeping Docetism, precisely by denying the true humanity of Jesus Christ.[38]

Barth's more specific charge against Bultmann is that his insistence upon an existentialist interpretation places interpreters in "Heideggerian

36. This section refers to Bultmann's insistence that the world-picture of the New Testament cannot be accepted by modern people. Bultmann is often accused of using the modern scientific world-picture as the criterion for judging the New Testament, even though Bultmann himself denies this in his essay "Zum Problem der Entmythologisierung" (1952), 184. Barth himself admits that this characterization of Bultmann may be misleading: "The old Rationalists, after D. F. Strauss, *believed* in a modern world-picture . . . Bultmann does not. He knows that it is relative. It has for him only de facto, not de jure authority." Barth, *Rudolf Bultmann: Ein Versuch, ihn zu verstehen*, 42; emphasis in original.

37. Ibid., 30–31.

38. Ibid., 33–34.

armor." In order to demythologize the New Testament kerygma on Bultmann's terms, it is first necessary to understand certain Heideggerian concepts. First, one must understand that all understanding is concerned with the individual's own self-understanding. Second, Heidegger has a specific way of understanding self-understanding, in that self-understanding is caught between authenticity and inauthenticity, between past and future. Thus the New Testament is primarily concerned with anthropology, and more specifically this anthropology must be understood in an existentialist fashion if it is to be understood properly. Barth sees only one place in all of Bultmann's theology that is not utterly dependent on Heidegger, and that is in Bultmann's treatment of the transition from unfaith to faith, from inauthentic to authentic existence, as an act of God. Here, and only here, in Barth's opinion, does Bultmann act independently as a theologian.[39]

In a letter dated June 8th, 1928, Bultmann responds with a blistering critique of Barth's supposed independence from philosophy:

> You have a sovereign scorn for modern work in philosophy, especially phenomenology. What point is there in saying occasionally that the dogmatician must also be oriented to philosophical work if the presentation finds no place for this orientation . . .? It seems to me that you are guided by a concern that theology should achieve emancipation from philosophy. You try to achieve this by ignoring philosophy. The price you pay for this is that of falling prey to an outdated philosophy. For because faith is the faith of a believer, i.e., an existent person (I can also say: because the justified person is the sinner), dogmatics can speak *only in existential-ontological terms.*[40]

Barth, in response, outlines two specific problems with Bultmann's definition of myth and his method of demythologizing. The first is philosophical, and the second (and more serious) is theological. First, Barth refuses to concede that myth can be interpreted exclusively as the expression of a particular self-understanding. He cites numerous varieties of myth—Teutonic, Egyptian, Greek, Modern (the myths of Marxism or the Christian West), etc.—to support his resistance to the assumption that all myths in all times and in all places have attempted exclusively to express a particular understanding of human existence. Are all myths anthropological in nature, recognizing and speaking exclusively to the human subject

39. Ibid., 37–38.

40. Jaspert and Bromiley, *Karl Barth/Rudolf Bultmann Letters*, 38–39; emphasis mine.

alone? But it is the second, theological question that is far more serious for Barth. He worries what will become of the Christian kerygma if it is "so tightly clamped in this vice," asking only about the self-understanding of the human being. Are we not refusing to allow the New Testament to proclaim the act of God in Jesus Christ when we refuse to admit that such things as the New Testament proclaims are really possible?[41]

Barth attempts to offer an explanation of Bultmann's intentions in his program of demythologizing. He concedes that several options are available, although none seems accurately to fit. First, Barth offers the explanation that Bultmann is quite simply a Rationalist, a new David Friedrich Strauss. The emphasis on demythologizing casts Bultmann in this light, as it appears that everything in Christianity is abandoned that is not acquitted in Reason's court. But for Bultmann demythologizing is only a secondary concern. The point of demythologizing, Barth thinks, is only to clear a path for existentialist interpretation. The difference between Bultmann and the Rationalists lies in the difference in their world-pictures. The Rationalists truly *believed* in the modern world-picture, but Bultmann does not. He recognizes that this world-picture, as all world-pictures, is contingent and relative, so he uses it as a tool rather than as the final criterion of truth.

Perhaps Bultmann is an apologist, in the tradition of Schleiermacher's attempts to make religion palpable to the "cultured despisers."[42] Bultmann's work does exhibit a certain pastoral concern for the modern person, and he is deeply concerned with making the gospel intelligible to modern people. Barth admits, however, that Bultmann would bristle at the use of the term "apologist" to describe him and his work, and he also admits that Bultmann's apologetics are at best only a by-product of his work.[43]

---

41. Barth, *Rudolf Bultmann: Ein Versuch, ihn zu verstehen*, 39–40. Here Barth appears to have misunderstood Bultmann. He largely ignores Bultmann's emphasis on the kerygma as an event in the life of the hearer. The emphasis on human existence and self-understanding serves to place the emphasis on the word of proclamation as an *event* here and now. The kerygma is a life-altering word addressed to the individual, and the true force of this word can be understood only in terms of the hearer's own self-understanding. Existentialism is not the only tool available to the expositor, and it certainly does not exhibit the characteristics of totalitarianism that Barth ascribes to it. Existentialism *is* an important resource for Bultmann's theology, but more central is the Word of God and the transformation of the individual hearer, i.e., the justification of the sinner.

42. See Schleiermacher, *Über die Religion*. ET: *On Religion*.

43. Here, perhaps, David Congdon's suggestion that Bultmann should be understood as a missionary to modernity is more apt than Barth's suggestion of "apologist" to describe Bultmann's theological project.

Perhaps he is simply a historian standing in the tradition of the nineteenth century. Is he a scholar divesting himself of his prejudices in order to study the New Testament as a document of a particular time and place, concluding that the genuine form of the kerygma is to be found in the Pauline epistles and interpreted in a Johannine framework? Is it Bultmann *the historian* who, as an unprejudiced interpreter of Scripture, has discovered the true intention of the New Testament—to express a particular understanding of human existence—and that demythologizing and existentialist interpretation are relevant even from a strictly academic perspective? His works *Geschichte der synoptischen Tradition*[44] and *Das Urchristentum im Rahmen der antiken Religionen*[45] exhibit Bultmann's capacity for historical research, and it is possible to read these texts without accepting his existential interpretation. But Bultmann is not merely a historian. His work cannot be read without taking seriously his devotion to the tasks of theology. Bultmann, even Bultmann the historian, never simply asks "what happened," but is always concerned with the implications of historical research for dogmatics, exegesis, and preaching. For Bultmann historical judgments are never the final judgments, and history serves its purpose only as a resource for doing theology.

Perhaps, Barth continues, the secret to Bultmann lies in his discovery of a new philosophical tool for theology. Is Bultmann's greatest contribution to theology his rigorous application of existentialism to theological investigations? Bultmann discovered existentialism after meeting Heidegger in Marburg, after which he began to apply this new philosophical tool to his theological work. Is this something new in Bultmann? Did not Thomas use Aristotle, Augustine Neoplatonism, and Strauss Hegel? Certainly Bultmann is no different. And yet Barth is convinced that Bultmann is largely misunderstood because he places such exclusive emphasis on existentialism that it appears as though he had discovered the only key to theology, even though Bultmann repeatedly emphasizes that he uses existential philosophy *only as a tool*. Just as it is inaccurate to regard Bultmann primarily as a historian, so too is it inaccurate to regard him primarily as a philosopher.

Finally, Barth suggests that perhaps Bultmann is simply a Lutheran *sui generis*, as Barth notices a striking affinity between Bultmann's system

44. Bultmann, *Geschichte der Synoptischen Tradition*. ET: *History of the Synoptic Tradition*.

45. Bultmann, *Das Urchristentum im Rahmen der antiken Religionen*. ET: *Primitive Christianity*.

and Melanchthon's *Loci Communes*.[46] Bultmann himself cites Melanchthon's famous dictum, "To know Christ is to know his benefits, not to look upon his nature and mode of incarnation," as legitimization for his program of demythologizing.[47] Melanchthon's reluctance to ground faith in historical knowledge likewise finds expression in Bultmann's thought. As Melanchthon puts it in the German version of the Augsburg Confession, "We must also explain that we are not talking here about the faith possessed by the devils and the ungodly, who also believe the historical facts that Christ suffered and was raised from the dead. But we are talking about true faith, which trusts that we obtain grace and forgiveness of sin through Christ."[48] Melanchthon's (and Luther's) work, like Bultmann's, moves about within the anthropological triangle of law, sin, and grace, with the Pauline epistles being promoted to the status of a canon within the canon. Bultmann himself has suggested that his program of demythologizing is a consistent application of the Lutheran-Pauline doctrine of justification by faith to epistemology.[49] His nuanced distinction between the sacred and the secular, his emphasis on anthropology, the central position of the word of proclamation in his theology, and his characteristic insistence on the *sola fide* all belie a Lutheran heritage. Even his fondness for existentialism can be traced back to the Lutheran father of existentialism, Søren Kierkegaard. Bultmann's work is inconceivable apart from his Lutheran background; therefore Barth cautions those who wish to strike at Bultmann, "lest they accidentally meet Luther, who in Bultmann is somehow also on the scene."[50]

In a letter dated November 11th–15th, 1952, Bultmann responds to Barth's criticisms of him in *Rudolf Bultmann: Ein Versuch, ihn zu verstehen*.[51]

---

46. Melanchthon, *Loci Communes*. ET: *Melanchthon on Christian Doctrine*.

47. Melanchthon, quoted in Bultmann, "Zum Problem der Entmythologisierung" (1952), 184–85. This dictum also could be cited in favor of Bultmann's insistence that the quest for the historical Jesus is theologically unnecessary.

48. "Die augsburgische Konfession," 79–80. ET: "Augsburg Confession."

49. Bultmann, "Zum Problem der Entmythologisierung" (1952), 207.

50. Barth, *Rudolf Bultmann: Ein Versuch, ihn zu verstehen*, 48.

51. This is in part a response to an appendix to Barth's essay on Bultmann. In the appendix, written immediately after receiving the second volume of *Kerygma und Mythos*, Barth reacts to what he perceives as an impasse in the Bultmann discussion. He regrets the unwillingness of Bultmann's students to engage in serious debate over their teacher's program, and two of Bultmann's students specifically attack Barth in their essay in the volume. See Hartlich and Sachs, "Kritische Prüfung der Haupteinwande Barths gegen Bultmann." The Hartlich and Sachs essay is in response to a selection from the second part of the third volume of Barth's *Kirchliche Dogmatik* (pp. 531–37), in which Barth

Bultmann concedes that the root of their disagreement is their respective attitudes toward philosophy and its usefulness for theology. He is convinced that philosophical (and particularly existential-ontological) reflection is necessary for theology, and he suggests that the reason Barth does not understand him is because Barth does not fully understand the importance and indeed the necessity of philosophy for theology. In Barth's response to Bultmann's letter (dated December 24th, 1952), he admits that he cannot and will not take existential philosophy seriously. Barth writes, "The most triumphant expansion of that philosophy over the whole earth could not make the slightest impression on me . . . I am not an enemy of philosophy as such, but I have hopeless reservations about the claim to absoluteness of any philosophy, epistemology, or methodology."[52]

A second problem lies in Barth's misperception of the importance of translation. Bultmann stresses that, if the proclamation of the church is to be intelligible to modern people, it must be extricated from a dated world-picture. This is the justification for demythologizing. Modern people are increasingly aware that they cannot achieve full self-understanding with the outdated world-picture of the Bible, but must adopt a modern world-picture in order to fully understand themselves; hence the need for existential philosophy. Bultmann believes that the fundamental issue is that the situation of the modern person demands existential interpretation of the kerygma. It is because Barth cannot see this problem in the same light that he fails to understand Bultmann.

In terms of the specific sections of Barth's essay, Bultmann offers equally specific rejoinders in his letter. Bultmann corrects Barth's judgment of his interpretation of faith as understanding.[53] He clarifies this statement to mean that understanding is only understanding of the question of decision that is posed to the expositor. The "Yes," in which understanding becomes faith and exposition becomes preaching, can be understood only

---

offers the five "Bultmannian axioms" (discussed above). In his appendix to *Rudolf Bultmann: Ein Versuch, ihn zu Verstehen*, Barth reacts sarcastically to this jointly written essay, which he describes as an attempt to "finish him." See Barth, *Rudolf Bultmann: Ein Versuch, ihn zu verstehen*, 54.

52. Jaspert and Bromiley, *Karl Barth/Rudolf Bultmann Letters*, 104–8.

53. Barth discusses the relationship between the hearer and the messenger, between the believers and the disciples, writing, "And so understanding can take place only in participation in the life of this, their message. Their understanding is always already faith, and their exposition itself is already preaching." Barth, *Rudolf Bultmann: Ein Versuch, ihn zu verstehen*, 5.

as a gift of the Spirit, not as a result of the expositor's own effort alone.[54] Expositors cannot enter into the task of exposition with a feeling of obligation to believe. Nor can they offer their own exposition as *direct* preaching. The expositor can only labor to show that the questions of decision posed in the text are also posed to the hearer, and in this way exposition becomes *indirect* preaching.

Barth understands Bultmann's attempt at making the New Testament kerygma accessible to moderns to proceed first through understanding it in its original historical form, and then translating it into other (i.e., modern) forms. Bultmann disagrees with the "first . . . then" in Barth's analysis. He understands the New Testament message to be historical knowledge in union with the original historical form, and thus he suggests that the work of translation was already begun in the New Testament itself. He prefers to think of the work of translation as happening simultaneously with understanding the message. I hear the message in my own existence, and in understanding it I am already translating it precisely because I can only understand it within my own situation. Again, the understanding of the question of existence is identical with translation, but the believing "Yes" is the gift of the Spirit. There is thus a crucial distinction here between the work of theology and the leap of faith.

Bultmann sees the question of translation as a natural consequence of work done in form criticism,[55] which illuminates the difficulty of precisely defining the kerygma. Theology can only ever be presented in controversy, in specific antitheses. Dogmatic formulations are only ever provisional, and the content of theological reflection must continuously be translated in order to speak effectively to the present situation.

The offense of the kerygma is the crucial element in Bultmann's program. But what is the offense of the New Testament? Barth asks, "May a faithful translation of the New Testament to modern hearers conceal the

54. In his letter to Bultmann dated December 24, 1952, Barth relates to Bultmann that his best and most peaceful thoughts of him are of Bultmann attempting a theology of the third article. Barth wishes Bultmann would make a more serious effort at clarifying the relationship between the second and third articles, while maintaining the dignity and distinction of both. If only Bultmann could accomplish this, their discussion could be much more fruitful. Barth admits that he would no longer be forced to oppose Bultmann so vehemently, and that he might even *"heideggern"* a little with him. At least the whale and the elephant would at last have a common theme. Jaspert and Bromiley, *Karl Barth/ Rudolf Bultmann Letters*, 104–8.

55. See Bultmann, *Die Erforschung der synoptischen Evangelien*, for his contribution to the development of form criticism.

hard fact that the difference of New Testament thought is something other, something opposed to that which is familiar?"[56] Bultmann responds that this is not the case at all, but that everything depends on what is understood by the "hard fact" of the offense. The offense that the New Testament is mythological is significant only in that it shows modern people that the offense it causes is a false offense. The New Testament world of thought is indeed substantially different from the modern world of thought, but this is not the true offense of the New Testament. The mythology of the New Testament attempts to objectify that which cannot be objectified,[57] and modern people likewise attempt the same objectification in an effort to understand their own existence. The genuine offense of the New Testament to modern people is that they are not supposed to think of themselves by means of objectifying thinking, which is ultimately an attempt to find security. The offense of the New Testament is that it shatters security by demonstrating that authentic existence can be found only in the surrender of security to the grace of God. This surrender for the sake of authentic existence therefore demands an existential interpretation. The New Testament must be interpreted existentially, for Bultmann, in order to show that the New Testament kerygma is in utter opposition to my own inauthentic existence. Translation must demonstrate that God has acted *pro me*, because modern people cannot understand the mythologically formulated expressions of this act in the New Testament as being relevant to their existence unless they are translated.

Bultmann now turns to Barth's treatment of the Christ event in Bultmann's theology, in which Barth attempts to determine Bultmann's exact understanding of the relationship between Christ and the kerygma.[58] Bultmann insists that Christ, insofar as he is relevant *pro me*, *is* the kerygma, because he is Christ only as he is Christ *pro me*, and as such he is encountered only in the kerygma. If Christ were not really present in the kerygma and in faith, then "Christ" would be a mere mythical figure. Thus Christology

---

56. Barth, *Rudolf Bultmann: Ein Versuch, ihn zu verstehen*, 13.

57. At a later point in his letter, Bultmann argues that the decisive point in demythologizing is not that the New Testament world-picture is outdated, but that all myth is objectifying. He insists that he does not replace mythical thinking with an objectifying science, but that he attempts to eliminate objectification altogether. Barth, in his letter of December 24, 1952, conversely blames Bultmann for unduly favoring a consistent "subjectivizing."

58. See Barth, *Rudolf Bultmann: Ein Versuch, ihn zu verstehen*, 17ff, for this discussion.

and soteriology form a substantial unity (perhaps we may even label this blending of the two loci "soterology").

Bultmann admits that God's act in Christ precedes faith and that the kerygma is a *verbum externum*, but it need not follow that Christology must precede soteriology in theological analysis and explication. Barth criticizes Bultmann for refusing to admit that there is an "inherent significance" in the cross that precedes faith.[59] Bultmann affirms this criticism, arguing that he cannot understand the term "inherent significance" because he can only understand significance in terms of relation. The cross is only significant to me because I have a relation to it. It is significant only insofar as it is significant *pro me*.

The discussion of the act of God proceeds from the discussion of the significance of the cross, and here Barth and Bultmann debate the meaning of "eschatological." Bultmann reads Barth's interpretation of the resurrection as "eschatological" as an unclear formulation, and it is precisely the definition of "eschatological" that poses the problem. For Bultmann, the "eschatological" event begins in time, but it is not an event that can be fixed in time; it is an event that is always present in proclamation. It is an event outside of time, in that it puts an end to secular time. The paradox of the event is that it puts an end to time while beginning at a certain point in time while also continuing in time. The paradox may also be described as the event in which God's time enters secular time. It is impossible to establish first that Christ's crucifixion is the saving event and then to believe in it as such, because one would first have to accept that Jesus is the Christ before actually believing him to be so. For Bultmann, the crucifixion can be regarded as the saving act of God only in faith. To have faith in Christ and to understand the crucifixion as God's saving act, as the salvation-event, are identical.

The remainder of Bultmann's letter primarily discusses Barth's various criticisms of his emphasis on "pre-understanding." Barth argues that it is illegitimate to approach the New Testament with a set of pre-conceived notions about its content. The reader must allow the New Testament to say what it wants on its own terms. Anything else simply is bad exegesis.[60] Bultmann counters that this effort to read the New Testament without presuppositions is impossible for a historically-contingent, historically-existing

59. Ibid., 20.
60. Ibid., 30ff.

person.[61] Even the attempt to maintain that the only presupposition is the lack of presuppositions is not valid, because every reader will approach a text with a personal history. Perhaps as an illustration of that last point and in a sign that he regrets the acrimony of their debate,[62] Bultmann closes with a quotation from *Figaro*: "How can I be angry? My heart speaks for thee! . . . Sorrow be forever banned!"[63]

In the years following the Second World War, Bultmann's students and sympathizers (most notably Ernst Käsemann, Gerhard Ebeling, Ernst Fuchs, Friedrich Gogarten, Walter Sachs, and Christian Hartlich) inherited the questions of myth, history, and the historical Jesus. Käsemann and Ebeling retreated from Bultmann's position that the quest for the historical Jesus is theologically irrelevant, instead suggesting that questioning behind the kerygma to the historical Jesus who is proclaimed in it is not only possible but also necessary. Others argued that Bultmann did not reach the logical conclusions suggested by his own work and pushed Bultmann's thoughts further by attempting to demythologize even the "act of God."

The debate between Barth and Bultmann ended with Barth's death in 1968, but the questions they raised and the responses they offered continued to influence the work of successive generations. The questions of myth and history, the role of existential philosophy in theological discussions, and the relationship between the Jesus of history and the Christ of faith remained important topics for research and debate for a generation after Barth and Bultmann.

In the years following the Barth-Bultmann debate, theologians of the next generation continued to wrestle with the questions of myth, history, kerygma, and faith that had occupied their teachers. Existential philosophy continued to play an important role in these discussions, but theologians attempted to develop their own theologies of existence rather than rely on previously determined categories. Left- and right-wing Bultmannians pushed the limits of Bultmann's position, focusing on demythologizing the act of God on the one hand, and renewing attempts to question behind the kerygma to the historical Jesus on the other. The relationship between myth and history remained a challenge and the resurrection

61. See Bultmann, "Ist voraussetzungslose Exegese möglich?"; and Bultmann, "Das Problem der Hermeneutik." ET: "Problem of Hermeneutics."

62. Bultmann writes that he finds Barth's appendix (Barth, *Rudolf Bultmann: Ein Versuch, ihn zu verstehen*, 54–56) painful, because it was obviously written in irritation.

63 Bultmann's letter dated November 11–15, 1952, Jaspert and Bromiley, *Karl Barth/ Rudolf Bultmann Letters*, 87–104.

remained a focal point of the debates. The questions remained the same; only the responses changed.

Three post-Bultmannian theologians offer significant contributions to the discussion of the resurrection and the role of myth and history. Wolfhart Pannenberg examines the nature of history, historical method, and the place of historical criticism in theological method; Eberhard Jüngel investigates the christological implications of the debate over the resurrection; and Ingolf Ulrich Dalferth explores the possibility of theology moving beyond the categories of myth and logos in order to develop a theological grammar of the awakened Crucified. It is to these next generations that we now turn.

After Bultmann

CHAPTER FIVE

Wolfhart Pannenberg on History and the Resurrection

WOLFHART PANNENBERG (1928–2014)[1] SPENT much of his career investigating the relationship between theology and history in Protestant systematic theology. His work includes studies of revelation,[2] theological anthropology,[3] Christology, historical method, and the concept of universal history. In terms of the present discussion, Pannenberg is particularly interested in the relationship between theology and history in theological explication of the resurrection of Jesus of Nazareth.

For Pannenberg, the chief issue at stake in these debates is the use of the historical-critical method to analyze the biblical accounts of the resurrection. He operates with a precise definition of historical method, which he discusses in essays on hermeneutics and universal history. For Pannenberg, the history of Jesus can be interpreted properly only in terms of a "universal history" (*Universalgeschichte*), which includes in it the history of Israel and what he calls "Yahwistic" history, or the history of God's relationship with Israel. Because Jesus and his disciples were Jews, their messianic understanding, their conceptions of the resurrection of the dead, and their theological world-picture must be understood in terms of Israel's theology of history.[4] Based on this understanding of historical consciousness,

---

1. At the time of his death Pannenberg was Emeritus Professor of Systematic Theology at the Protestant Theological Faculty in Munich.

2. See especially Pannenberg, "Offenbarung und 'Offenbarungen.'" For his discussion of the relationship between myth and faith in the revelation, see "Die Weltgründende Funktion des Mythos und der christliche Offenbarungsglaube."

3. See especially *Anthropologie in theologischer Perspektive*. ET: *Anthropology in Theological Perspective*.

4. See Pannenberg, "Heilsgeschehen und Geschichte," ET: "Redemptive Event and

Pannenberg argues for a universal-historical approach to New Testament interpretation that includes everything from Israel's historical conscious-ness to the New Testament inheritance of that historical consciousness and also our contemporary historical consciousness, all conceived as an overarching unity.

Pannenberg recognizes a significant problem in New Testament interpretation, namely the relationship between history and hermeneu-tics. These two disciplines actually combine to represent a single theme for Pannenberg, but each discipline requires a distinct treatment and a specific understanding. In terms of the interpretation of texts, Pannenberg recognizes that a gulf has opened up between the literal meaning of the texts and the events they describe, on one side, and the distance between those events and the contemporary situation, on the other.[5] He highlights the development of a "tendency critique," in which the interpreter seeks to go behind the texts to gain an impression of the general tendency of the events they describe, as a move toward the necessary recognition of the immense distance between the thought-world of the New Testament and that of the contemporary world. This awareness of the distance be-tween the New Testament and the present created the central hermeneuti-cal problem of the modern era: that of intelligibly spanning this distance between the New Testament world and the present.[6] It is precisely for this reason that Pannenberg carefully distinguishes between the tasks of his-torical research and hermeneutics.

The historical task is to go behind the texts to the events they describe, while the hermeneutical task is to bridge the chasm between these texts and the present. The question for Pannenberg is whether the totality of this task is best described as history or hermeneutics. Insofar as the attempt to go behind texts arises only when these texts are interpreted, the task is pri-marily a task of hermeneutics. But insofar as historical questioning of the

---

History," for his discussion of the relationship between the understanding of history in the New Testament and in Israel. Here Pannenberg argues that Bultmann fails to recog-nize this relationship, due especially to his "eschatologizing" of history and his emphasis on the apocalyptic nature of the New Testament conception of history. Pannenberg ar-gues that the New Testament operates with a specifically Jewish understanding of history and that the eschatological and apocalyptic character of the New Testament need not stand in opposition to the historical consciousness of Israel.

5. Pannenberg, "Hermeneutik und Universalgeschichte," 90. ET: "Hermeneutic and Universal History."

6. Ibid., 91.

texts includes the task of interpreting the texts in light of universal history (which includes the life of the interpreter), the task is primarily historical.

The hermeneutical approach, according to Pannenberg, moves exclusively between the past text and the present interpreter,[7] whereas the historical approach involves a "detour" behind the texts to the events they describe. This detour is required by the texts themselves, in that they speak of an event that lies behind the texts. Historical work always implies the problem of universal history, because these texts have a significance in the present. They are not simply dead remnants of the past, so that the task of the historian becomes analogous to a caretaker of a cemetery.[8] The fact that the meaning of texts is never exhausted when they are understood merely as remnants of the past is the basis of the relative independence of hermeneutics from historical research. But because contemporary historical science continues to regard universal history as a peripheral issue rather than its central task, history ought to be subsumed into hermeneutics.[9]

At the same time, Pannenberg recognizes a fundamental unity between theological and historical hermeneutics. It is a reality inherent in hermeneutics that the same text will yield a plurality of interpretations. While this multiplicity of interpretations is of interest to theologians, it is not the primary interest of theological hermeneutics to consider these various interpretations. A multiplicity of interpretations, for Pannenberg, ought to be considered more a source of embarrassment than of satisfaction for theologians. Nevertheless, the task of theology is to examine and interpret these various interpretations, because the theologian is concerned with the ultimate validity of the truth about which theology is concerned. Theologians, faced with a plurality of interpretations, search for criteria that allow these interpretations to be measured against the source of the Christian tradition. This search leads the theologian to inquire into the relationship between historical and theological knowledge.

While the theologian seeks to measure the plurality of interpretations against the source of the Christian tradition (whether that source is the already pluralized early Christian proclamation of Christ or the historical Jesus himself), the historian seeks to measure the plurality of historical

---

7. Ricoeur has argued that it is the task of hermeneutics to approach the "world in front of the text," rather than move behind it to understand the intention of the author. In this way the interpreter recognizes that the text itself is a new creation, and the text is allowed to speak on its own terms. See Ricoeur, "Task of Hermeneutics."

8. Pannenberg, "Hermeneutik und Universalgeschichte," 93.

9. Ibid., 95.

interpretations against the facticity of the subject matter, which is inherent in the object of inquiry. Historical interpretations, however, must recognize that there is a meaning and a significance that is not exhausted by the facticity of the subject matter. It is because of the meaning and significance of the event that historical interpretation is expressed in a multiplicity of forms, and this multiplicity requires ongoing discussion and interpretation.[10]

For Pannenberg, then, theological and historical hermeneutics meet precisely at the point of the historical person of Jesus of Nazareth. Historical hermeneutics is interested in this person as a historical person, while theological hermeneutics is interested in this person as the source of the Christian tradition. Because this historical person constitutes in his person a central theme in universal history, the distinction between historical and theological hermeneutics remains a crucial one. The issue here highlights the importance of the responsibility of hermeneutics to the present, and this responsibility itself requires the hermeneutical efforts at bridging the chasm between the New Testament and the present.

In terms of the historical-critical method and New Testament interpretation, Pannenberg recognizes a fundamental antithesis between the biblical history of God and the world-picture of the historical-critical method, ascribing to the latter an "anthropocentric character."[11] The modern historical-critical method is marked by anthropocentricity, because this methodology removes from its interpretation any vestiges of divine causality as a matter of methodological principle. Historical events are caused by human beings and thus can and must be reconstructed by analogy to the universally human.[12] Historical events cannot be investigated as isolated events, but must be investigated as events that are reciprocally connected to other historical events. Because this is so, Pannenberg regards any attempts at relegating biblical events to "primal history" (*Urgeschichte*) or at separating salvation history (*Heilsgeschichte*) from secular history as inconsistent on both theological and historical grounds.[13] Instead, he acknowledges no necessary opposition between historical method and a theology of history.

---

10. Pannenberg, "Über historische und theologische Hermeneutik." ET: "On Historical and Theological Hermeneutic."

11. Pannenberg, "Heilsgeschehen und Geschichte," 260.

12. See especially Troeltsch, "Über historische und dogmatische Methode in der Theologie."

13. Pannenberg, "Heilsgeschehen und Geschichte," 261.

The key to the relation between historical method and theology, in his opinion, lies in the principle of analogy in historical understanding, which is the foundation of the historical method.[14] The principle of analogy, in essence, is that something difficult to understand is to be understood by historians in terms of something that lies closer to their own experience of the world. There is an anthropocentric bias inherent in this method, because something that is unknown or unintelligible can only be discovered and interpreted in terms of what is already known in human experience. Pannenberg accuses modern historians of focusing too narrowly on the general and the typical in history at the expense of the individual and the novel in history. These historians, operating with a bias toward the typical, threaten to ignore the particularity of phenomena on which genuine historical interest should be focused. He specifically accuses Heidegger's existential analysis of sacrificing the particular in favor of his attempt to understand historical processes as expressions of various modes of human existence.[15]

Pannenberg insists that theology must take a "burning interest" in historical method, but because of the activity of the transcendent God, who is constantly creating something new, theology must be interested primarily in the particular, the unique, and the novel in history.[16] In this sense, application of analogies is a vital tool for theological reflection. These analogies should be employed not as expressions of uniformity, but rather precisely to determine the limits of analogy as a methodological tool. However, because something in history eludes analogy does not mean that it is entirely without analogy. In this case, the historian has no right to declare this datum's reality impossible. Rather, this case requires an analogy with "forms of consciousness that do not measure up to reality [*nicht realitätsgerechten Bewußtseinsformen*]."[17]

Pannenberg highlights the investigations of the historical Jesus as a central issue in the relationship between theological and historical hermeneutics. He admits that the fundamental hermeneutical problem of theology is the bridge between the New Testament thought-world and the thought-world of the present, as well as the evolution of the Christian tradition that is rooted in this New Testament thought-world. The phrase "Word of God"

14. Ibid., 263.
15. Ibid., 265.
16. Ibid., 266.
17. Ibid., 267.

has become the catchphrase for this process of evolution. Pannenberg asserts that this phrase merely designates the process without providing the means by which to accomplish it. Rather than use this formula as proof of its own orthodoxy, theology should devote itself to clarifying the problems designated by this term and take as its theme the problem of transmitting the Christian tradition into the present age. At the same time, theology should refrain from focusing too narrowly only on the transmission phase of the Christian tradition, which diverts attention away from the problems inherent in the distance between the New Testament and the present. Thus, for Pannenberg, theological and historical hermeneutics must coexist in theological reflection if this process of transmission is to succeed.[18]

The process of the transmission of the Christian tradition must overcome two methodological obstacles if it is to succeed: first, the historical-hermeneutical obstacle of understanding the texts of the Bible in their original world-context; and second, the theological-hermeneutical obstacle of applying the interpretation of these texts to the present. Many interpreters of Scripture have undertaken these attempts with varying degrees of success, but Pannenberg focuses his attention Rudolf Bultmann and his existentialist interpretation of the New Testament.[19]

Bultmann reads the New Testament as a document that expresses something significant about human existence. To this end, he assumes that the existential structure of human existence is characterized a priori by the fact that interpreters work as those who question, precisely because it is questionability that characterizes human existence. This questionability of the text informs Bultmann's concept of pre-understanding as well, because interpreters will read the New Testament with the questions of human existence always in mind, with a desire to relate the subject matter of the text to their own life. Pannenberg accuses Bultmann of unintentionally weakening and limiting the possibilities of the text by looking only for what the text can say of human existence. While it is true that the New Testament speaks

18. Pannenberg, "Über historische und theologische Hermeneutik," 129–30.

19. Michael Welker, for example, applauds Pannenberg's efforts to move the post-Bultmannian discussion in a decidedly different direction. See Welker, *God the Revealed*, 113–17. In this work Welker seeks alternatives to what he perceives as a distorted, modern version of "faith" that has its roots in the ultimately anthropocentric approaches of Kant, Schleiermacher, and Kierkegaard and their attention to the "inner self" at the expense of the objective givenness of divine transcendence. Welker names Bultmann as a particularly compelling example of this anthropocentrism in modern theology, to which Pannenberg presents a more compelling alternative. Ibid., 44–46.

of human existence, Pannenberg hastens to add that the New Testament also speaks of many other subjects. He emphasizes that the New Testament is concerned primarily with God and God's interaction in and with the world and its history, and anything the New Testament says about human existence must be conditioned by this primary concern.

Bultmann, according to Pannenberg, reads the New Testament in reverse order. Rather than read what the New Testament says about existence as conditioned by its primary task of speaking of God and the world, Bultmann, because of his pre-understanding, reads the New Testament as speaking of God and the world only as *expressions* of an underlying understanding of human existence. Pannenberg agrees with Bultmann that God can only be thought of as the One who is asked about in the questionability of human existence, but God must nevertheless be understood as the indispensable presupposition of human existence rather than the expression of the human being's questionability. To that extent, understanding of God logically precedes understanding of the self. This logical privileging of the self over God in Bultmann's pre-understanding, Pannenberg believes, is symptomatic of Bultmann's "anthropological narrowing of the question."[20]

Because of this existential narrowing of the hermeneutical task, an additional problem arises of how the historical distance between the text and the reader can be retained in all its profundity. If this historical distance is ignored on the a priori grounds of an existentialist reading, as Pannenberg discerns in Bultmann's approach, then the attempt to build a hermeneutical bridge between the text and the present cannot succeed. Pannenberg suggests that Bultmann could not see this danger because he was not aware of the importance of universal history. If a text can make a claim on interpreters, then interpreters cannot place a priori limits on this claim, but must take seriously and unqualifiedly the particularity of that which is past. The interpreter must recognize, acknowledge, and respect the distance between past and present while affirming their relatedness.

20. Pannenberg, "Hermeneutik und Universalgeschichte," 100–101. This does not mean that Bultmann actually does logically privilege the self over God, however. In fact, Bultmann understands the two types of knowledge to be mutually conditioned and productive, and in this, at least, he could appeal to Calvin as an ally, as Calvin famously opens the *Institutes* with a declaration that "nearly all the wisdom we possess, that is to say, true and sound wisdom, consists of two parts: the knowledge of God and of ourselves. But, while joined by many bonds, which one precedes and brings forth the other is not easy to discern." In fact, for Calvin, as for Bultmann, knowledge of self and knowledge of God are mutually conditioned and productive. Calvin, *Institutes of the Christian Religion*, 1:35.

If the historical distance of that which is past is retained, then the connection between past and present cannot be found anywhere else than in the context of history, and in this way the hermeneutical question is subsumed into the universal-historical question. Bultmann did not make this step, in Pannenberg's estimation, because his pre-understanding is not related to the historical context, and the claim of the text is restricted to the formal "either-or" of the inauthenticity or authenticity of existence. In fact, the historical character, the "what" of the claim, is not important for Bultmann; the mere "that" is the decisive matter.[21]

Nevertheless, Pannenberg does credit Bultmann's use of existential philosophy for emancipating historicity from history:

> The emancipation of historicity from history, the reversal of the relationship between the two to a grounding of history from the historicity of humanity, appears to be the final peak of the way that began when modern people made humanity instead of God the bearer of history. When the historicity of humanity is set up in opposition to the continuity of the course of history, the last possible step is taken along this way, before the experience of history as well as that of historicity must be lost.[22]

This emancipation is accomplished in Bultmann's understanding of eschatology. Jesus Christ, as eschatological event, is the end of history. Believers no longer live in a universal-historical framework; they now live an eschatological life. For Bultmann, the course of history as a universal-historical process is finished. But Pannenberg argues that this end of history is only *anticipated* in history, in Jesus Christ. The meaning of the belief that in Jesus Christ history has ended can itself be understood only with the help of an apocalyptic conception of history, and thus the framework of history remains intact. Pannenberg suggests that for Bultmann an understanding of history as a whole is now made possible because the end of history is already present. The problem in this schema, for Pannenberg, is that no one can make the eschaton the key to history, because it has been revealed to us in such a mysterious, incomprehensible way through the resurrection of Jesus.[23]

---

21. Pannenberg, "Hermeneutik und Universalgeschichte," 103–4.

22. Pannenberg, "Heilsgeschehen und Geschichte," 232–33. Pannenberg uses "*Geschichte*" and its variations throughout this passage for "history" and "historicity."

23. Ibid., 236–37.

Pannenberg is especially interested in the role of historical method-ology and the relationship between theological and historical hermeneu-tics in the interpretation of the resurrection of Jesus and he recognizes several distinct problems confronting any theological interpretation of the resurrection. First, historical-critical methodology presents a series of obstacles for the Christian historian when the object of interpretation is the resurrection. Second, the resurrection of Jesus presents a specific and unique historical problem. And third, the results of these interpreta-tions often present a separate series of problems when they are applied to Christian proclamation.

Pannenberg confronts these problems in an essay titled "History and the Reality of the Resurrection."[24] The Christian proclamation of the resurrection of Jesus continues to meet with disbelief and derision in the present, just as it did when it was first proclaimed. The reason for this deri-sion concerns differing outlooks on reality. Christians presuppose a specific understanding of reality when they proclaim Jesus risen from the dead, but this particular outlook on reality is not shared by everyone. The Christian belief in the resurrection of Jesus is informed by another belief in the future general resurrection of the dead. Because this general resurrection has not yet occurred, the fact that one person has already experienced resurrection is extremely unlikely, and therefore Christian proclamation of just such an event is met with derision and disbelief.

Pannenberg detects a certain a priori suspicion against the resurrec-tion of the dead operative in many historical investigations of the New Testament. The prejudice against the resurrection of the dead is presup-posed before the investigation of the text even begins. The general popu-lation operates with this suspicion as a matter of course, but Pannenberg laments the fact that Christian historians and theologians operate with similar suspicions in their own work. Christian historians must approach the texts of the New Testament with the same critical eye and method-ological procedure as any historian approaches any text, not only in their claims to historical facticity, but also in their reconstruction of the course of events that emerge from historical analysis. These historians operate with the tools available to them, but Pannenberg notes that the historical-critical method is not infallible and the criteria and tools of historical judg-ment are not beyond dispute. Pannenberg is willing to admit that there is no threat in the use of these criteria and tools for biblical exegesis and

24. Pannenberg, "History and the Reality of the Resurrection."

he concedes the appropriateness of making judgments based on historical analyses. The threat emerges when the historian attempts to reconstruct the course of events based on the application of these criteria and tools. Here the historian is called to engage secular history in a debate concerning the nature of reality. The Christian historian should and must claim exemption from the presuppositions of historical-critical methodology at this point, because secular historical understanding differs from Christian historical consciousness at precisely this point. The Christian *historian* is unable to be a *Christian* historian and subscribe to a conception of reality that a priori excludes divine intervention in the course of history.

The secular historian approaches the resurrection of Jesus with a particular presupposition of the nature of reality that excludes any act of God or the possibility of a dead man returning to life. This presupposition leads to prejudice in dealing with the texts of the Easter tradition. Pannenberg argues that "the negative judgment on the bodily resurrection of Jesus as having occurred in historical fact is *not a result* of the historical critical examination of the Biblical Easter tradition, *but a postulate* that precedes any such examination."[25]

Christian historians operating with this preconceived, secular conception of reality attempt to establish alternative explanations of the event of Easter because they are convinced that it is the task of the historian to apply the (secular) historical method to the story of Easter. Pannenberg disagrees: "Precisely at this point a historian who happens to be a Christian should take exemption from a procedure that for a priori reasons imposes upon the Christian story a secularist reading."[26]

What Pannenberg appears to be suggesting here is that "religious" and "secular" history are not, all things considered, the same type of history, or at the very least that Christian historians should not preclude the possibility of supernatural intervention or miracles before they have even begun to investigate the past. He is not suggesting that we can *know* that such events happened, but he is suggesting that it is arrogant to dismiss the *possibility* out of hand at the very start of historical analysis of the traditions that appear to assert just such a possibility. He turns to contemporary physics to suggest that the standard presupposition against the possibility of the resurrection of the dead might not be as universally accepted in the scientific community as the more liberal historical critics might assume, citing

25. Ibid., 321.
26. Ibid.

the work of American physicist Frank Tipler to support his claim that it is no longer scientifically unfeasible to believe in the resurrection of the dead in the midst of human history.[27] Pannenberg stresses that it is not necessary for theologians to consider work such as Tipler's as established facts of science; it is enough to recognize that such considerations are no longer completely foreign to a scientific world-picture. The importance of this allowance is that theological investigations of the New Testament resurrection accounts can now investigate these texts in a purely historical fashion, without the need for certain a priori presuppositions. He emphasizes his conclusion that negative judgments on the possibility of the resurrection of Jesus should not be presented as purely objective judgments based on careful historical scrutiny, but as the result of a prejudice against the possibility of resurrection that precedes historical examination of the texts.

It should be possible to accept the proclamation of the resurrection of Jesus as a historical event while also maintaining the role of historical reason, in Pannenberg's summation. The key to this coexistence is for the historian to allow a place for God in the course of historical processes. The limitations of human knowledge cannot exclude the possibility of God's actions within human history, so it is the task of the Christian historian to challenge historical positivism, to clear a place for God in modern historical consciousness in order to achieve a "more appropriate" understanding of reality.[28]

If the bodily resurrection is granted as a historical possibility, its meaning is not exhausted by that historicity; rather, it must be proclaimed in its significance. Pannenberg treats the issue of Christian proclamation and its relationship to historical investigation in an essay on the kerygma and history in a *Festschrift* for Gerhard von Rad.[29] In this essay, Pannenberg investigates the fundamental characteristics of "kerygma theology" as a phenomenon in the history of theology. He cites the work of Martin Kähler, particularly *Der sogennante historische Jesus und der geschichtliche, biblische Christus*, as the source of this new theology. Kähler's assertion that "the real Christ is the preached Christ"[30] may well be regarded as the main theme of kerygma theology, particularly of its anti-historical expressions. Not only kerygma theology's aversion to inquiries into the life of the

---

27. Tipler, *Physics of Immortality*.

28. Pannenberg, "History and the Reality of the Resurrection," 319–26.

29. Pannenberg, "Kerygma und Geschichte." ET: "Kerygma and History."

30. Kähler, *Der sogenannte historische Jesus*, 44.

historical Jesus, but also its emphasis on proclamation originates at least partly in Kähler's work. One of kerygma theology's chief concepts is the "Word of God," and it is not surprising that it owes its genesis partly to the development of dialectical theology, which also called itself a "theology of the Word of God." While Karl Barth does take proclamation as his point of departure, kerygma theology finds its most developed expression in the theology of Rudolf Bultmann.[31]

Pannenberg understands kerygma theology as an attempt to stress the character of the biblical writings as a *witness*, in opposition to two other ways of dealing with historical material: the quest for general truth and a particular form of historical research.[32] He turns to historical investigation within liberal Protestant theology at the beginning of the twentieth century for clarification. Historical investigation at this time did not often attend to the particularity of the events the Bible describes. Liberal theologians and historians instead studied the biblical texts as documents of human religiosity in terms of analogies and uniformity rather than particularity and individuality. These historians could not speak of particular acts of God because of certain presuppositions concerning the historical method. Kerygma theology recognized the error of these presuppositions and developed in conscious opposition to them. The failure of nineteenth-century historical methodology was especially evident in the nineteenth-century Lives of Jesus, for which there was no clear connection between the historical person of Jesus and the apostolic witness to Jesus the Christ. Kähler recognized this fact and attacked these studies, realizing that the gospels speak of the risen Christ and do not attempt to provide biographical reports of the man Jesus. Kerygma theology likewise recognized that when the Bible is read as a collection of documents describing secular events and human religiosity, their genuine content—their witness to the acts of God—remains obscured from view. In Pannenberg's estimation, while kerygma theology correctly noted this failure of nineteenth-century liberal theology, kerygma theology also failed in that it overcompensated and lost sight of the historical foundation of the biblical witness.

---

31. For Pannenberg's discussion of Bultmann within the broader context of twentieth-century Protestant theology, see "Die Auflösung der Dialektischen Theologie bei Rudolf Bultmann."

32. For Bultmann's own discussion of general truths in terms of Christian proclamation, see Bultmann, "Allgemeine Wahrheiten und christliche Verkündigung." ET: "General Truths."

Because Pannenberg stresses that the kerygma does have a historical foundation, he criticizes kerygma theology for rejecting any attempt to go behind the kerygma and verify its object through historical research. For kerygma theology, faith must be satisfied with the kerygma and must not seek security by inquiring into the historical facticity of the events it describes. Pannenberg argues that the word alone, with its claim to truth, is not sufficient ground for faith. The message of Jesus requires historical legitimization, which it received through the resurrection of Jesus from the dead.[33] To highlight this, he inquires into the validity of the kerygma theologians' distinction between fact and meaning. He asks, "Does not the meaning of an event belong to the event itself insofar as it is to be understood only its own historical context?"[34] He blames form-critical research with annihilating the unity of fact and meaning by elevating the kerygma over against its historical foundation. Kerygma theology's efforts to make the primitive Christian kerygma, rather than the events behind that kerygma, the focus of historical inquiry resulted in relegating to obscurity the events to which it bears witness. Through form-critical research, every layer of the New Testament can be traced to some testimony of the earliest Christians, while the life, words, and deeds of Jesus himself remain largely untouched. Thus the question of the life of the historical Jesus became meaningless because it was altogether lost.

With the introduction of Heidegger's existential philosophy into the theological enterprise, the Gospels lost their significance as testaments to the life of Jesus and became early Christian expressions of an understanding of human existence. Bultmann especially championed this method of interpreting scripture, but in order to pursue it he was forced to abandon Kähler's view of scripture as the record of salvation history in favor of an eschatological origin of the New Testament kerygma. The goal of exegesis became uncovering the eschatological understanding of existence, and to this end not the "what," but only the "that" of the origin of Easter faith and the kerygma is important.[35]

In his study of Christology, *Grundzüge der Christologie*, Pannenberg seeks the "what" of the Easter event through historical investigation in an

33. This is precisely where Bultmann, and Wilhelm Herrmann before him, most passionately disagree because, for them, to require historical legitimation for faith through historical research amounts to epistemological works righteousness.

34. Pannenberg, "Kerygma und Geschichte," 133.

35. Ibid., 133–34.

essay on the resurrection of Jesus as a historical problem.[36] The tradition of the resurrection of Jesus can be divided into two distinct strands: the traditions of the appearances of the risen Lord, and the traditions of the discoveries of Jesus' empty tomb. The process of the assimilation of these two traditions is already at work in the New Testament itself: Mark and Paul each contain only one strand, while John contains both in striking proximity. In the oldest layers of the tradition, however, both strands remain quite distinct: Mark contains only the empty tomb tradition, and Paul contains only the appearances tradition.[37]

Because the Gospel accounts of the appearances of the risen Jesus have been overlaid with several layers of myth and legend, Pannenberg admits that it is difficult to discover any kernel of the historical in them.[38] Because this is so, he focuses his discussion on the appearances tradition as found in the letters of Paul. Paul enumerates the list of witnesses of the risen Lord in 1 Cor. 15 in an effort to provide historical proof of Jesus' resurrection. Although this attempt at proof might be questionable in terms of modern standards for determining historical proof, such an attempt is perfectly legitimate according to the standards of Paul's time.

Pannenberg suggests that Paul's discussion of the resurrection of Jesus in the first verses of 1 Cor. 15 combines personal testimony and older, codified formulations. Paul adds his own personal testimony of his experience of an appearance of the risen Lord to an already-accepted formulation that dates from a time very close to Jesus' death, using both in an attempt to provide historical proof of Jesus' resurrection to the Corinthian Christians. Unfortunately, these formulations and testimonies do not convey any sense of the specific nature and quality of these appearances. It is precisely at this point that difficulties arise, because the New Testament appearances tradition is so complex.

First, the New Testament records events that might be described as "extraordinary visions" that might not have been visible to everyone. To label something a "vision," in Pannenberg's estimation, is not to dispute the reality of the event experienced in this form, but is only to express

36. Pannenberg, *Grundzüge der Christologie*. See especially his section on "Die historische Problematik der Auferstehung Jesu," 85–103, in his third chapter, "Die Auferweckung Jesu als Grund seiner Einheit mit Gott," 47–112. ET: *Jesus*.

37. For more on the textual history and theological significance of these two strands and their complex interrelation, see Marxsen, *Resurrection of Jesus of Nazareth*.

38. For Pannenberg's discussion of myth in the biblical and Christian tradition, see Pannenberg, *Christentum und Mythos*.

something about the subjective mode of this experience. Pannenberg attacks as utter failures Strauss's (and others') explanation of the Easter tradition as the result of certain mental and historical presuppositions at work in the minds of the disciples. To maintain that the appearances were produced solely through the imagination of the disciples is to miss entirely the point of these appearances: the Easter appearances are not to be explained from the faith of the disciples, but rather the faith of the disciples is to be explained from the appearances of the risen Lord. Pannenberg points to the gradual development of the Easter tradition as evidence that this tradition was not simply concocted by the disciples as a result of their sorrow over Jesus' catastrophic demise (*pace* Reimarus). The historian is still required to reconstruct the course of these events based on the textual evidence, and the success or failure of this enterprise rests on the historian's understanding of reality. If the historian approaches the text with the presupposition that the dead do not rise, then Jesus has not risen. If, on the other hand, the historian recognizes that an event such as the resurrection is within the scope of reality in terms of the apocalyptic expectation of first-century Judaism, then the historian must consider this expectation and the hope of resurrection as genuine possibilities when reconstructing these events.[39]

Pannenberg concludes from this discussion that the resurrection of Jesus can be designated a historical event if the following applies: if the emergence of primitive Christianity can be understood, in spite of all critical examination of the tradition, *only* in light of contemporary eschatological hope in the resurrection of the dead, then that which is described as such *is* a historical event, even if the historian can know nothing more about it. An event that is capable of being expressed only in eschatological language is nonetheless to be asserted as a historical event. For Pannenberg, the sheer unlikelihood of Christianity emerging and thriving if what it claimed to be the foundation of its faith were nothing more than deception or an illusion (à la Reimarus and Strauss) is enough to prove that early Christians really did mean to speak of the resurrection as an objective historical event, and thus Christians today must likewise assume that it was

39. Despite Pannenberg's efforts to present a stark contrast here, it is difficult to see in what way understanding how a first-century author and audience thought about the possibility of resurrection from the dead has any bearing on determining whether such a thing actually happened. It would seem that in this case we would be making an a priori assumption that such things can and do happen, just as Pannenberg blames most contemporary historians for making an a priori assumption that they cannot and do not happen.

an objective historical event, even if historians cannot provide support or proof of that event.

It is customary to object theologically to the possibility that the resurrection of Jesus could be a historical event, that the resurrection is the beginning of a new time. The reality of the new time cannot be judged or perceived in terms of the old time, however, but the historian must make claims within the standards of this old time and can therefore say nothing at all about the resurrection of the dead. Pannenberg admits that there is some truth to this argument. Because the life of the risen Lord involves the reality of a new creation and a new time, he is no longer perceptible as one object among others in this world. He can therefore only be encountered through an extraordinary experience (e.g., a visionary experience), and only in metaphorical language. In this way, through extraordinary experiences, the risen Lord made himself known in the midst of this reality to specific people, at a specific time in history, in a specific place. Because these experiences took place in human history, they are to be affirmed or denied also as historical events. If the interpreter abandons the concept of historical event when investigating the resurrection, then it is no longer possible to affirm that the resurrection of Jesus or his appearances really happened at a specific time and place. There is absolutely no justification for affirming Jesus' resurrection as an event if it cannot be affirmed as a *historical* event. The historical validity and facticity of this event cannot be apprehended by faith alone, but through historical research.[40]

The traditions about the empty tomb originally circulated independently of the traditions about the appearances of the risen Jesus, but investigation of these traditions will ultimately inform conclusions about the Easter tradition taken as a unity. Pannenberg insists that the empty tomb tradition is not found in Paul's letters because he did not need such a tradition to affirm Jesus' resurrection. Geographical distance from Jerusalem as well as the scope and focus of Paul's theological arguments made mention of the empty tomb unnecessary in Paul's letters, but for the original Christian community in Jerusalem the situation was quite different. For the Christians in Jerusalem, any proclamation of the resurrection of their Lord inevitably led back to the tomb of Jesus. Pannenberg asks, how could the disciples in Jerusalem proclaim Jesus' resurrection if they were in constant

---

40. For a more detailed discussion of faith, see Pannenberg, *Systematic Theology*, vol. 3. See especially the sections "Faith as Trust," "Faith and Knowledge," "Faith and Historical Knowledge," "The Ground of Faith and the Thoughts of Faith," and "Faith as Assurance of Salvation," 136–72.

danger of being refuted by viewing the tomb in which Jesus' body still lay interred? The early Christian proclamation of Jesus' resurrection would have been inconceivable had not the empty tomb been assumed. Pannenberg cites the fact that the empty tomb is the only common factor in all four synoptic gospels to be overwhelming evidence for its historical probability.

Given the partial but not complete overlapping of the traditions of the empty tomb and the appearances of the risen Jesus, what can we know about their historicity? Contemporary scholarship assumes that the appearances (supposedly) occurred in Galilee, while the empty tomb (supposedly) was discovered in Jerusalem. The question about the disciples' journeys is decisive: did the disciples return to Galilee immediately after Jesus was taken prisoner, or did they remain in Jerusalem until after Jesus' death? If they left Jerusalem after Jesus' arrest, then the empty tomb would have been discovered in their absence, meaning the two traditions would have developed independently. If, however, the disciples remained in Jerusalem until after Jesus' death, then they themselves would have discovered the empty tomb and it would have been this discovery that led them to Galilee. Pannenberg tends to accept the former hypothesis, that the disciples returned to Galilee before Jesus' death, and that the tradition of the empty tomb developed independently of the tradition of the appearances.[41] This assumption is vitally important for Pannenberg. If it is assumed that these two traditions developed independently of one another, then by their mutually complementing one another they make the assertion of the reality of Jesus' resurrection appear historically very probable. Pannenberg emphasizes the fact that in historical inquiry, the historical probability of something always means that it is then to be presupposed until contrary evidence appears. In another essay he asks,

> Does not the postulate of the principal uniformity of all events form the chief argument against the historicity of the resurrection of Jesus, for example? But if that is so, does not the opinion, which has come to be regarded as nearly self-understood, that the resurrection of Jesus cannot be a historical event, rest on a remarkably weak foundation? Only the particular nature of the reports make possible a judgment about the historicity of the resurrection, not the prior judgment that all events must be principally uniform.[42]

41. He is able to say this because he concludes that the appearance narratives in the four gospels are so thoroughly shaped by legendary elements that they scarcely count as historical reports. Pannenberg, *Grundzüge der Christologie*, 92.

42. Pannenberg, "Heilsgeschehen und Geschichte," 266, n. 22.

Thus, for Pannenberg, the resurrection of Jesus is a historical event, one that can be determined to have occurred within time and space, and as such is open, in theory if not always in practice, to historical inquiry.[43]

Pannenberg represents a more conservative Christian response to Bultmann's project, particularly with respect to the relationship between history and Easter faith. Whereas Bultmann was willing to abandon the attempt to secure a firm foundation for Christian faith through historical research, Pannenberg insists that the historicity of the bodily resurrection of Jesus constitutes a confessional Rubicon that should not be crossed unless one is willing to jettison the core of the church's faith and witness to the risen Christ. And yet there are significant weaknesses in Pannenberg's position, ironically exposed in the very place he supposes is its strongest point. He insists that the resurrection of Jesus must be understood as a historical event because without that assumption the Christian faith is meaningless. And yet in order to make sense of that historical event we must first accept the apocalyptic view of history and eschatology without which the resurrection makes no sense. But at the same time, he proposes that if the resurrection is a historical event then it should in theory be accessible to historical investigation regardless of one's own religious commitments or lack thereof. Gregory Dawes succinctly summarizes the only logical conclusion to be drawn from these inconsistencies:

> Pannenberg's claim that the resurrection can be established historically—a claim that he modifies but never openly abandons—lies in ruins. A history that requires one to accept from the outset the apocalyptic view of the world is no history at all, but a highly tendentious theology. Insofar as history is a public discipline which does not involve a prior commitment to particular religious views, there is no sense in which Pannenberg's argument could be presented as "historical." For one would need to be a believer (that is to say, to have already accepted belief in the resurrection of the dead) before this argument would become convincing.[44]

Despite these weaknesses (and perhaps because many do not agree that they are indeed weaknesses), Pannenberg's project has been highly regarded in many theological circles, but his is not the only trajectory leading from Bultmann to the present. Other German voices have contributed to the conversation about the relationship between myth, history, and the

43. Pannenberg, *Grundzüge der Christologie*, 85–103.
44. Dawes, *Historical Jesus Question*, 341.

resurrection that, in many ways, are more sympathetic to Bultmann's project while also intending to respond faithfully to questions newly framed in new times. We turn to two such voices now.

CHAPTER SIX

Two Contemporary Approaches to Myth, History, and the Resurrection

Eberhard Jüngel

EBERHARD JÜNGEL[1] HAS WRITTEN extensively on the doctrine of the Trinity, ecclesiology, Christology, Christian freedom, the intersections of theology and philosophy, among many other topics.[2] In terms of Christology, his work has focused on the relationship of faith to the historical Jesus, the proclamation of Jesus, and the early Christian proclamation as formulated in the letters of Paul.[3] He is also interested in the truth of myth and the necessity of demythologizing[4] and the relationship between Christology and historical understanding.[5]

In terms of the resurrection of Jesus and the concepts of myth and history, Jüngel approaches the problem from a hermeneutical perspective rather than taking a strictly historical approach. In his essay on the process of historical understanding as an introduction to Christology, Jüngel quotes a Swabian proverb that appears in Hegel's Jena diary:

> In Swabia people say of something that took place long ago that it is so long since it happened that it can hardly be true anymore.

---

1. Jüngel (b. 1934) is Emeritus Professor of Systematic Theology and the Philosophy of Religion in the Faculty of Evangelical Theology at the University of Tübingen.

2. A *Festschrift* for Jüngel with essays covering these and other aspects of his work was recently published as Malysz, *Indicative of Grace*.

3. See Jüngel, *Paulus und Jesus*.

4. Jüngel, "Die Wahrheit des Mythos und die Notwendigkeit der Entmythologisierung."

5. Jüngel, "Die Wirksamkeit des Entzogenen." ET: "Effectiveness of Christ Withdrawn."

> So Christ died for our sins so long ago that it can hardly be true anymore.[6]

This proverb highlights a specific hermeneutical problem raised by historical reflection, namely that the temporal distance between a historical event and the present seems to rob that past event of its significance in and for the present. This poses a potentially fatal problem for Christology because the theologian must ask not only who Jesus *was*, but also, and more importantly, who Jesus Christ *is*. This is the essence of the christological question: what is the relationship between the past tense *was* and the present tense *is* when speaking of Jesus the Christ? This question poses two problems for Jüngel. First, there is a hermeneutical problem concerning the relationship of the present to the past, namely the possibility of those in the present being confronted and addressed by something from the distant past. Second, there is a theological problem, namely the fact that a truth that is considered divine is said to be apprehended in a historical event, meaning it must therefore be understood in terms of the temporality of history.

The first question about the relationship between the past and the present becomes an existential one for Jüngel, as he places the emphasis on the relationship between our historical existence in the present and those events that occurred long before we existed. Historical existence is related to time in a special way. For example, the fact that a square has four sides is true regardless of the time in which any particular square exists. Time is indifferent to this truth, just as this truth is indifferent to time. Historical existence, however, relates to time quite differently. Temporal distance can, it seems, make a past event seem somehow truer or somehow less true. But what is the relationship between historical existence, time, and truth? As historical creatures, we exist at a certain point in history: we exist in time. In other words, to exist historically is to exist in time. Because we exist in time, we are connected in this way to all historical existence. This is so both in terms of the past and in terms of the future. As long as we live, we will share a common "tomorrow" with everything else that exists at the present. When we reach that tomorrow, it will become "today," and we will find a new "tomorrow" on the horizon. Only in death, in the cessation of our existence, do we become "past." For Jüngel there are really two different questions that are inseparably related: first, what is the relation of the past to our own present; and second, what is our relation to the past?

---

6. Hegel, quoted in Jüngel, "Die Wirksamkeit des Entzogenen," 15.

Our relation to the past can be accomplished by means of a conscious act, such as historical research. There are dangers involved in historical research because historical research always involves choices and thus includes an inescapable arbitrariness. Historical interest is always interest in some particular aspect of the past. A particular person, event, institution, movement, or phenomenon is the focus of historical interest, and the historian attempts to make sense of these particular historical "artifacts" in terms of the present, bringing them, as it were, into the present from the past. The future, on the other hand, is always impinging on us in the present. It constantly presents itself at the same rate at which the past recedes from the present. In this way those in the present can be aware that what is past was once also present, and even future, for another time. This makes historical reflection both necessary and interesting.

Jüngel wonders, however, if then the task of historical research merely would be to relegate the past permanently to the past, to file it away as something past and not present: put differently, to relieve the present of the past. This task, however, would only serve to reveal the fact that the present remains burdened with the past. This is so because the past never remains past, but is significant and influential for the present and the future. The past refuses to remain past.[7] Thus the present must maintain a dual perspective, with one eye toward the future and another toward the past. Jüngel argues that the compulsion to work through the past in the present is a constitutive moment of historical existence. In this way we can define the present as "working out the future by working through the past [*Verarbeitung von Vergangenheit als Erarbeitung von Zukunft*]."[8] This historical work can never be finished, because the past is never static; it continues to withdraw as the present proceeds into the future. Thus for every item of history there is a "consequent history" (*Nachgeschichte*) or what might also be called a "history of effects" (*Wirkungsgeschichte*),[9] which serves to influence the meaning of the event of which it is consequence and effect. Any mastery of the past is impossible, because the past is never complete; there is always more "past." The past is meaningful for the present only when those in the present recognize that they are affected—and effected—by the

7. Or as William Faulkner famously put it in *Requiem for a Nun*, "The past is never dead. It's not even past," 92.

8. Jüngel, "Die Wirksamkeit des Entzogenen," 23.

9. Ibid., 24. The term *Wirkungsgeschichte* is particularly important in Hans-Georg Gadamer's hermeneutics.

past, that they do not stand above or beyond or outside the past and its enduring influence.

There is a second question for Jüngel, namely the question of the relation of the past to the present. Hegel's quotation of the Swabian proverb expresses the belief that the truth can become outdated. This implies that historical existence or historical events are not true merely because of their facticity. The truth of historical existence exceeds facticity, because the assertion of facticity can either be correct or incorrect. Either something is factual, or it is not; there is no third alternative. However, Jüngel suggests that to say of something that it soon may no longer be true is to uncover a third alternative, namely the potentiality of actuality. Any actuality (the mere existence of a person, for example) always has the potential to be more than simply actual. A mere fact always has the potential of becoming more than a mere fact; it has the potential to become significant beyond its actuality. The actuality of the past cannot be repeated, but the potentiality of the past, the possibilities from which it arose and the possibilities that the past has opened up, remain.[10]

This issue of potentiality and effectiveness leads Jüngel back to his original hermeneutical (and specifically christological) problem. It is the nature of the past to recede, and as such many particulars within the totality of history are forever lost. This is true even in the case of Jesus of Nazareth. Because there are very few historically verifiable details of his life available to historical research, we must recognize and concede that much of the particularity of his historical existence is forever lost. Or as Wilhelm Bousset once remarked, "what we know of the pragmatic context of [the life of Jesus] is so little that it would fit on a slip of paper."[11] It is not enough to recognize and accept the scantiness of historical details about Jesus, however, because the early Christians attempted to portray the salvific meaningfulness of Jesus' historical existence and even developed a new literary genre to accomplish just this goal: the gospel. The gospels are much more than accounts of the mere chronological unfolding of the life of Jesus, because it was much more important for them to portray the particular *effect* of Jesus' life: the proclamation of salvation for those whom he addressed.

10. Ibid., 25–27. To put this a different way, we might say that *Historie* always has the potential to be more than mere *Historie*; it has the potential to become *Geschichte*.

11. Bousset, "Die Bedeutung der Person Jesu für den Glaube," 294. ET: "Significance of the Personality of Jesus for Belief." See also Hege, "Jesus Christ as Poetic Symbol."

For this reason the gospels are not concerned with all the details of Jesus' life, because what they include is enough to present him as a salvific unity.[12]

Jüngel appropriates three theses of Hans-Georg Gadamer to explicate this "effective-historical hermeneutic" in terms of the history of Jesus:

1. It is necessary and possible to elaborate the historical horizon belonging to the situation of the historian.

2. It is necessary and possible to sketch the historical horizon of the object of historical investigation.

3. It is necessary and possible to incorporate the historical horizon of the object of investigation into the historical horizon of the existence of the historian, so that in this process of understanding there is a "fusion of horizons" (Horizontverschmelzung), which means that as one historical horizon is projected it is simultaneously fused with the other historical horizon and thus, in a real sense, removed.[13]

It is part of historical existence for the historical to recede further into the past, and it is also part of historical existence for the historical to have an effect on the present through this passing away. In the case of Jesus, his effectiveness consists of his death—what Jüngel calls his "withdrawal"— which faith in his resurrection confirms. Jüngel emphasizes his thesis that the *death* of Jesus evoked faith in Christ, and that the absence of Jesus allowed the New Testament to develop as a testimony to his presence.[14]

Building on this question of the relation of truth to history, in a later article on the dogmatic significance of the historical Jesus for faith Jüngel begins his discussion with the same Swabian proverb quoted in Hegel's Jena diary. But in this essay Jüngel's position appears to evolve when he proposes that not only the *death* but also the *life* of the historical Jesus is significant for faith. It is the task of dogmatics to recognize that its responsibility is more than historical; it is far more responsible to the possibility of faith in Jesus Christ. Therefore dogmatics must concern itself with the historical Jesus if it is to avoid the charge of replacing historical reality with mythology or ideology. To this end, Jüngel proposes three lines of thought: first, the dogmatic necessity of the quest for the historical Jesus; second, the

---

12. Jüngel, "Die Wirksamkeit des Entzogenen," 28.

13. Gadamer, *Wahrheit und Methode*, 283. ET: *Truth and Method.*

14. Jüngel, "Die Wirksamkeit des Entzogenen," 28–32.

connection between the kerygma and the historical Jesus; and third, the question of the personal identity of Jesus Christ.

The question of the dogmatic importance of the historical Jesus leads to the center of theological thinking, because theological thinking is realized in the tension between historical knowledge and dogmatic responsibility. Jüngel emphasizes this tension in terms of methodology. To know something historically means to analyze "what it became [*Gewordensein*], what it was [*Gewesensein*], and its effects," while to know something dogmatically means to represent its effects in their significance in and for the present.[15] But historical knowledge cannot be the foundation of dogmatic responsibility because theological matters must by their very nature as *theo*-logical be understood in terms of God. Because God cannot be known through historical or scientific research, God can be known only through God's revelation, which requires faith. Thus, for Jüngel, dogmatic responsibility (i.e., the responsibility to explicate the conviction of faith) cannot be grounded in historical knowledge.[16] This does not mean that dogmatic responsibility does not have an interest in history, however, because God's revelation occurs in historical events. Furthermore, faith in God is always itself a historical event and is thus accessible to historical knowledge.[17]

In terms of the historical Jesus, there is much about him that we do not know *historically*. Therefore, his life was much more than the sum of what we now know about him. Dogmatically, however, we know much more about Jesus *the Christ* because that is how he is proclaimed and believed in the Christian church. Jüngel suggests that dogmatic responsibility in the matter of the historical Jesus begins with this "Christological *as*."[18] He cites Bultmann's question posed to Barth (how do we understand that the proclaimer Jesus becomes the proclaimed Christ?[19]) as the decisive question that leads from the historical to the dogmatic formulation of the question. Historical research alone cannot answer the question of why the man Jesus of Nazareth has been so consistently proclaimed as

15. Jüngel, "Zur dogmatischen Bedeutung der Frage nach dem historischen Jesus," 214. ET: "Dogmatic Significance." Emphasis in original.

16. Ibid., 215.

17. Marxsen makes a similar distinction between historical access to the resurrection itself and historical access to the faith that is awakened and expressed in the proclamation and confession that Jesus is risen. *The Resurrection of Jesus of Nazareth*, 119ff.

18. Jüngel, "Zur dogmatischen Bedeutung," 215.

19. Bultmann, letter to Karl Barth, dated December 10, 1926, Jaspert and Bromiley, *Karl Barth/Rudolf Bultmann Letters*, 28.

the Christ to the point that the name "Jesus" and the title "Christ" have become one phrase: Jesus Christ.

Jüngel argues that a confession (such as the confession of Jesus as the Christ) says as much about the confessors as it says about the one who is confessed.[20] The confession that Jesus is the Christ is really a statement on behalf of the confessors that the human Jesus is to be thought of as God. And, as Jüngel has demonstrated, because God cannot be known through historical research, Jesus *as the Christ* also cannot be understood through historical research, but can only be confessed through the power of the Spirit. To make this point he enlists Martin Kähler and Wilhelm Hermann, both of whom attacked the nineteenth century Life of Jesus movement for attempting to ground faith in historical knowledge.[21]

Bultmann renewed this critique in the early twentieth century, but in doing so he radicalized the earlier critique to the point that historical facts and historical knowledge (i.e. *Historie*) became completely irrelevant for faith in Jesus Christ. Bultmann insisted that it is illegitimate to move behind the kerygma in order to find proof for faith—to seek security— which is a fruitless attempt to know Christ "after the flesh."[22] He developed this further by insisting that only the "that" of Jesus' life, not the "what," is significant for faith. It is in the context of making the kerygma intelligible to modern people that Bultmann proposes his program of demythologizing. In an essay on myth,[23] Jüngel proposes that it is specifically because there is truth inherent in myth that demythologizing is a necessary and fruitful project.[24]

20. Bousset made a similar point in his groundbreaking work, *Kyrios Christos*, first published in 1913. Bousset, *Kyrios Christos*.

21. For an extended treatment of Kähler's and Hermann's significance in this discussion, see Jüngel, *Paulus und Jesus*, 71ff. See also Hege, *Faith at the Intersection*, specifically the second chapter.

22. See Bultmann, "Die Bedeutung des geschichtlichen Jesus für die Theologie des Paulus." ET: "Significance of the Historical Jesus." See also Jüngel, *Paulus und Jesus*, 78ff, for an extended discussion. Here Jüngel highlights Bultmann's radicalization of the positions of Kähler and Hermann. Bultmann's insistence on understanding the significance of the Word allowed the possibility of questioning the relationship between Jesus and his word and from there also the origin of Christology. Even though Bultmann himself did not explore this question (largely due to his emphasis on the irrelevance of the historical Jesus for faith), his students inherited the question and took it more seriously, producing rich reflections on these issues in their own work.

23. Jüngel, "Die Wahrheit des Mythos."

24. Congdon devotes a significant portion of *The Mission of Demythologizing* to

Jüngel argues that there are two means of receiving myth: a mythical reception of myth, and a reception of myth that consciously critiques myth. This distinction is important, because in mythically receiving myth, one becomes aware of myth's truth, while in critically receiving myth, one operates with a preconceived suspicion of myth. It is only through mythically receiving myth *as myth* that one can then work through the myth in order to recognize its truth. Jüngel speaks of truth in this context because in the mythical reception of myth one is aware of the truth of myth, while in the critical reception of myth one immediately critiques the myth without first recognizing its truth.[25] But how can one speak simultaneously of the truth of myth and the necessity of demythologizing?

We can speak of both because myth is distanced from truth not only in content but also in form. This distancing of myth does not lead to its rejection, however. Because of this distancing, myth must be understood as the Other, whether this otherness is conceived in terms of separation from logos,[26] separation from reality, separation from the gospel, or separation from faith. It is when myth is perceived as the Other that its significance is appreciated. Demythologizers operate with the assumption that there is a truth in myth that is hidden by its objectifying language. Demythologizers are correct in this assumption, because through this program it is possible to recognize the distance of myth and so to uncover its truth.

However, Bultmann's insistence that the problem of myth is its objectification of that which is unobjectifiable is no longer acceptable if one recognizes that the point of myth is precisely to objectify the unobjectifiable. Jüngel suggests that the point of the christological myths of the New Testament is to emphasize the striking difference between creator and creatures, between God and humans. This is evident because the culmination of the New Testament Christ myth is the portrayal of God's becoming incarnate in Jesus of Nazareth. This portrayal locates the transcendent God within the world, and as such God becomes objectified. The point is not to collapse the distinction between God and humans, but precisely

---

Jüngel's critical appropriation of Bultmann, as well as Jüngel's analysis of the debate between Bultmann and Barth. For the former, see especially pp. 440–66; for the latter, see especially pp. 14–34.

25. Jüngel, "Die Wahrheit des Mythos," 42–43.

26. See Dalferth, *Jenseits von Mythos und Logos*, for a discussion of the possibility of theology moving beyond the dichotomy of myth and logos.

to emphasize the striking dissimilarity, or the "infinite qualitative distinction," between God and creation.[27]

Jüngel agrees with Bultmann that the power of myth is its ability to express something fundamental about human existence, and for this reason it is necessary to demythologize the Christ myths of the New Testament. Demythologizing recognizes and reveals the intention of myth to place human existence in the context of its greater life with God, specifically by localizing the Christian life "in Christ." While myth accomplishes this by making the world the location or context of God, demythologizing intends to make God the location or context of true human existence.[28] Insofar as this is the intention of myth, and more specifically the Christ myth of the New Testament, it is important for theology to understand these myths in terms of what they say about God and about human existence.

For Bultmann, this meant that it is theologically unnecessary to know anything about the historical Jesus of Nazareth beyond the mere fact of his existence as the locus of God's incarnation and revelation. However, several of Bultmann's students, most notably Ernst Käsemann[29] and Gerhard Ebeling,[30] retreated from Bultmann's radical position and suggested that questioning back from the kerygma to the historical Jesus is not only theologically possible but also indispensable. They emphasized the fact that it was one particular man, Jesus of Nazareth, whom God made the Christ, and that for that very reason faith must be interested to know all it can about this person. They hastened to add that this inquiry into the life of the historical Jesus is not an attempt to ground faith in historical knowledge, but rather to protect faith from Docetic misunderstandings.

Jüngel makes much of Ebeling's suggestion that it is dogmatically responsible to know all that can be known about the historical Jesus in order to guard against faith's self-contradiction. As Ebeling puts it, "Either the question of the historical Jesus destroys Christology, or else the question of the historical Jesus must show itself to be identical with the christological problem—there is no third option."[31] Therefore dogmatics has a

27. Jüngel, "Die Wahrheit des Mythos," 54.

28. Ibid., 54–55.

29. See Käsemann, "Das Problem des historischen Jesus."

30. See Ebeling's essay "Das bloße 'Daß,'" 115–16. See also Ebeling, "Die Frage nach dem historischen Jesus und das Problem der Christologie." ET: "Question of the Historical Jesus."

31. Ebeling, "Die Frage nach dem historischen Jesus," 16.

responsibility to expose to historical-critical investigation everything that is christologically relevant. Even Easter faith can be examined historically, as it is beyond historical doubt that confessing Jesus as the Christ is inseparably bound to Easter faith. This Easter faith is faith in the resurrection of the crucified Jesus from the dead. Because God has raised *this man* from the dead, historical inquiry into the earthly life of Jesus is necessary. Jüngel largely agrees with Ebeling and Käsemann on this point, suggesting that although faith in Jesus as the Christ cannot be *grounded* in the historical Jesus, it must nevertheless find *support* in him.[32] Thus the question remains: how did Jesus understand himself, and how does this self-understanding relate to faith in Jesus as the Christ?

Jüngel suggests that in his self-understanding Jesus understood himself to be at one with God's will. The "Amen" placed at the beginning of his statements in which he asserts God's will (especially in the Gospel of John) expresses his eschatological unification with the will of God.[33] Jesus

32. Jüngel, "Zur dogmatischen Bedeutung," 219. See Jüngel, *Paulus und Jesus*, 80ff, for Jüngel's discussion of the various efforts of Bultmann's students to investigate the relationship between the historical Jesus and the proclaimed Christ.

33. Jüngel, "Zur dogmatischen Bedeutung," 236. See also Ebeling, "Jesus und Glaube," ET: "Jesus and Faith," for a discussion of the concept of faith in the Old and New Testaments, and the relationship between this concept of faith and the person of Jesus of Nazareth. Ebeling notes that in the Septuagint, the root πιστ- most often corresponds with the Hebrew אמן. He suggests that the most significant meaning of the correspondence is expressed in the Nifal form נאמן, which he translates as "a thing corresponding to what it promises to be." In other words, a thing does not disappoint the expectation it raises. In this way אמן (and αμην) is employed to express God's faithfulness and, in terms of God's work, to express its becoming a reality, being valid, and taking place. Therefore, the use of αμην, as much as it means "it is true" or "it is valid," also means "it happens" and "it becomes a reality." Ebeling includes a paragraph from Hans von Soden's essay "Was ist Wahrheit," in which he discusses the Hebrew concepts of truth and reality: "The peculiarity of the Hebrew concept of truth is . . . on the one hand its temporal determination, its specifically historical character. It is always a case of something that has happened or will happen, not of something that by nature is, is so, and must be so. To that extent, reality and truth would here not be distinguishable at all, but truth is reality seen as history. Truth is not something that lies somehow below or behind things and would be discovered by penetrating their depths or their inner meaning; but truth is what will emerge in the future. The opposite of truth would, so to speak, not really be illusion, but essentially disillusion (as we tend to use this word). What is lasting and durable and has a future is true, particularly the eternal as the imperishable, everlasting, final, ultimate. The law of events would be truth for the Hebrew not in the sense of a regularity or natural law that is always confirmed in all events, but in the sense of the fulfilled determination of its unique course, of its divinely appointed rightness. . . . The second thing to be emphasized is that questions of truth for the Hebrew are not really questions about whether things

understood God's will as the decision for the unity of humanity with God, expressed most powerfully in Jesus' proclamation of the coming reign of God. Jüngel suggests that Jesus understood his identity as the one who accomplishes this unity between humanity and God. This unity is accomplished through Jesus' call to decision—everyone who acknowledges him will be acknowledged before God (Luke 12:8, etc.) —and in this way Jesus acknowledges himself as an eschatological phenomenon.[34] Here Jüngel cites Bultmann's observation that Jesus' call to decision implies a Christology.[35]

It is significant, however, that nowhere in the life of Jesus can one find an explication of this implicit Christology. Jüngel argues that the Easter confession of Jesus as the Christ was possible only *because* Jesus never claimed any "christological dignity" for himself.[36] At this point dogmatic responsibility first begins, namely when these christological statements (even the confession of the resurrection of Jesus from the dead) are affirmed by the early church as constitutive elements of Jesus' personal identity. Jüngel suggests that "dogmatically the historical Jesus is significant precisely to the degree that the mystery of his personal identity points beyond the story of his earthly life and suffering, and thus beyond his death. That this has indeed happened is shown clearly in the way the title *Christ* has become part of the name of the person: *Jesus Christ.*"[37]

Jüngel attempts to answer the question of the personal identity of Jesus Christ in terms of the language of relation (*Beziehung*). Personal being is being in relation, and this includes relation to God, relation to others, and

---

are so or not, but questions about the existence or non-existence of the persons who are interested in it." Soden, "Was ist Wahrheit?," 10–11. Pannenberg also cites this essay in his own treatment of the concept of truth. See Pannenberg, "Was ist Wahrheit?"

34. This is not to be confused with suggesting that Jesus proclaimed himself to be God, as few contemporary New Testament scholars are willing to allow that Jesus ever made such claims for himself.

35. Bultmann, *Das Verhältnis der urchristlichen Christusbotschaft zum historischen Jesus*, 16. ET: "Primitive Christian Kerygma." See also Jüngel, *Paulus und Jesus*, 81, for a treatment of the relationship between Jesus' own proclamation and the proclamation of Jesus as the Christ. Jüngel refers to the work of Ebeling as well as Ernst Fuchs, both of whom attempt to show that the proclamation of Jesus as the Christ as the *content* of faith is hermeneutically related to the historical Jesus as the *ground* of faith. Just as the presence of Jesus Christ *in* the Word went into the proclamation of Jesus as the Christ, so the past relationship of Jesus *to his own word* went into his own proclamation.

36. Jüngel, "Zur dogmatischen Bedeutung," 237.

37. Ibid.

relation to oneself. In short, to exist as a human being is to exist in relation.[38] Furthermore, to exist in relation is realized in events, which means that to exist is to have a history. As long as a person lives there are relations and when these relations end, life ends. The state of relationlessness (*Beziehungslosigkeit*) is death. Furthermore, the destruction of relations that are constitutive of human being means the loss of peace, which includes a fractured relationship to God: "there is no peace for the godless" (Is. 48:22).[39] Jüngel illustrates that on the basis of Jesus' own self-understanding and on the basis of the Easter kerygma, the person of Jesus Christ can be understood as the one who creates peace in the midst of a fractured relationship to God, to others, and to oneself. The Easter kerygma therefore proclaims the death of Jesus as the ultimate peace-making event.[40]

The Easter kerygma, the proclamation of the death and resurrection of Jesus as this peace-making event, presumes the identity of the risen one with the crucified one, the risen Christ with the earthly Jesus.[41] Jüngel suggests that the decisive knowledge that the resurrection of Jesus provides for faith is that the one who lives in such a way lives completely from God. To be raised from the dead means to live from God, and without the God who raises the dead, Jesus would simply be dead. The event of the resurrection is thus a *creatio ex nihilo*. As Paul writes to the Romans, the God who raises the dead is the God who calls into existence the things that do not exist (Rom. 4:17).[42] Therefore faith recognizes in Jesus what he already was in a hidden way: the one who "ek-sisted completely from God."[43] As Ivor Davidson points out, for Jüngel

---

38. Ibid. This line of thinking is radicalized by Carter Heyward, who goes so far as to define God as "our power in mutual relation." Heyward, *Redemption of God*.

39. Jüngel, "Zur dogmatischen Bedeutung," 237.

40. Ibid.

41. For more on these themes in Jüngel's thought, see Davidson, "Crucified One," which pays special attention to Jüngel's attempts to reconcile Luther and Barth on the theology of the cross.

42. Jüngel, "Zur dogmatischen Bedeutung," 238. Małysz notes a reciprocal focus in Jüngel's treatment of the resurrection as an event that occurs in the life of humanity but also in the life of God. As he points out, for Jüngel the resurrection "constitutes divine openness to the new humanity, to human agency in correspondence to God." Małysz, "Resurrection as Divine Openness," 145–46.

43. Here, Jüngel borrows Heidegger's terminology of "ek-sistence" to indicate the unique quality of the human.

The resurrection is overwhelmingly epistemic in its force. It does not reverse Jesus's suffering and death; it discloses what his suffering and death are all about. Its power is not, it should be noted, to 'explain' the mystery of the cross, for mystery that remains; but the resurrection is, as the obverse side of the same mystery, the exposition of that event in all its wonder.[44]

In this respect Jüngel argues that the event of the resurrection is the revelation of that which Jesus already was, namely the one who "ek-sisted" completely from God and who insisted on the will of God.[45] For Jüngel, "it is precisely in Jesus' humanity that he is the Son of God; that is, in wanting to be and in actually being nothing other than the human person in correspondence to God, he *is* the Son of God."[46] Furthermore, it is precisely this "liberating" radical *distinction* between humanity and God, revealed in the life, death, and resurrection of Jesus, that, paradoxically, makes possible the strictest *unity* between God and humanity.[47]

Jüngel, far more than Pannenberg, is sympathetic to Bultmann's aims in his theological project and in significant ways represents a continuation of that project. At the same time, Jüngel offers promising constructive options beyond what Bultmann proposed, especially in Jüngel's precise and penetrating investigation of the meaning of myth and history for Christology and in his Trinitarian-soteriological grounding of the resurrection. As Derek Nelson points out in an invitation to Jüngel's theology, American theologians and pastors have much to learn from Jüngel, even though, as George Newlands laments, in our context Jüngel has more often been respected than read.[48] Nelson's essay is one attempt to amend that situation, and two relatively recent monographs in English have introduced Jüngel's

---

44. Davidson, "Crucified One," 44. Davidson goes on to critique Jüngel for having a deficient pneumatology, such that it is difficult to understand how Jüngel supposes that the cross can indeed be the revelatory event *for us* that he proclaims it to be. Welker agrees: "such reference to God's 'selflessly' opening self-relation cannot really adequately or clearly articulate the salvific power of the resurrection and the Holy Spirit." Welker, *God the Revealed*, 179. In an earlier book Welker attempts to address these pneumatological deficiencies, as he understands them. See Welker, *God the Spirit*.

45. See Jüngel's section on the crucified Jesus Christ as a vestige of the Trinity in Jüngel, *Gott als Geheimnis der Welt*, 470–505. ET: *God as Mystery of the World*.

46. Jüngel, "Zur dogmatischen Bedeutung," 239. There are shades here of Schleiermacher's focus in the *Glaubenslehre* on Jesus' "perfect God-consciousness."

47. Ibid., 240.

48. George Newlands, quoted in Nelson, "Indicative of Grace," 177.

theology to a wider audience.[49] Another contemporary theologian sympathetic to Bultmann's (and Jüngel's) project is Ingolf Ulrich Dalferth, to whom we now turn.

Ingolf Ulrich Dalferth

Ingolf Ulrich Dalferth,[50] after completing his doctoral degree under Jüngel at Tübingen, has written on the topics of semiotics, philosophy of religion, ecumenism, and the problem of evil. For the purposes of this discussion we will focus on Dalferth's work in Christology and hermeneutics.

In an essay on myth and demythologizing, Dalferth describes his work on this subject with the subtitle, "a recollection of the indispensable task of theology."[51] The task of recognizing and interpreting myth is indispensable for theology because every culture, past and present, has its myths, which cannot be eliminated or ignored. Myths are not simply pre-rational products of primitive societies, but are ubiquitous in every culture, past and present; they persist because no living culture has a closed "background of meaning" (*Sinnhintergrund*).[52] According to Dalferth, "the vigor of culture is an expression of its power to integrate various traditions into its background of meaning and to meld these into a new and continuously evolving unity."[53] Each culture therefore contains within itself the potential to evolve, and this potential is expressed especially powerfully in the culture's myths. A culture will privilege one type of myth while criticizing another, and these myths themselves are balanced by various "counter-myths" in which "our" myth is understood to be superior to other myths (e.g., the Christian

---

49. See DeHart, *Beyond the Necessary God*; and Małysz, *Trinity, Freedom and Love.*

50. Dalferth (b. 1948) is Danforth Professor of Philosophy of Religion at Claremont Graduate University and Emeritus Professor of Systematic Theology, Symbolism, and Philosophy of Religion in the Theological Faculty of the University of Zürich.

51. Dalferth, "Von der Mythenkritik zur Entmythologisierung."

52. There is no adequate phrase in English to capture the complexity of meaning in Dalferth's term *Sinnhintergrund*. *Sinn* in this context can be translated as sense, meaning, consciousness, etc. All of these shades of meaning should be noted when reading *Sinnhintergrund*. A living culture's background of meaning is never closed, precisely because the culture is living and still evolving. Only when the culture dies will its background of meaning be closed. In this sense *Sinnhintergrund* is analogous to *Geschichte*, which will never be fully understood until history itself has come to an end.

53. Ibid., 58.

myth versus pagan myths in the ancient church). Thus myths, for Dalferth, become a linguistic expression of a culture's background of meaning.

In the form of narratives, these myths express what is self-understood and often taken for granted as self-evidently obvious in that particular culture. Myth expresses a culture's "self-understandability," not in terms of our culture's exceptionalism and absoluteness such that it cannot be otherwise, but rather the myths obscure and therefore seek to minimize our awareness of the contingency of our own and every other culture. Myths offer empirical and historical rationalizations of things as they are, not as facts, but rather as what Dalferth calls "counterfacts": "As such they do not so much narrate what was or is, but rather what could and should be, so that they call to mind 'what never happened but is always valid.'"[54] In other words, myths create the ideological framework that allows us to take our culture for granted as the only way things could (and should) be.

Myths are convincing, but only when they remind us of something of which we are already convinced. Thus the convincing power of myth lies not so much in the details of the narrative itself but rather in its ability to evoke our approval or consent in the context in which and for which the story is told. Myths bring to expression through narrative what is commonly held to be self-understood, and thus they serve as a reminder of what is always valid. And so, where myths relate historical experiences, their purpose is not to communicate the past to the present, but rather they remind us of what we should never forget.[55] The emphasis is always on the present, understood with the aid of the dominant myths of a particular culture. So the question for Dalferth is not "how long we should live with myths, but rather with what myths we should continue to live."[56] He quotes Hegel's sentiment that myths belong to the maturation of the human race; when humanity grows up, there is no more need for myths.[57] Dalferth notes that Hegel's confidence sounded just as anachronistic then as it does today, because Hegel himself was operating within a mythical structure: the myth of the Enlightenment. This is the myth of the displacement of myth with and through logos, resulting in myths being relegated further into the past in favor of a more rational worldview.[58]

---

54. Ibid., 59. Dalferth is quoting Sallust in the last portion of the passage.

55. Ibid.

56. Ibid., 60

57. Hegel, *Vorlesungen über die Philosophie der Religion*, quoted in ibid.

58. Although Dalferth does not make this connection, much the same progression is

Dalferth suggests that there is no such irreversible process as the transformation "from myth to logos." Each culture is enmeshed in its own myths and exists in light of its particular background of self-understanding, which provides the context both for its questions and its search for answers. The relationship between myth and logos should not be considered from the perspective of "earlier or later," but rather from the perspective of "simultaneity." The difference between myth and logos is a difference that developed historically in the process of what Dalferth calls "the self-clarification of the logos."[59] Especially in the eighteenth and nineteenth centuries, scholars assumed that sustained rational criticism of myth would separate the rational from the mythical in a unidirectional linear progression in such a way that myth was interpreted in terms of logos, but logos was not interpreted in terms of myth. But in our own time logos is no longer perceived as the antithesis of myth, but is now understood to participate in its own myth, namely the myth of the Enlightenment: the Western myth of the sovereignty and autonomy of absolute reason. Dalferth concludes that this myth of absolute reason shows that the relationship between myth and logos is primarily a relationship of simultaneity because it is precisely reason itself that is being understood mythically.[60]

But what are the implications of this discussion for theology? Dalferth suggests that there are two implications. First, each theology has its own particular context and therefore its own mythical influence due to its particular cultural location. This situation requires theologians to engage in a critical debate with the myths of its time. Second, theologians must not relegate myths to the darkness of the past, thinking they have succeeded in demythologizing them by introducing the clarity of rational thought. In theology there is always a tension between the mythological language of faith, which is simultaneously susceptible to criticism and remythologizing, and demythologized dogmatic discourse, which seeks to explicate faith in critical distinction from its mythological forms of expression, thereby becoming susceptible to an uncritical rationalism. Dalferth argues that these two tasks—the critical engagement with myth *and* logos—occur

---

outlined in Kant's famous essay, "Beantwortung der Frage," ET: "An Answer to the Question," in which Kant proposes that the motto of the Enlightenment ought to be "*Sapere aude!* [Dare to use your own understanding]" and suggests that enlightenment consists in "throwing off the yoke of immaturity."

59. Dalferth, "Von der Mythenkritik zur Entmythologisierung," 60.

60. Ibid., 60–61.

simultaneously and that together they combine to form the foundation of Christian theology.[61]

Theology cannot completely free itself from the mythology of its language of faith without losing its religious foundation and the phenomenal basis of its reflection on faith. In no way do myths belong only to the primitive origin of theology. Critical engagement with myth has been, since the beginning of theology, the foundation of Christian self-understanding. Ancient Greek theology tended to take the side of logos against myth by understanding the polar tension between logos and myth as the contrast in which theology itself stood in opposition to myth. Christian theology inherited this contrast and enlisted the aid of the philosophical logos, setting "Christian reason" in opposition to "pagan myth." Only in the Enlightenment did this situation begin to change. The conflict in theology ceased to be an external conflict between Christian reason and pagan myth and became an internal conflict between myth and logos in theology itself. Dalferth argues that it is not myth, but rather the criticism of myth that is the origin of theology.[62]

In light of the historical-critical appropriation of the category of myth, contemporary theologians can no longer insist on the antithesis between myth and logos. Hermeneutically, theologians must recognize that mythical thought permeates the biblical texts. Dogmatically, theologians must be aware of the mythological elements of theology and of how extensively theology relies on mythical forms and functions, especially in light of our awareness of the ubiquity of myth. The central problem in the theological debate with the question of myth today is no longer the demarcation of Christian logos from myth, but rather the hermeneutical and dogmatic issue of the inevitable presence of mythical thought and forms of speech in Christianity itself. Dalferth suggests that the question theology should now investigate is how the eschatological truth claims of Christian faith can be interpreted dogmatically without hermeneutically having to disavow or ignore the mythological character of Christian discourse.[63]

Dalferth's preferred solution to this problem is a hermeneutic of myths. The interpretation of myth demonstrates that myth itself is an interpretation and that myth operates with a hermeneutical structure lying beneath the surface of the narrative. If a text is interpreted as myth, then

---

61. Dalferth, *Jenseits von Mythos und Logos*, 36.

62. Ibid., 37.

63. Dalferth, "Von der Mythenkritik zur Entmythologisierung," 76.

the text must itself be understood as an interpretation of another myth. If this is so, then there can be no interpretation other than a continuation of its mythical meaning in other forms. Only when the interpretation is of something that is *not* mythical can it be understood as mythological speech about the non-mythological. In the latter case myths or mythological texts can be demythologized and interpreted non-mythologically. But the question remains whether a myth is understood hermeneutically as a mythical interpretation of the mythical or as a mythological presentation of the non-mythical.[64] In the first case each attempt at a non-mythical meaning of the mythical interpretation would fail because the object of interpretation is myth all the way down. In the second case the non-mythical meaning of mythological speech is available, which also allows for a non-mythological meaning.[65] This is the possibility that Rudolf Bultmann examined through his demythologizing project.

Since the New Testament itself, Christians have insisted that Christian discourse expresses something non-mythical; at the same time, this message is expressed mythologically. As Dalferth puts it, "this message does not relate something that never happened but somehow remains valid, but rather it proclaims that something totally new has taken place in history: that through the power of the Spirit God has acted in Jesus Christ."[66] It was to understand this proclamation that Bultmann developed his program of demythologizing. The purpose of demythologizing was not to isolate and eliminate the mythical elements of the Christian tradition, but rather to interpret the mythological elements of the Christian proclamation, which "in, with, and under mythical forms of speech says something non-mythical."[67] This program of demythologizing is not only legitimate, but it is commanded, because the New Testament kerygma itself already critiques and demythologizes its contemporary world-picture and its accompanying self-understanding, and it does this by speaking *mythologically* but not *mythically*. The program of demythologizing at-

---

64. The distinction between the terms "mythical" and "mythological" is an important one in this discussion. "Mythical" (*mythisch*) describes something that is itself a myth. In contrast, "mythological" (*mythologisch*) describes speech, narrative, or thought that describes or interprets something *as* a myth, even though the object of the interpretation might be non-mythical.

65. Dalferth, "Von Mythenkritik zur Entmythologisierung," 76–77.

66. Ibid., 78.

67. Ibid. Notice Dalferth's use of "in, with, and under" here, which mirrors Luther's language for the real presence of Christ in the Eucharist.

tempts to demythologize the New Testament kerygma in order to guard against mythical misunderstandings of Christian faith, and as such it performs a necessary function of Christian theology.[68]

Dalferth suggests that if Christianity hopes to contribute authentically to a pluralist religious conversation, it must speak in its own distinctive voice, which is Christology. He argues that Christology is more than one locus within theology: Christian theology *is* Christology, through and through.[69] Dalferth proposes what he calls "fields of reference" for christological discussions: the witness of the life of Jesus, the specific witness of Easter, and the spiritual witness of the Christian community. In these three fields of reference Christian theology can maintain its distinctive voice, its historical identity, and its present relevance. But if these christological discussions are to succeed, Dalferth proposes that theology must move beyond the alternatives of myth and logos. If theology protests too vociferously against myth by means of philosophical logos, then religion protests against the rationalistic trivialization and conceptual overcompensation of theology. If theology decries logos too vigorously, then it faces the philosophical or scientific accusation of religious obscurantism. In the first case, theology succumbs to the temptation to suffocate its distinctive voice and witness; in the second case, the temptation is to renounce any claim to speak coherently at all.[70]

The only way to avoid these accusations is to move beyond the categories of myth and logos and to relieve the tension between the two. Dalferth proposes that it is not theology itself, but rather the horizons of thought and understanding in which these categories originally evolved that are to blame for this tension. In order to relieve the tension of this polarization of myth and logos in Christian theology, Dalferth suggests the development and clarification of a "christological grammar of the Christian life of faith." Only if this development is successful, in Dalferth's estimation, can Christian theology present itself as an independent and relevant voice in the ongoing religious and philosophical conversation.[71]

Through an analysis of the etymological origins of the terms "myth" and "logos," Dalferth discovers that both terms have surprisingly similar origins. Both terms originally described a process of transmission, with

68. Ibid., 79.

69. Dalferth, *Jenseits von Mythos und Logos*, 3.

70. Ibid., 6.

71. Ibid.

"myth" describing that transmission that took place in a religious context, and "logos" describing that transmission that took place in an academic context. The difference between myth and logos is not an original, internal difference, but a difference that was invented by modern European intellectuals and read back onto the history of these terms and their use in the past. This invented contradiction does not represent past realities, but represents a European cultural development in which religion and science were placed in opposition.[72] In this context the difference between myth and logos developed as a practical difference of orientation. Logos achieved a position of superiority, so that myth was always understood in terms of logos, while logos was understood independently of myth. The distinction between myth and logos thus emerged in the process of the self-clarification of logos, with myth always giving way to logos in a process of maturation.[73] However, an irreversible linear progression from myth to logos is not possible, in Dalferth's estimation, because each time is enmeshed in its own myths, both past and present. Rather than dismiss these myths in an attempt to move forward into enlightenment by means of logos, it is the task of theology to take both myth and logos seriously and to enter into critical dialogue with them.[74]

In the New Testament, myth and logos are employed with equal frequency. The opposition between the two concepts in the New Testament is not so much an opposition between narrative and conceptual thought forms, because the Christian logos appears just as frequently as myth; the evangelists use both concepts. The difference between the two lies not in *how* something is described, but rather in *what* is described, if it is "experienced truth" or "invented pseudo-truth." Precisely because the logos also speaks of faith it can be misunderstood as myth. In logos, a truth comes to expression as history, but in myth a truth (or a pseudo-truth) is expressed in the form of a story, which can then (often wrongly) be interpreted away as nothing more than allegorical speech.[75]

In modern theology the task of identifying and interpreting myths becomes critical. Before myths can be interpreted, they need to be identified. A further distinction among myths is made so that theology recognizes a relationship between myth and history as well as a

72. Ibid., 19.
73. Ibid., 23.
74. Ibid., 36.
75. Ibid., 73.

relationship between myth and truth. Both questions remain important in current theological discussions, as the interpretation of these relationships requires theology's use of the historical-critical method. In earlier theological applications of the historical-critical method (e.g. Reimarus), the biblical texts were typically understood as expressing either fact *or* fiction, myths *or* history. Strauss and Bultmann recognized this problem in modern theology, and both Strauss's critical project and Bultmann's program of demythologizing highlighted one of the most important hermeneutical questions in modern theology by problematizing the relationship between myth, history, and truth.[76]

Based on his interpretation of Strauss and Bultmann, Dalferth proposes a new way of approaching the question of the relationship between myth and logos. He understands Bultmann's greatest contributions to be in the area of language and anthropology, but he also suggests that Bultmann's solution stopped short of success. Bultmann remained at an impasse in terms of the role of language and metaphor, which is the point of departure for Dalferth. Dalferth suggests that Bultmann found himself at a crossroads in terms of language: either religious symbols and images can only be interpreted by means of other symbols and images, in which case the interpretation is for all intents and purposes open-ended and uncontrollable, or the interpretation of symbols and images is limited and defined, in which case the interpretation must be existential. In both cases, Dalferth believes, Bultmann was too quick to discard the images, symbols, and metaphors in favor of translating them into contemporary thought forms.

Dalferth suggests a third option: it is possible to make the New Testament images, symbols, and metaphors intelligible to contemporary people by reconstructing the grammar of the New Testament images, symbols, and metaphors themselves.[77] The task of interpretation then would not

76. Ibid., 115.

77. Ibid., 153. Bultmann, however, does treat this issue briefly in "Zum Problem der Entmythologisierung" (1961), in which he asks if there is a limit to demythologizing. He notes that it is often said that neither religion nor the Christian faith can dispense with mythological speech. Bultmann disagrees, but not without noting that such speech does provide images and symbols for cultic and liturgical language. He emphasizes, however, that the decisive thing about these images and symbols is that they conceal a meaning that theology and philosophy must reveal. This meaning cannot be remythologized, because it too will require interpretation, *ad infinitum*. The claim that myth (and images and symbols) is indispensable assumes that there are some myths that cannot be interpreted existentially. If these myths cannot be interpreted existentially, then it must mean that in some cases it is necessary to speak of God in objectifying terms. This is

be to make a distinction between mythological forms of presentation and the kerygmatic intention of the New Testament texts based on existential analysis. It would instead be an inquiry into the function of New Testament images, so that these images are able to provide guidelines for Christian discourse in the present. The task of Christian dogmatics in light of this proposition would be an effort to understand the grammar of Christian image-discourse, rather than existential interpretation of the New Testament texts. This means, then, that rather than seeking out the meaning of the kerygma *behind* the images, symbols, and metaphors, the images, symbols, and metaphors themselves are the object of inquiry and analysis as bearers of the kerygma. Theology's task in this case is to analyze and clarify the function of these images, symbols, and metaphors in the life and discourse of the early Christian communities and to construct a grammar by which the patterns and rules of this discourse are made available and normative for Christian faith today.[78]

This, Dalferth suggests, is a promising way out of the tension between myth and logos because it posits Christian theology as a third way, a way of thinking and speaking that is truly *sui generis* because the subject matter of Christian theology is itself *sui generis*.[79] For Dalferth, as for Bultmann, the central theme of Christian theology is the eschatological act of God in Jesus Christ. Dalferth suggests that the truth of the Christian confession of faith stands or falls with its confession of this salvific act. To this end he

---

precisely the problem of myth for Bultmann. He proposes that instead of using objectifying language to speak of God, we use analogical language instead. But even in the use of analogy one is returned to the field of existential analysis, for analogy uses what is known to the human as its referent. So for Bultmann it is not possible to avoid existential analysis, which means that it is not possible to retain the use of myths, images, or symbols that have not been thoroughly demythologized and interpreted existentially. Bultmann's work maintains its validity and its importance for Dalferth, however, because Bultmann's true intention in demythologizing was not to eliminate myth, but rather to clarify the kerygma and its expression of the salvific act of God.

78. The efforts of modern theology to clarify the relationship between myth and logos have led us to realize that theology must move beyond myth and logos if it is to make its eschatological truth-claims. Dalferth argues that the subject matter of Christian faith cannot be expressed without the symbolic, metaphorical, and mythological medium of our language. In light of this reality, it is the task of dogmatics to develop itself as a grammar of the Christian life of faith, specifically to understand, interpret, and speak appropriately using the rich symbolic and metaphorical language and imagery of the Christian tradition. Dalferth, *Jenseits von Mythos und Logos*, 163.

79. See Dalferth, preface to the English edition, *Crucified and Resurrected*.

justifies the claim with which he began his work: that all Christian theology is primarily Christology.[80]

In his monograph *Der auferweckte Gekreuzigte*, Dalferth sketches a grammar of Christology based on his earlier discussion in *Jenseits von Mythos und Logos*.[81] He maintains that the Christian proclamation that Jesus is the Son of God is grounded in the understanding that Jesus is the crucified one whom God awakened from the dead (*der von Gott von Tode auferweckten Gekreuzigten*).[82] The logical conclusions for Christology of this understanding and Dalferth's precise formulation of it is that this christological confession must always reconstruct its content as a statement about the awakened crucified one. This means that the theme of christological confession is not the historically conceivable (*historisch faßbare*) Jesus of Nazareth, but rather the one whom God awakened from the dead: Jesus Christ, the *Christus praesens* of the kerygma. This orientation is rooted in the Easter proclamation of God's eschatological act, by which God awakened Jesus from the dead, and the entire New Testament is a collection of various expressions of this one central theme. Indeed, "the confession that God raised the crucified Jesus from the dead is the theological foundation and basic judgment of the Christian faith, behind which one cannot go. When one speaks of Jesus, one speaks of the one awakened by God."[83]

The meaning of this confession is by no means obvious and self-evident because it combines several separate claims. First, the awakened one is the crucified Jesus of Nazareth. Second, the confession speaks of an eschatological event that concerns all humanity. And third, it is *God* who awakened Jesus from the dead.[84] The confession that it was *Jesus of Nazareth* whom God awakened from the dead requires an investigation into the personal history of Jesus. The gospels are quite clear that Jesus' primary mission was to proclaim the advent of the reign of God. Through his words and deeds, Jesus made available the nearness of God, and his proclamation

---

80. Dalferth, *Jenseits von Mythos und Logos*, 312–13.

81. As Dalferth mentions in his preface to *Der auferweckte Gekreuzigte*, this material was originally the second half of *Jenseits von Mythos und Logos* but was ultimately published separately and by a different press.

82. Dalferth, *Der auferweckte Gekreuzigte*, 23. Dalferth consistently uses the term *Auferweckung* ("awakening") rather than *Auferstehung* ("resurrection") to emphasize that what happened to Jesus was *not* bodily resuscitation. See Dalferth, "Volles Grab, leerer Glaube?," for a more extensive discussion of this and related questions.

83. Dalferth, *Der auferweckte Gekreuzigte*, 24.

84. Ibid., 24–25.

of God and of God's power to transform the world is the foundation of the early Christian confessions. At the center of Jesus' proclamation lies the message of the inbreaking of the reign of God. This message provided the first Christians with the interpretive key to their understanding of the passion, cross, and appearances of Jesus after his death.

The first Christians understood the life of Jesus, which had ended in his death on the cross, in light of his proclamation of the coming reign of God. Consequently, the disciples believed that God remained near to Jesus even in death and because that was the case, Jesus' death had significance beyond his life: "the merciful love of God that Jesus had proclaimed proved to be stronger than death itself and established the reality that God, not death, had the last word in Jesus' history."[85] The first Christians understood this to mean that God had initiated in Jesus what would eventually become a reality for them: they too would be raised to eternal life by the God who raised Jesus from the dead. This salvific act has universal significance because it was expressed once and for all that it is not humanity's distance from God in sin and death, but rather God's love for us and God's proximity to us that is the ultimate reality in our lives.[86]

The central confession of the first Christians was that the cross of Jesus was an eschatological act of God for the salvation of the world, an event that profoundly altered not only the life of Jesus, but their own lives as well; above all, this confession was soteriological. As Dalferth puts it, "the Christian confession of the awakening of Jesus is in essence more than a confession of the meaning of the cross of Jesus; it is a confession of the eschatological act of God in the history of Jesus Christ and it is also a confession of God's loyalty to us for our salvation."[87]

Dalferth is especially concerned with the word of the cross and awakening of Jesus as the point of departure for his Christology, as he proposes that "the Christian faith stands and falls with the confession of the awakening of Jesus by God."[88] There is no word from the cross without the resurrection, but this word does not belong to the cross itself: "the cross is silent and can do nothing but silence. God remained silent, Jesus died, and the disciples fled. There is nothing more to understand in the cross in the context of human experience. The cross itself cannot lead to the proclamation

85. Ibid., 25–26.
86. Ibid., 26.
87. Ibid.
88. Ibid., 31.

of the awakening, for the cross is soteriologically silent."[89] To understand the cross in its soteriological significance means to understand it first in terms of the life of God and therefore also in terms of human life. It is in the identification and interpretation of the cross as the cross of *Jesus Christ* that the cross becomes the salvation event. The proclamation of the awakening of Jesus brings the truth of the cross to speech. The word of the cross is the word that God is near to us and that we are near to God even in death. The Easter proclamation is only properly understood as nothing other than the word of the cross, which brings to speech the reality of the cross as salvation event. "Only the word accomplishes this: the cross as such remains forever silent. Only when this word is interpreted through the word of the gospel in the context of the life of God does it begin to speak . . . This word does not so much say who and what God is . . . as much as it tells us who and what we are, what the world is, what death is."[90]

What the word of the cross tells us is that we are being transformed from self-centeredness to God-centeredness, and that this transformation therefore effects a shift in our relation to God, from a theoretical or intellectual understanding of God as an abstraction to a practical, lived relationship with the God whom Jesus called "merciful Father." This transformation is not accomplished by repeating the historical fact of the cross, but it is accomplished by presenting us with a concrete event in our own history, in order to initiate something completely new in us: becoming receptive within our life and death to God's life, so to make us "truly free in the midst of all the imperfections and incompleteness of our lives."[91]

In order for this word to come to expression in its saving significance, four tendencies toward belittlement (*Verharmlosungstendenzen*)[92] of the cross must be avoided. First is the historical belittlement, which presents the cross primarily or exclusively as an event in the life of Jesus, as the last event of his earthly life. Second is the ethical belittlement, which pres-

---

89. Ibid., 44.

90. Ibid., 44–45.

91. Ibid, 48.

92. *Verharmlosung* is a difficult word to translate. The literal sense of *Verharmlosung* is "trivializing" or "downplaying." For example, when a teenager borrows the family car and hits a tree, the teenager might tell the parents that it is only a small scratch. This is an example of *Verharmlosung*. In the sense in which Dalferth uses it, Jo Bennett has translated it as "belittlement," such that the true scandal or power of the cross is belittled, in the sense of being both minimized, downplayed, and trivialized. Dalferth, *Crucified and Resurrected*, 49.

ents the cross primarily or exclusively as a standard or model of Christian behavior. Third is the symbolic belittlement, which reduces the cross to a human experience or attitude. And fourth is the religious belittlement, which moves too quickly from Good Friday to Easter and thereby diminishes the importance of the cross in order to emphasize the importance of the resurrection.[93]

Dalferth recognizes that the act of God constitutes the central theme of the resurrection confession. He outlines the debate between Karl Barth and Rudolf Bultmann over the resurrection, in which Bultmann declares the resurrection not to be a historical event but rather to be the emergence of faith in the disciples and in which Barth argues that the resurrection is a historical event in the life of Jesus rather than the emergence of Easter faith in the disciples.[94] Dalferth proposes that it is not the reality or facts of the resurrection itself but the act of God, which cannot be described as such but only confessed and believed by those who are included in and transformed by this act, that should be the central issue in discussions of the resurrection. Against both Barth and Bultmann, Dalferth proposes that the act of God in the awakening of Jesus is neither a historical event limited to the life of Jesus nor something reducible to the subjective impressions of the disciples; rather, the act of God in the awakening of Jesus is first and foremost the divine creative act in the cross for the benefit of all humanity. Only by privileging God's act in the cross can those four "tendencies toward belittlement" be avoided.[95]

God, by awakening Jesus from death to life, opens several possibilities to us. First, God reveals the immovable permanence of God's creative presence; second, God establishes the point of God's presence (to be ever-present and ever-creating); third, God reveals the character of God's divine creativity (love); and fourth, God establishes that God remains present even in death. God's act in the cross reveals that God is the God who creates, that God is creative love. In this hindsight onto the cross God's act is understood to be a *creatio ex nihilo*: "a being from not-being, a new being from the old being, a being-with-God from a being-distanced-from-God, an eternally-being-with-God from a being-separated-from-God."[96] This creative act of God is a *Trinitarian* act, as it is understood christologically

---

93. Dalferth, *Der auferweckte Gekreuzigte*, 48–50.

94. Ibid, 55.

95. Ibid., 56–57.

96. Ibid., 58.

in terms of Jesus, theologically in terms of God, and pneumatologically in terms of the salvation of humanity. The God who acts is the triune God whose threefold act in the cross encompasses creation, reconciliation, and completion.[97] "If this is the case," Dalferth concludes, "then all the historical [*historisch*] statements about the historic [*geschichtlich*] Jesus, his life, teaching and death, as well as the statements about us and our world, come to expression as moments in the comprehensive reality of God."[98]

How did this early Christian proclamation of the awakening of Jesus develop? Dalferth argues that the Christian proclamation of Jesus' awakening was by no means an obvious, self-evident truth; "it was—especially for those who experienced firsthand the death of Jesus on the cross—in fact completely unbelievable."[99] So what prompted the first Christians to proclaim Jesus risen from the dead, in spite of the doubt and ridicule with which their confession was met?

Dalferth proposes that it was not possible for the disciples to argue from a commonly held belief in the general resurrection of the dead,[100] nor could they argue based on previous cases of resurrection. They had no precedent whatsoever upon which to base their claims, except to confess that Jesus' resurrection was a mighty act of God. The believability of their claim did not rest in their powers to convince those to whom it was proclaimed; rather, they understood that their proclamation did not rest on the testimony of human beings at all, but was proclaimed through the power of the Spirit of the God who awakened Jesus from the dead.[101]

The eyewitness reports of the appearances of Jesus did not make the proclamation more believable or acceptable, as the story of Thomas in the Gospel of John illustrates (John 20:24–29). The only ones convinced by the appearances were the ones who encountered God in Jesus himself, the ones who came to faith firsthand.[102] For those who did not know Jesus in his earthly life, faith in his resurrection is possible only through the Spirit, in

97. Ibid., 59.

98. Ibid., 59–60.

99. Ibid., 62.

100. Compare Pannenberg, especially his section on the conception of the resurrection of the dead in Judaism and early Christian expectation of the general resurrection of the dead in *Grundzüge der Christologie*, 69–85.

101. Dalferth, *Der auferweckte Gekreuzigte*, 63.

102. Dalferth seems to be overlooking Paul here, who, according to Paul himself, did not know the earthly Jesus but nevertheless came to faith thanks to a vision of the risen Christ.

the community of those who gather in Jesus' name.[103] But Dalferth argues that the central problem of the Easter confession lies not in the convincing power of these first witnesses, but in the content of the confession itself.[104]

Historically, there are only two facts (*Tatsachen*)[105] in the Easter confession: that Jesus was crucified in the vicinity of Jerusalem, and that the disciples reported that the living Lord had appeared to them. Therefore "it is not the resurrection of Jesus as a historical event in itself, but the Easter experience of the disciples that is the determining historical circumstance [*Sachverhalt*] on which the proclamation is based."[106] This Easter experience brings to expression their witness to the appearances of Jesus, not the other way around. There was indeed an element of cognitive dissonance in their experience of the appearances of Jesus: Jesus died on the cross, and yet they had experienced him as the one who lives. The disciples solved this dissonance by appealing to an act of God. Yes, Jesus was dead, but he now lives, because he was awakened by God. Dalferth studiously avoids the temptation to ground the reality of the resurrection in the empty tomb because, in his estimation, any theological discussion or debate about the empty tomb of Jesus is irrelevant because the only available historical facts are the death of Jesus on the cross and the disciples' reports of appearances of the living Lord. Nowhere in the New Testament is the event of the resurrection itself described as it happened, and Paul does not even mention the empty tomb and yet confessed that Jesus was risen, so for Dalferth any conjectures about the event of the resurrection itself, as well as the empty tomb, are theologically irrelevant.[107]

Historical questions about the empty tomb and the nature of Jesus' body are ultimately irrelevant because, for Dalferth, the awakening of Jesus from the dead is not a historical event because it is not a mundane event at all, but an eschatological, creative act of God. "The awakening of Jesus is not a historical event *in* the world, which as such stands alongside other historical events. Much more than that, it is rather an eschatological event

103. This claim is reminiscent of Schleiermacher's analysis in the *Glaubenslehre* of faith as mediated by the Christian community's response to and expression of the impression first received from Jesus and his perfect God-consciousness.

104. Dalferth, *Der auferweckte Gekreuzigte*, 64.

105. For a discussion of the history of the concept of *Tatsache* in Christian theology, see Staats, "Der theologiegeschichtliche Hintergrund des Begriffes 'Tatsache.'"

106. Dalferth, *Der auferweckte Gekreuzigte*, 66.

107. See Dalferth's article "Volles Grab, leerer Glaube?" for a discussion of the relationship between the resurrection and the empty tomb.

on the world."[108] This is so because all historical events, Dalferth suggests, "have their place in this world and thus are essentially mundane; the awakening of Jesus, however, is essentially divine. It marks the boundary and the end of our world."[109]

The Easter faith of the disciples can only be understood in terms of a twofold grounding: it is grounded in the history of Jesus *and* in the history of the ones who confessed him to be awakened from the dead. This twofold grounding manifests itself in the confession that Jesus is the Christ who was awakened by God and that the disciples' faith emerged through the power of the Spirit:

> *God alone* awakened Jesus from the dead, *God alone* elected and called those who witnessed this unbelievable deed of God, and *God alone* made it possible through the Spirit to believe this witness and to join in the confession of the message of the awakening. The content, the execution, and the success of the message of the awakening were likewise understood as the *free deed and act of the creative love of God*, which required no human corroboration—faith does not rest in any sense on the human message but entirely on the power of God.[110]

Thus the disciples' confession of the act of God came to speech in a Trinitarian formulation. Dalferth explicates this Trinitarian formulation in terms of the revelation of God, which was itself Trinitarian in nature. First, it is the revelation that Jesus is the Christ, the Son of God. Second, it is the revelation that God is the Father who has awakened Jesus from the dead. And third, it is the revelation of the divinity of the Spirit, insofar as it is through the power of the Spirit that this revelation occurs and is accepted in trusting faith.[111] The awakening of the crucified one must therefore always be understood as an act of God. As Dalferth puts it, "There is no awakened one and likewise no faith in the awakened one unless God effects both."[112] This is revealed in the word of the cross, which is the word of the gospel. It is in the gospel, the kerygma of the church, that this revelation becomes revelation *to us*, and it is through this proclamation that we meet the crucified one whom God awakened from the dead. It is through this encounter

---

108. Dalferth, *Der auferweckte Gekreuzigte*, 80; emphasis in original.
109. Ibid., 79.
110. Dalferth, "Volles Grab, leerer Glaube?," 387; emphasis in original.
111. Dalferth, *Der auferweckte Gekreuzigte*, 81.
112. Dalferth, "Volles Grab, leerer Glaube?," 404.

that we come to Easter faith in the triune God, and it is the task of theology to provide a grammar for this Easter discourse.

Dalferth, like Jüngel, is largely sympathetic to Bultmann's project while also pushing it in new and promising constructive directions. What distinguishes Dalferth's work on the resurrection is its compelling practical, even pastoral, sensitivity. Being far more than a purely intellectual exercise, Dalferth's critique of the modern stalemate between myth and logos and his thoroughly Trinitarian grounding of the cross and resurrection of Jesus reveal a deep desire to proclaim the gospel in all its power to our own time and place, all while taking with utmost seriousness the promise and the perils of our postmodern situation. Despite his recent move to Claremont Graduate University in California and his publication of several books in English, Dalferth remains relatively unfamiliar to American audiences.[113] Given his broad interests and his powerful writing, it is to be hoped that this regrettable situation will soon change.

Above all, Dalferth is a theologian of the Christian life, and so it is fitting to end this last section with a passage from Dalferth's preface to the new English translation of his book on the resurrection, in which he summarizes the relationship between the task of theology and the faith that theology seeks to explicate. In his words we can hear echoes of Bultmann as well:

> The problems of our world are not solved in or by theology, but Christian theology aims at helping Christians to engage in identifying and solving the problems of our time by providing guidelines and signposts for orientation. A grammar book is not to be confused with a discourse or a practice that enacts that grammar, and while Christian theology seeks to outline the grammar of a Christian life of faith, it is in the actual practice of this faith in the manifold areas of human life in our contemporary world that this grammar is enacted. We must not expect theology to do what can only be done in the life and practice of faith. Theologies come and go, and no theological view ought to be confused with the eschatological reality that it seeks to unfold ... What is decisive about human life from a Christian point of view is not what we think and do but that this life is the locus of God's creative and transforming presence, whether we believe it or not. Accordingly, the crucial question is not about our theologies but rather the question of

---

113. At this time there are still no studies in English devoted specifically to Dalferth's theology.

whether our life is actually transformed from a life of unfaith and self-love to a life of faith and the love of God and neighbor.[114]

---

114. Dalferth, preface to *Crucified and Resurrected*, xvii.

CHAPTER SEVEN

Some Concluding Remarks

CHRISTIANITY STANDS OR FALLS with its proclamation that God raised the crucified Jesus from the dead, such that without the resurrection there would be no Christian church. But what does this mean? What are the theological implications of such a statement? Several inexhaustible topics for theological reflection emerge from this one statement: Who is God? Who was Jesus? Who is Jesus the Christ? What is the significance of the cross? What is the meaning of the resurrection? How ought this to be proclaimed? And finally, what does all of this mean for us? The presumption that Christianity stands or falls by its proclamation of the resurrection requires theological attention to the implications and possibilities inherent in this confession.

Good questions never die; only the responses change. Not only is the question of the resurrection a good question, it is also perhaps the most important question for Christian theology. The responses to these questions must evolve because the context in which the questions are raised is also always evolving. What was the most faithful response for the ancient church might not be the most faithful response for the church at the beginning of the twenty-first century. It is the task of theology to evaluate its context and develop faithful responses that address that same context. Without this continuous revision of its responses, theology risks becoming irrelevant, and because each new generation has its own specific problems and possibilities, theology must continue to engage itself and its generation in critical reflection and dialogue.

The perennial question of the resurrection is an exemplary illustration of the continuity of the theological enterprise. As each new generation poses its questions and discovers new insights, theologians apply these insights to its discussion of the resurrection in light of their present context.

For example, Hermann Samuel Reimarus took a decidedly rationalist approach to the resurrection, while David Friedrich Strauss investigated the question of resurrection in terms of the newly discovered importance of myth. Rudolf Bultmann emphasized the significance of eschatology and the quest for authentic human existence in his treatment, while Wolfhart Pannenberg resisted the prevailing tendency to downplay the historicity of the resurrection. Eberhard Jüngel pushed Bultmann's insights on myth and history further than Bultmann himself was willing or able to do, while Ingolf Ulrich Dalferth suggested that theology finally move beyond the false dichotomy of myth and logos to establish a third option: the grammar of Christian images, symbols, and myths. Without this tension between myth and logos, Strauss would have no means by which to launch his analysis, and yet Dalferth views this tension as a hindrance to theology. And while Ernst Troeltsch insisted that theologians also be impartial historical critics, Pannenberg argued that Christian historians must take leave of secular historical methods when approaching the resurrection.

Each generation of theologians provides a foundation for the theologians of the ensuing generations; without the work of the former, the latter would have no ground on which to stand. Without earlier generations' use of historical-critical methods, Pannenberg would have no foundation for his own reorientation of theology toward "universal history." Without Strauss's insistence on the tension between myth and logos, Dalferth would have no cause to suggest that theology can find a better way. At the center of these debates stands Rudolf Bultmann. His own work continues to shape the present conversation, so that no one can investigate the resurrection without confronting his looming presence. His responses continue to be controversial and contested, yet his questions remain as important for theology now as when he first raised them. What is the resurrection, and what is its significance for us here and now?

Bultmann's insistence that the resurrection is significant precisely because it is significant *for us* and for our existence informs his methodology as well as his conclusions. It is quite natural that he should enlist the help of existential philosophy, because it is precisely this philosophy that allows him to clarify his theological claims concerning human existence. Because of his attention to the precariousness and contingency of historical existence, Bultmann likewise understands and interprets history from an existential perspective. But it is his work as a New Testament theologian that earns Bultmann's ranking among the great theologians of the twentieth century. His efforts at demythologizing, as he himself contends, are a consistent application of the Lutheran-Pauline doctrine of justification by faith to epistemology. His insistence on the indispensability of the proclamation has important consequences for homiletics, and his work in hermeneutics and exegesis continues to influence the way we read and interpret biblical texts as historical documents with significance for the present.

Post-Bultmannian discussions of the resurrection acknowledge Bultmann's significance while attempting to move beyond his own assumptions and conclusions. Karl Barth and Wolfhart Pannenberg both regret Bultmann's radical criticism of the New Testament texts as well as his reliance on (or subjugation to) secular existential philosophy. Eberhard Jüngel appreciates Bultmann's recognition of the mythological framework of the New Testament, but he believes that Bultmann was not insistent enough on the inherent truth of myth. Both Jüngel and Gerhard Ebeling, while affirming Bultmann's emphasis on the "that" of Jesus' life, nevertheless cannot affirm Bultmann's claim that the historical Jesus of Nazareth has little or no relevance for faith and theology. Ingolf Ulrich Dalferth treats Bultmann quite extensively in his own work, praising Bultmann's contributions to the discussion of the resurrection, but Dalferth also ultimately disagrees with Bultmann's conclusions. The common sentiment among those sympathetic to Bultmann's work is that Bultmann asked the right questions but did not always offer the best conclusions in his responses to those important questions. These post-Bultmannians offer their own responses to Bultmann while also raising new questions, such that their contributions will doubtless become another generation's foundation. The implications of these post-Bultmannian discussions open up new trajectories for theology in the twenty-first century, thus deserving our attention.

Pannenberg has argued that the relationship between theology and the historical method is of crucial importance, and he offers a schema of "universal history" as his solution to the problem of theologically interpreting history while remaining a part of history. At the same time, his efforts also reveal an emphasis on a sometimes insular theological method over against the historical. In terms of the resurrection, Pannenberg insists that this is a historical event, but at the same time he refuses to open this event to historical criticism. He collapses the distinction between *Historie* and *Geschichte*, making the two identical, such that something that is enduringly significant must be historical. Pannenberg's conclusions have revealed a complicated relationship between theology and history, inviting further investigations of this relationship in order to create space for more fruitful conversations between these methods.

Jüngel has argued that there is a truth inherent in myth and that there is therefore also a legitimate case for demythologizing. The pressing issue for Jüngel is the relationship between myth and truth and how this relationship can be maintained in light of demythologizing. In terms of the resurrection, Jüngel is particularly interested in the christological implications of the discussions of the resurrection. He investigates the relationship between Christian proclamation of the resurrection and Jesus' own proclamation of the coming reign of God, so that resurrection and proclamation form a complex unity. The Christian hope of the resurrection includes the conviction that, just as God remained near to Jesus even in death, so will God remain near to us even in our own death. The resurrection of Jesus is the re-establishment of humanity's relationship with God, as it was precisely in his humanity that Jesus was the Son of God. The implications of these conclusions for theological anthropology in particular are still being worked out by a new generation of theologians.

Finally, Dalferth has sought to provide theology with an alternative to the long-simmering tension between myth and logos. He examines myth in a much broader context than Bultmann, including within his presentation the modern myth of the Enlightenment, which he cites as the origin of this tension between myth and logos. Dalferth proposes that we must move beyond the dichotomy of myth and logos in order to construct a theology in which the grammar of images, symbols, and metaphors is developed and deployed for orienting Christian faith and life. He investigates the possibility of theology constructing a christological grammar of the Christian life of faith and the implications of this grammar for contemporary intrareligious and interreligious dialogues. He argues that theology must concern itself with the grammar of its reflection rather than the internal debate between myth and logos if it is to present a coherent theological system. In terms of the resurrection, Dalferth emphasizes the inherent tension of the phrase "the awakened crucified one" and the implications of this tension for his grammatical project. To this end, he is especially concerned with the word of the cross and the eschatological character of the act of God in the resurrection. There is an intentionally kerygmatic character in Dalferth's presentation, for it is through the proclamation of the word of the cross that the salvation event comes to human speech within the framework of a christological grammar. It is through our encounter with this proclamation that we come to faith in the triune God who awakened Jesus from the dead.

These three theologians—Pannenberg, Jüngel, and Dalferth—have inquired into the meaning and significance of the resurrection of Jesus in light of post-Bultmannian theological developments, and yet each in his own way remains in conversation with Bultmann. Future theological discussions of the resurrection will likewise return to Bultmann. As Jüngel has suggested, as long as human beings exist, we exist in relationships. Our relationship to ourselves, to each other, to God, and to the crucified and risen Lord changes as our own situation changes, and it is the task of Christian theology to ask the appropriate questions and to formulate coherent and faithful responses so that the proclamation of the resurrection continues to meet people in the midst of their own concrete existence, as Bultmann himself tirelessly professed.

What are the implications of these post-Bultmannian discussions? What areas of research have they opened up for us, and what new questions and problems have arisen? Pannenberg has posed a significant challenge to historians and theologians alike; because Christianity is a historical phenomenon, and because all theology occurs within a specific historical context, historical reflection is an integral component of any theological discussion. Therefore it is the indispensable task of historical theologians to investigate and explicate the problems and possibilities imbricated within this relationship. This task is all the more significant thanks to more recent developments in theology, specifically the renewed appreciation of historicism and of the influences of social location (in terms of sex, gender, race, class, nationality, etc.) on theologizing.

Jüngel has focused our attention on the christological implications of examinations of the resurrection for the Christian life. He disagrees with Bultmann about the irrelevance of historical investigations into the life of Jesus, and his discussions of the relationship of Jesus to God offer fruitful possibilities for a richer understanding of the Christian life. He proposes that it was precisely in his humanity that Jesus was the Son of God, and therefore it is precisely in our full humanity that we become human beings in correspondence to God. Because Jesus is the one who accomplishes the unity of humanity with God, Jüngel emphasizes the importance of relationships in his Christology. Jesus Christ is the one who repairs fractured relationships, such that through him we are offered the possibility of becoming children of God. This emphasis on relationships and the correspondence of

Jesus' own self-understanding to Christian understanding of him presents a challenge to the historical theologian. Because faith can and must find support in the historical Jesus of Nazareth, it is necessary to investigate his life with every scholarly tool available to us, despite the significant challenges such investigations have encountered and will continue to encounter. Many liberation theologians have taken this cue to return our attention to the historical Jesus, not simply to provide a secure foundation for Christian faith but more significantly to ground and inspire liberative praxis consistent with Jesus' radical love for the poor and marginalized.

Finally, Dalferth's insistence that theology is capable of moving beyond the tension between myth and logos opens inviting possibilities for new theological discussions of the resurrection and more broadly for rethinking the relationship between "Athens and Jerusalem." Rather than maintain the classical dialectic between myth and logos in these discussions (a dialectic that will severely limit the introduction of anything new into the discussion), Dalferth suggests that theology concentrate instead on developing a grammar of the Christian life, based on the awakening of the crucified one by God. Because the Christian church stands or falls on its confession of the resurrection of Jesus, Dalferth suggests that theology should focus on the grammar of this confession rather than the event of the resurrection itself. Investigations of the resurrection are possible and necessary, but he has argued that it is not enough to investigate the resurrection as a historical question. The resurrection is meaningful and significant only if it is significant for us, and this is only embodied and enacted within the framework of a grammar of the Christian life of faith. Dalferth's work thus provides new areas of research for theological hermeneutics, semiotics, historical theology, and practical theology.

Pannenberg, Jüngel and Dalferth have illustrated that it is difficult (if not impossible) to investigate the resurrection of Jesus of Nazareth without confronting Rudolf Bultmann. To paraphrase Karl Barth, whoever wants to investigate the resurrection of Jesus must take caution, for Bultmann is always somehow also on the scene. Bultmann's greatest success was not necessarily in the solutions he offered, but in his formulations of the questions of the resurrection of Jesus, human existence, and Christian faith. His work and the work of his predecessors have provided rich soil and sturdy roots for their theological descendants to flourish.

Theology at the beginning of the twenty-first century is confronted with a world that is becoming increasingly secularized. The role of science and technology has revolutionized modern understandings of reality and theology must address this new understanding in its own reflections as well as in its public confessions. Bultmann believed that one of the most important tasks of theology is to make the New Testament kerygma intelligible and meaningful in the lives of contemporary women and men. This task is just as important and necessary now as it was for Bultmann, so that successful translation of the New Testament kerygma continues to determine the theological agenda of this and every age.

Bultmann and Dalferth especially emphasize the importance of the word. Bultmann stresses the transformative character of the preached word, while Dalferth proposes the development of a christological grammar rooted in the word of the cross as Christianity's unique and indispensable contribution to humanity's religious life. This emphasis has significant implications for homiletics and for preaching. Theologians must continue to consider and clarify the relationship between theological analysis and proclamation of the word in the context of worship (in other words, the relationship between second-level and first-level theological discourse). The Lutheran tradition has always emphasized the importance of the preached word, and this emphasis is only intensified in light of Bultmann and of post-Bultmannian contributions. Bultmann has argued that the risen Lord is encountered in the preached word and nowhere else. This bold claim requires serious reflection on the role of preaching in theology and worship, but there are additional implications for the church's witness if we take a broader, more holistic view of the meaning of "proclamation" to include other, nonverbal examples such as liturgy, the arts, and the church's work for justice.

Another area opened up by these discussions concerns the nature and function of religious language. Bultmann's attention to myth and kerygma, especially the truth of the cross brought to speech in the proclaimed word, privileges language as the medium of God's revelation. Theology too, whatever else it is, is done in words. Recent decades have witnessed a linguistic turn in debates about theological method, including the status of religious truth claims and the implications of conceiving of religious language as mythical, symbolic, or metaphorical statements rather than as propositional statements. Gary Dorrien, in *The Word as True Myth*, goes so far as to say that "one way to interpret the history of modern theology is therefore through its attempts to deal with the cluster of questions that the myth question contains,"[1] and this question continues to stalk contemporary theology as well.

The method of theology itself has been the topic of considerable discussion in the years following Bultmann and the collapse of dialectical theology, including David Tracy's proposal of a revisionist theological method rooted in the analogical imagination,[2] Gordon Kaufman's description of theology as imaginative construction,[3] and Sallie McFague's insistence on a remythologizing of religious language in a metaphorical theology, to name just a few of many examples.[4] More theologians, it would appear, are comfortable with myth, image, symbol, and metaphor than ever before; surely Bultmann's influence has played an important role in this conceptual shift, even for those who explicitly wish to transcend his own method and conclusions.

Jüngel and Dalferth represent two intriguing contemporary German examples of a reevaluation of myth and religious language that moves beyond the dichotomy between myth and logos,[5] and, as such, invite dialogue with Anglophone theologians doing similar work in their own contexts.[6] Jüngel's and Dalferth's insistence that the Christian faith is grounded in the divine reality that impinges upon us and graciously discloses itself to us in what Gerhard Ebeling has called a "word-event," such that the thinking subject is displaced as the sole claimant to define and to know the real, recalls similar efforts to "chase the Cartesian *cogito* from the field"[7] in the various post-critical Continental philosophical traditions that have been enjoying a renaissance in the last decades. Such points of contact suggest that the so-called "turn to religion" in Continental philosophy might benefit from including these and similar German theological voices in the conversation.

1. Dorrien, *Word as True Myth*, 1.

2. See Tracy, *Analogical Imagination*, and *Plurality and Ambiguity*.

3. See Kaufman, *Essay on Theological Method*, and *In Face of Mystery*.

4. See McFague, *Metaphorical Theology*, and *Models of God*.

5. Jüngel himself presents several theses summarizing his views on the usefulness of metaphor for a hermeneutics of narrative theology in an essay entitled "Metaphorische Wahrheit." ET: "Metaphorical Truth." Curiously, he argues for a reading of metaphor that is at the same time literal, but literal in a quite specific sense. This effort to transcend what are traditionally mutually exclusive conceptions of religious language mirrors Dalferth's effort to transcend the traditional dichotomy of myth and logos.

6. Dorrien's analysis of the question of myth in modern theology offers just this type of perspective on the work of theologians on both sides of the Atlantic.

7. Webster, Introduction to Jüngel, *Theological Essays*, 2.

* * * * * * * *

The impetus for this present study was the claim that Christianity stands or falls with its confession that God raised Jesus from the dead. Rudolf Bultmann's work offers tantalizing possibilities for further research and post-Bultmannian discussions have reformulated these possibilities and projected them into our current century. It is the task of this and future generations of theologians to appropriate this tradition, to inherit its questions, and to formulate fresh and faithful responses for the sake of the church's proclamation of Jesus Christ, the Crucified and Risen One.

Bibliography

"The Augsburg Confession." Translated by Charles P. Arand et al. In *The Book of Concord: The Confessions of the Evangelical Lutheran Church*, edited by Robert Kolb and Timothy J. Wengert, 27–105. Minneapolis: Fortress, 2000.

Backhaus, Gunther. *Kerygma und Mythos bei David Friedrich Strauss und Rudolf Bultmann*. Theologische Forschung 12. Hamburg: Reich, 1956.

Badiou, Alain. *Saint Paul: La Fondation de l'Universalisme*. Collection Les Essais du Collège International de Philosophie. Paris: Presses Universitaires de France, 1999.

———. *Saint Paul: The Foundation of Universalism*. Translated by Ray Brassier. Cultural Memory in the Present. Stanford, CA: Stanford University Press, 2003.

Baird, William. *History of New Testament Research*. Vol. 1, *From Deism to Tübingen*. Minneapolis: Augsburg Fortress, 1992.

Barth, Karl. *Church Dogmatics*. Vol. III/2, *The Doctrine of Creation*. Edited by G. W. Bromiley and T. F. Torrance. Translated by H. Knight et al. New York: T. & T. Clark, 2004.

———. *Church Dogmatics*. Vol. IV/2, *The Doctrine of Reconciliation*. Edited by G. W. Bromiley and T. F. Torrance. Translated by G. W. Bromiley. New York: T. & T. Clark, 2004.

———. *Die Auferstehung der Toten: Eine akademische Vorlesung über 1. Kor. 15*. Munich: Kaiser, 1924.

———. *The Epistle to the Romans*. Translated by Edwyn Hoskyns. London: Oxford University Press, 1968.

———. *Kirchliche Dogmatik*. Vol. III/2, *Die Lehre von der Schöpfung*. Zollikon: Evangelischer, 1948.

———. *Kirchliche Dogmatik*. Vol. IV/2, *Die Lehre von der Versöhnung*. Zollikon: Evangelischer, 1955.

———. *Protestant Theology in the Nineteenth Century: Its Background and History*. Translated by Brian Cozens and John Bowden. New ed. Grand Rapids: Eerdmans, 2002.

———. *The Resurrection of the Dead*. Translated by H. J. Stenning. New York: Revell, 1933.

———. "Rudolf Bultmann: An Attempt to Understand Him." Translated by Reginald H. Fuller. In *Kerygma and Myth: A Theological Debate*, edited by Hans-Werner Bartsch, 2:83–132. London: SPCK, 1962.

———. *Rudolf Bultmann: Ein Versuch, ihn zu verstehen*. Theologische Studien 34. Zollikon: Evangelischer, 1952.

———. *The Word of God and the Word of Man*. Translated Douglas Horton. New York: Harper, 1957.

Barton, John. *The Nature of Biblical Criticism*. Louisville: Westminster John Knox, 2007.

Bartsch, Hans-Werner. *Der gegenwärtige Stand der Entmythologisierungsdebatte*. Hamburg: Reich, 1954.

———. "The Present State of the Debate." Translated by Reginald H. Fuller. In *Kerygma and Myth: A Theological Debate*, edited by Hans-Werner Bartsch, 2:1–82. London: SPCK, 1962.

Berger, Peter L. *Questions of Faith: A Skeptical Affirmation of Christianity*. Religion in the Modern World. Malden, MA: Blackwell, 2004.

Betz, Hans Dieter. "The Concept of the 'Inner Human Being' (ο εσω ανθροπος) in the Anthropology of Paul." *NTS* 46, no. 3 (2000) 315–41.

Bousset, Wilhelm. "Die Bedeutung der Person Jesu für den Glaube: Historische und rationale Grundlagen des Glaubens." In *Fünfter Weltkongress für Freies Christentum und Religiösen Fortschritt: Protokoll der Verhandlungen*, edited by Max Fischer and Friedrich Michael Schiele, 291–305. Berlin: Protestantischer Schriftenvertrieb, 1910.

———. *Kyrios Christos: A History of the Belief in Christ from the Beginnings of Christianity to Irenaeus*. Translated John E. Steely. Nashville: Abingdon, 1970.

———. *Kyrios Christos: Geschichte des Christusglaubens von den Anfängen des Christentums bis Irenaeus*. 5th ed. Göttingen: Vandenhoeck & Ruprecht, 1965.

———. "The Significance of the Personality of Jesus for Belief." In *Fifth International Congress of Free Christianity and Religious Progress: Proceedings and Papers*, edited by Charles W. Wendte and V. D. Davis, 208–21. Berlin: Protestantischer Schriftenvertrieb, 1911.

Bultmann, Rudolf. "Allgemeine Wahrheiten und christliche Verkündigung." *ZThK* 54 (1957) 244–54.

———. "Die Bedeutung des geschichtlichen Jesus für die Theologie des Paulus." In *Glauben und Verstehen*, by Rudolf Bultmann, 1:188–213. Tübingen: Mohr/Siebeck, 1933.

———. "Der Begriff der Offenbarung im Neuen Testament." In *Glauben und Verstehen*, by Rudolf Bultmann, 3:1–34. Tübingen: Mohr/Siebeck, 1962.

———. "Der Begriff des Wortes Gottes im Neuen Testament." In *Glauben und Verstehen*, by Rudolf Bultmann, 3:268–93. Tübingen: Mohr/Siebeck, 1962.

———. "The Christian Hope and the Problem of Demythologizing." *ExpT* 65, nos. 8–9 (1954) 228–30, 276–78.

———. "Die christliche Hoffnung und das Problem der Entmythologisierung." In *Glauben und Verstehen*, by Rudolf Bultmann, 3:81–90. Tübingen: Mohr/Siebeck, 1962.

———. "The Concept of Revelation in the New Testament." In *Existence and Faith: Shorter Writings of Rudolf Bultmann*, edited and translated by Schubert M. Ogden, 58–91. Cleveland: World, 1960.

———. "The Concept of the Word of God in the New Testament." Translated by Louise Pettibone Smith. In *Faith and Understanding*, edited by Robert W. Funk, 286–312. Fortress Texts in Modern Theology. Philadelphia: Fortress, 1987.

———. *Die Erforschung der synoptischen Evangelien*. Aus der Welt der Religion 4. Gießen: Töpelmann, 1925.

———. "Die Eschatologie des Johannes-Evangelium." In *Glauben und Verstehen*, by Rudolf Bultmann, 1:134–52. Tübingen: Mohr/Siebeck, 1933.

———. "The Eschatology of the Gospel of John." Translated by Louise Pettibone Smith. In *Faith and Understanding*, edited by Robert W. Funk, 165–83. Fortress Texts in Modern Theology. Philadelphia: Fortress, 1987.

———. *Das Evangelium des Johannes*. Kritistch-exegetischer Kommentar über das Neue Testament 2/10. Göttingen: Vandenhoeck & Ruprecht, 1941.

———. "General Truths and Christian Proclamation." Translated by Schubert M. Ogden. In *History and Hermeneutic*, edited by Robert W. Funk, 153–62. Journal for Theology and the Church 4. New York: Harper, 1967.

———. *Geschichte der synoptischen Tradition*. 2nd ed. Forschungen zur Religion und Literatur des Alten und Neuen Testaments N.F. 12. Göttingen: Vandenhoeck & Ruprecht, 1931.

———. "Geschichte und Eschatologie im Neuen Testament." In *Glauben und Verstehen*, by Rudolf Bultmann, 3:91–106. Tübingen: Mohr/Siebeck, 1962.

———. "Die Geschichtlichkeit des Daseins und der Glaube: Antwort an Gerhardt Kuhlmann." *ZThK* 11 (1930) 339–64.

———. *The Gospel of John: A Commentary*. Translated by G. R. Beasley-Murray et al. Johannine Monograph. Eugene, OR: Wipf & Stock, 2014.

———. "History and Eschatology in the New Testament." *NTS* 1, no. 1 (1954) 5–16.

———. *History and Eschatology: The Presence of Eternity*. New York: Harper, 1962.

———. *History of the Synoptic Tradition*. Translated by John Marsh. 2nd ed. New York: Harper, 1976.

———. "Is Exegesis without Presuppositions Possible?" In *New Testament & Mythology and Other Basic Writings*, edited and translated by Schubert M. Ogden, 145–53. Philadelphia: Fortress, 1984.

———. "Ist voraussetzungslose Exegese möglich?" In *Glauben und Verstehen*, by Rudolf Bultmann, 3:142–50. Tübingen: Mohr/Siebeck, 1962.

———. *Jesus*. Berlin: Deutsche Bibliothek, 1926.

———. *Jesus and the Word*. Translated by Louise Pettibone Smith and Erminie Huntress Lantero. New York: Scribner, 1989.

———. *Jesus Christ and Mythology*. New York: Scribner's, 1958.

———. "Karl Barth, *Die Auferstehung der Toten*." In *Glauben und Verstehen*, by Rudolf Bultmann, 1:38–64. Tübingen: Mohr/Siebeck, 1933.

———. "Karl Barth, *The Resurrection of the Dead*." Translated by Louise Pettibone Smith. In *Faith and Understanding*, edited by Robert W. Funk, 66–94. Fortress Texts in Modern Theology. Philadelphia: Fortress, 1987.

———. "Neues Testament und Mythologie: Das Problem der Entmythologisierung der neutestamentlischen Verkündigung." In *Kerygma und Mythos I: Ein theologisches Gespräch*, edited by Hans-Werner Bartsch, 15–48. 4th ed. Hamburg: Reich, 1960.

———. "New Testament and Mythology." In *New Testament & Mythology and Other Basic Writings*, edited and translated by Schubert M. Ogden, 1–43. Philadelphia: Fortress, 1984.

———. "On the Problem of Demythologizing" (1952). In *New Testament & Mythology and Other Basic Writings*, edited and translated by Schubert M. Ogden, 95–130. Philadelphia: Fortress, 1984.

———. "On the Problem of Demythologizing" (1961). In *New Testament & Mythology and Other Basic Writings*, edited and translated by Schubert M. Ogden, 155–63. Philadelphia: Fortress, 1984.

————. "On the Question of Christology." In *New Testament & Mythology and Other Basic Writings*, edited and translated by Schubert M. Ogden, 116–44. Philadelphia: Fortress, 1984.

————. "The Primitive Christian Kerygma and the Historical Jesus." In *The Historical Jesus and the Kerygmatic Christ: Essays on the New Quest of the Historical Jesus*, translated and edited by Carl E. Braaten and Roy A. Harrisville, 15–42. Nashville: Abingdon, 1964.

————. "The Problem of Hermeneutics." In *New Testament & Mythology and Other Basic Writings*, edited and translated by Schubert M. Ogden, 69–93. Philadelphia: Fortress, 1984.

————. "Das Problem der Hermeneutik." In *Glauben und Verstehen*, by Rudolf Bultmann, 3:211–35. Tübingen: Mohr/Siebeck, 1962.

————. *Primitive Christianity in Its Contemporary Setting*. Translated by Reginald H. Fuller. New York: World, 1956.

————. "The Question of Wonder." In *Faith and Understanding*, edited by Robert W. Funk. Translated by Louise Pettibone Smith, 247–61. Fortress Texts in Modern Theology. Philadelphia: Fortress, 1987.

————. "Romans 7 and the Anthropology of Paul." In *Existence and Faith: Shorter Writings of Rudolf Bultmann*, edited and translated by Schubert M. Ogden, 147–57. Cleveland: World, 1960.

————. "Römer 7 und die Anthropologie des Paulus." In *Imago Dei: Beiträge zur theologischen Anthropologie, Gustav Krüger zum siebzigsten Geburtstage am 29. Juni 1932 dargebracht*, edited by Heinrich Bornkamm, 53–62. Giessen: Töpelmann, 1932.

————. "The Significance of the Historical Jesus for the Theology of Paul." In *Faith and Understanding*, edited by Robert W. Funk. Translated by Louise Pettibone Smith, 220–46. Fortress Texts in Modern Theology. Philadelphia: Fortress, 1987.

————. "Theologie als Wissenschaft." *ZThK* 81, no. 4 (1984) 447–69.

————. *Theologie des Neuen Testaments*. 2nd ed. Neue theologische Grundrisse. Tübingen: Mohr/Siebeck, 1954.

————. *Theologische Enzyklopädie*. Edited by Eberhard Jüngel and Klaus Müller. Tübingen: Mohr/Siebeck, 1984.

————. "Theology as Science." In *New Testament & Mythology and Other Basic Writings*, translated and edited by Schubert Ogden, 45–68. Philadelphia: Fortress, 1984.

————. *Theology of the New Testament*. 2 vols. Translated by Kendrick Grobel. New York: Scribner's, 1951.

————. *Das Urchristentum im Rahmen der antiken Religionen*. Zürich: Artemis, 1949.

————. *Das Verhältnis der urchristlichen Christusbotschaft zum historischen Jesus*. Sitzungsberichte der Heidelberger Akademie der Wissenschaften, Philosophisch-Historische Klasse 3. Heidelberg: Carl Winter Universitätsverlag, 1960.

————. "Welchen Sinn hat es, von Gott zu reden?" In *Glauben und Verstehen*, by Rudolf Bultmann, 1:26–37. Tübingen: Mohr/Siebeck, 1933.

————. "What Does It Mean to Speak of God?" In *Faith and Understanding*, edited by Robert W. Funk. Translated by Louise Pettibone Smith, 53–65. Fortress Texts in Modern Theology. Philadelphia: Fortress, 1987.

————. *What Is Theology?* Edited by Eberhard Jüngel and Klaus W. Müller. Translated by Roy A. Harrisville. Fortress Texts in Modern Theology. Minneapolis: Fortress, 1997.

———. "Zum Problem der Entmythologisierung" (1952). In *Kerygma und Mythos II: Diskussion und Stimmen zum Problem der Entmythologisierung*, edited by Hans-Werner Bartsch, 179–208. Hamburg: Reich, 1952.

———. "Zum Problem der Entmythologisierung" (1961). In *Glauben und Verstehen*, by Rudolf Bultmann, 4:128–37. Tübingen: Mohr/Siebeck, 1984.

———. "Zur Frage der Christologie." In *Glauben und Verstehen*, by Rudolf Bultmann, 1:85–113. Tübingen: Mohr/Siebeck, 1933.

———. "Zur Frage des Wunders." In *Glauben und Verstehen*, by Rudolf Bultmann, 1:214–28. Tübingen: Mohr/Siebeck, 1933.

Calvin, John. *Institutes of the Christian Religion*. 2 vols. Edited by John T. McNeill. Translated by Ford Lewis Battles. Library of Christian Classics 20–21. Philadelphia: Westminster, 1960.

Caputo, John D. *The Weakness of God: A Theology of the Event*. Indiana Series in the Philosophy of Religion. Bloomington: Indiana University Press, 2006.

Chapman, Mark D. *Ernst Troeltsch and Liberal Theology: Religion and Cultural Synthesis in Wilhelmine Germany*. Christian Theology in Context. New York: Oxford University Press, 2001.

Collins, John J. *The Bible After Babel: Historical Criticism in a Postmodern Age*. Grand Rapids: Eerdmans, 2005.

Congdon, David W. *The Mission of Demythologizing: Rudolf Bultmann's Dialectical Theology*. Minneapolis: Fortress, 2015.

———. *Rudolf Bultmann: A Companion to His Theology*. Cascade Companions. Eugene, OR: Cascade, 2015.

Dalferth, Ingolf Ulrich. *Der auferweckte Gekreuzigte: Zur Grammatik der Christologie*. Tübingen: Mohr/Siebeck, 1994.

———. *Crucified and Resurrected: Restructuring the Grammar of Christology*. Translated by Jo Bennett. Grand Rapids: Baker Academic, 2015.

———. *Jenseits von Mythos und Logos: Die christologische Transformation der Theologie*. Quaestiones Disputatae 142. Freiburg: Herder, 1993.

———. "Volles Grab, leerer Glaube? Zum Streit um die Auferweckung des Gekreuzigten." *ZThK* 95, no. 3 (1998) 379–409.

———. "Von der Mythenkritik zur Entmythologisierung: Eine Erinnerung an unverzichtbare Aufgaben der Theologie." In *Die Wirklichkeit des Mythos: Eine theologische Spurensuche*, edited by Volker Hörner and Martin Leiner, 57–81. Gütersloh: Gütersloher, 1998.

Davidson, Ivor J. "The Crucified One." In *Indicative of Grace—Imperative of Freedom: Essays in Honour of Eberhard Jüngel in His 80th Year*, edited by R. David Nelson, 29–49. New York: Bloomsbury, 2014.

Dawes, Gregory W. *The Historical Jesus Question: The Challenge of History to Religious Authority*. Louisville: Westminster John Knox, 2001.

Dawkins, Richard. *The God Delusion*. Boston: Mariner, 2008.

DeHart, Paul J. *Beyond the Necessary God: Trinitarian Faith and Philosophy in the Thought of Eberhard Jüngel*. AAR Reflection and Theory in the Study of Religion 15. Atlanta: Scholars, 1999.

"Die augsburgische Konfession." In *Die Bekenntnisschriften der evangelisch-lutherischen Kirche*, 31–137. 3rd ed. Göttingen: Vandenhoeck & Ruprecht, 1956.

Dixon, A. C., and R. A. Torrey, eds. *The Fundamentals: A Testimony to the Truth*. 12 vols. Los Angeles: Bible Institute of Los Angeles, 1910–1915.

Dorrien, Gary. *The Word as True Myth: Interpreting Modern Theology.* Louisville: Westminster John Knox, 1997.

Drews, Arthur. *The Christ Myth.* Translated by C. Delisle Burns. Westminster College— Oxford Classics in the Study of Religion. Amherst, NY: Prometheus, 1998.

———. *Die Christusmythe.* Jena: Diederichs, 1909.

Ebeling, Gerhard. "Die Frage nach dem historischen Jesus und das Problem der Christologie." *ZThK* 56 Beih. 1 (1959) 14–30.

———. "Jesus and Faith." Translated by James W. Leitch. In *Word and Faith*, by Gerhard Ebeling, 201–46. Philadelphia: Fortress, 1963.

———. "Jesus und Glaube." *ZThK* 55 (1958) 64–110.

———. "The Question of the Historical Jesus and the Problem of Christology." Translated by James W. Leitch. In *Word and Faith*, by Gerhard Ebeling, 288–304. Philadelphia: Fortress, 1963.

———. *Theologie und Verkündigung: Ein Gespräch mit Rudolf Bultmann.* Hermeneutische Untersuchungen zur Theologie 1. Tübingen: Mohr/Siebeck, 1963.

———. *Theology and Proclamation: Dialogue with Bultmann.* Translated by John Riches. Philadelphia: Fortress, 1966.

———. *Wort und Glaube.* 4 vols. Tübingen: Mohr/Siebeck, 1960–1995.

Eliade, Mircea. *Myth and Reality.* Translated by Willard R. Trask. Long Grove, IL: Waveland, 1998.

Faulkner, William. *Requiem for a Nun.* New York: Random House, 1951.

Gadamer, Hans-Georg. *Truth and Method.* 2nd rev. ed. Translated by Joel Weinsheimer and Donald G. Marshall. New York: Continuum, 1997.

———. *Wahrheit und Methode: Grundzüge einer philosophischen Hermeneutik.* 2nd ed. Tübingen: Mohr/Siebeck, 1965.

Gerrish, B. A. "Jesus, Myth, and History: Troeltsch's Stand in the 'Christ-Myth' Debate." *JR* 55 (1975) 13–35.

Grigg, Richard. *Beyond the God Delusion: How Radical Theology Harmonizes Science and Religion.* Minneapolis: Fortress, 2008.

Hammann, Konrad. *Rudolf Bultmann: A Biography.* Translated by Philip E. Devenish. Salem, OR: Polebridge, 2013.

———. *Rudolf Bultmann: Eine Biographie.* Tübingen: Mohr/Siebeck, 2009.

Harris, Horton. *David Friedrich Strauss and His Theology.* Monograph Supplements to the Scottish Journal of Theology. Cambridge: Cambridge University Press, 1973.

Harrisville, Roy A. "Bultmann's Concept of the Transition from Inauthentic to Authentic Existence." In *Kerygma and History: A Symposium on the Theology of Rudolf Bultmann*, translated and edited by Carl E. Braaten and Roy A. Harrisville, 212–28. Nashville: Abingdon, 1962.

Hartlich, Christian, and Walter Sachs. "Kritische Prüfung der Haupteinwände Barths gegen Bultmann." In *Kerygma und Mythos II: Diskussion und Stimmen zum Problem der Entmythologisierung*, edited by Hans-Werner Bartsch, 114–25. Hamburg: Reich, 1952.

———. *Der Ursprung des Mythosbegriffes in der modernen Bibelwissenschaft.* Schriften der Studiengemeinschaft der Evangelischen Akademien 2. Tübingen: Mohr/Siebeck, 1952.

Harvey, Van. "D. F. Strauss' *Life of Jesus* Revisited." *ChHist* 30 (1961) 191–211.

———. *The Historian and the Believer: The Morality of Historical Knowledge and Christian Belief.* Urbana: University of Illinois Press, 1996.

Hege, Brent A. R. "Contesting Faith, Truth, and Religious Language at the Creation Museum: A Historical-Theological Reflection." *Theology and Science* 12, no. 2 (2014) 142–63.

———. *Faith at the Intersection of History and Experience: The Theology of Georg Wobbermin*, Eugene, OR: Wipf and Stock, 2009.

———. "Jesus Christ as Poetic Symbol: Wilhelm Bousset's Contribution to the Faith-History Debate." *ZNThG* 16, no. 2 (2009) 197–216.

Heidegger, Martin. *Being and Time*. Translated by John Macquarrie and Edward Robinson. New York: Harper, 1962.

———. *Sein und Zeit*. 7th ed. Tübingen: Neomarius, 1953.

Herberg, Will. "Five Meanings of the Word 'Historical.'" *Christian Scholar* 47, no. 4 (1964) 327–30.

Herrmann, Wilhelm. *The Communion of the Christian with God Described on the Basis of Luther's Statements*. Edited by R. W. Stewart. Translated by J. S. Sandys Stanyon. 2nd ed. New York: Putman, 1906.

———. *Der Verkehr des Christen mit Gott im Anschluss an Luther dargestellt*. 4th ed. Stuttgart: Cotta, 1903.

Heyward, Carter. *The Redemption of God: A Theology of Mutual Relation*. 30th anniv. ed. Eugene, OR: Wipf and Stock, 2010.

Hitchens, Christopher. *God is not Great: How Religion Poisons Everything*. New York: Twelve, 2007.

Hume, David. *An Enquiry concerning Human Understanding and Other Writings*. Edited by Stephen Buckle. Cambridge Texts in the History of Philosophy. Cambridge: Cambridge University Press, 2007.

Jaspers, Karl. *Philosophy of Existence*. Translated by Richard Grabau. Works in Continental Philosophy. Philadelphia: University of Pennsylvania Press, 1971.

Jaspert, Bernd, and Geoffrey W. Bromiley, eds. *Karl Barth/Rudolf Bultmann Letters: 1922–1966*. Translated by Geoffrey W. Bromiley. Grand Rapids: Eerdmans, 1981.

Jüngel, Eberhard. "The Dogmatic Significance of the Question of the Historical Jesus." Translated by John B. Webster. In *Theological Essays*, 2:82–119. Edinburgh: T. & T. Clark, 2014.

———. "The Effectiveness of Christ Withdrawn: On the Process of Historical Understanding as an Introduction to Christology." Translated by John B. Webster. In *Theological Essays*, 1:214–31. Edinburgh: T. & T. Clark, 2014.

———. *Glauben und Verstehen: Zum Theologiebegriff Rudolf Bultmanns*. Sitzungsberichte der Heidelberger Akademie der Wissenschaften, Philosophisch-Historische Klasse, 1. Heidelberg: Carl Winter Universitätsverlag, 1985.

———. *God as Mystery of the World: On the Foundation of the Theology of the Crucified One in the Dispute between Theism and Atheism*. Translated by Darrell L. Guder. Grand Rapids: Eerdmans, 1983.

———. *Gott als Geheimnis der Welt: Zur Begründung der Theologie des Gekreuzigten im Streit zwischen Theismus und Atheismus*. Tübingen: Mohr/Siebeck, 1978.

———. "Metaphorical Truth: Reflections on Theological Metaphor as a Contribution to a Hermeneutics of Narrative Theology." Translated by John B. Webster. In *Theological Essays*, 1:16–71. Edinburgh: T. & T. Clark, 2014.

———. "Metaphorische Wahrheit: Erwägungen zur theologsichen Relevanz der Metapher als Beitrag zur Hermeneutik einer narrativen Theologie." In *Entsprechungen: Gott-*

Wahrheit-Mensch (Theologische Eröterungen II), 103–57. 3rd ed. Tübingen: Mohr/ Siebeck, 2002.

———. *Paulus und Jesus: Eine Untersuchung zur Präzisierung der Frage nach dem Ursprung der Christologie*. Hermeneutische Untersuchungen zur Theologie 2. Tübingen: Mohr/Siebeck, 1962.

———. "Die Wahrheit des Mythos und die Notwendigkeit der Entmythologisierung." *HoJB* 27 (1991) 32–50.

———. "Die Wirksamkeit des Entzogenen: Zum Vorgang geschichtlichen Verstehens als Einführung in die Christologie." In *Gnosis: Festschrift für Hans Jonas*, edited by Barbara Aland, 15–32. Göttingen: Vandenhoeck & Ruprecht, 1978.

———. "Zur dogmatischen Bedeutung der Frage nach dem historischen Jesus." In *Wertlose Wahrheit: Zur Identität des christlichen Glaubens (Theologische Erörterung III)*, 214–42. Beiträge zur evangelischen Theologie 105. Munich: Kaiser, 1990.

Kähler, Martin. *The So-Called Historical Jesus and the Historic Biblical Christ*. Translated and edited by Carl E. Braaten. Fortress Texts in Modern Theology. Philadelphia: Fortress, 1988.

———. *Der sogennante historische Jesus und der geschichtliche, biblische Christus*. 2nd ed. Edited by Ernst Wolf. Theologische Bücherei 2. Munich, Kaiser, 1956.

Kant, Immanuel. "An Answer to the Question: What Is Enlightenment?" Translated by H. B. Nisbet. In *Political Writings*, edited by Hans Reiss, 54–60. 2nd ed. Cambridge Texts in the History of Political Thought. Cambridge: Cambridge University Press, 1991.

———. "Beantwortung der Frage: Was ist Aufklärung?" *Berlinische Monatsschrift* (1784) 481–94.

Käsemann, Ernst. "Das Problem des historischen Jesus." *ZThK* 51 (1954) 125–53.

———. "The Problem of the Historical Jesus." In *Essays on New Testament Themes*, translated by W. J. Montague, 15–47. Studies in Biblical Theology 41. London: SCM, 1965.

Kay, James F. *Christus Praesens: A Reconsideration of Rudolf Bultmann's Christology*. Grand Rapids: Eerdmans, 1994.

Kaufman, Gordon D. *An Essay on Theological Method*. 3rd ed. Reflection and Theory in the Study of Religion. Atlanta: Scholars, 1995.

———. *In Face of Mystery: A Constructive Theology*. Cambridge, MA: Harvard University Press, 1993.

Kuhlmann, Gerhardt. "Zum theologischen Problem der Existenz: Fragen an Rudolf Bultmann." *ZThK* 10 (1929) 28–57.

Loisy, Alfred. *L'Évangile et l'Église*. Paris: Picard, 1902.

———. *The Gospel and the Church*. Translated by Bernard B. Scott. Lives of Jesus. Philadelphia: Fortress, 1976.

Longnecker, Bruce W., and Mikeal C. Parsons, eds. *Beyond Bultmann: Reckoning a New Testament Theology*. Waco, TX: Baylor University Press, 2014.

Lüdemann, Gerd. *The Great Deception and What Jesus Really Said and Did*. Amherst, NY: Prometheus, 1999.

———. *The Resurrection of Christ: A Historical Inquiry*. Amherst, NY: Prometheus, 2004.

Luther, Martin. "The Large Catechism." Translated by Charles P. Arand et al. In *The Book of Concord: The Confessions of the Evangelical Lutheran Church*, edited by Robert Kolb and Timothy J. Wengert, 377–480. Minneapolis: Fortress, 2000.

———. "Prefaces to the Old Testament." In *Luther's Works*, edited by E. Theodore Bachmann, 35:235–51. Philadelphia: Fortress, 1960.

Małysz, Piotr J. "The Resurrection as Divine Openness." In *Indicative of Grace—Imperative of Freedom: Essays in Honour of Eberhard Jüngel in His 80th Year*, edited by R. David Nelson, 143–53. New York: Bloomsbury, 2014.

———. *Trinity, Freedom and Love: An Engagement with the Theology of Eberhard Jüngel*. T. & T. Clark Studies in Systematic Theology. New York: T. & T. Clark, 2012.

Marxsen, Willi. *The Resurrection of Jesus of Nazareth*. Translated by Margaret Kohl. Philadelphia: Fortress, 1970.

McFague, Sallie. *Metaphorical Theology: Models of God in Religious Language*. Philadelphia: Fortress, 1982.

———. *Models of God: Theology for an Ecological, Nuclear Age*. Philadelphia: Fortress, 1987.

McKenzie, Steven L., and Stephen R. Haynes, eds. *To Each Its Own Meaning: An Introduction to Biblical Criticisms and Their Application*. Rev. ed. Louisville: Westminster John Knox, 1999.

Melanchthon, Philipp. *Loci Communes: Lateinisch-Deutsch*. Translated by Horst Georg Pöhlmann. Gütersloh: Mohn, 1993.

———. *Melanchthon on Christian Doctrine*. Translated and edited by Clyde L. Manschreck. A Library of Protestant Thought. New York: Oxford University Press, 1965.

Nelson, Derek. "The Indicative of Grace & the Imperative of Freedom: An Invitation to the Theology of Eberhard Jüngel." *Dialog* 44, no. 2 (2005) 164–80.

Nelson, R. David, ed. *Indicative of Grace—Imperative of Freedom: Essays in Honour of Eberhard Jüngel in His 80th Year*. New York: Bloomsbury, 2014.

Nestle, Wilhelm. *Vom Mythos zum Logos: Die Selbstentfaltung des griechischen Denkens von Homer bis auf die Sophisten und Sokrates*. Stuttgart: Kröner, 1942.

Nietzsche, Friedrich. "David Strauss: The Confessor and the Writer." Translated by R. J. Hollingdale. In *Untimely Meditations*, edited by Daniel Breazeale, 1–55. Cambridge Texts in the History of Philosophy. Cambridge: Cambridge University Press, 1997.

Ogden, Schubert. *Christ without Myth: A Study Based on the Theology of Rudolf Bultmann*. New York: Harper & Row, 1961.

———. "The Debate on 'Demythologizing'." *JBR* 27 (1959) 17–27.

Pannenberg, Wolfhart. *Anthropologie in theologischer Perspektive*. Göttingen: Vandenhoeck & Ruprecht, 1983.

———. *Anthropology in Theological Perspective*. Translated by Matthew J. O'Connell. Philadelphia: Westminster, 1985.

———. "Die Auferstehung Jesu—Historie und Theologie." In *Beiträge zur Systematischen Theologie*, 1:308–18. Göttingen: Vandenhoeck & Ruprecht, 1999.

———. "Die Auflösung der Dialektischen Theologie bei Rudolf Bultmann." In *Problemgeschichte der neueren evangelischen Theologie in Deutschland: Von Schleiermacher bis zu Barth und Tillich*, 205–32. Göttingen: Vandenhoeck & Ruprecht, 1997.

———. *Christentum und Mythos: Späthorizonte des Mythos in biblischer und christlicher Überlieferung*. Gütersloh: Mohn, 1972.

———. *Grundzüge der Christologie*. Gütersloh: Mohn, 1964.

———. "Heilsgeschehen und Geschichte." *KuD* 5 (1959) 218–37, 259–88.

———. "Hermeneutic and Universal History." Translated by George H. Kehm. In *Basic Questions in Theology*, 1:96–136. Philadelphia: Fortress, 1983.

———. "Hermeneutik und Universalgeschichte." *ZThK* 60 (1963) 90–121.

———. "The Historical Jesus as a Challenge to Christology." In *Beiträge zur Systematischen Theologie*, 1:287–95. Göttingen: Vandenhoeck & Ruprecht, 1999.

———. "History and the Reality of the Resurrection." In *Beiträge zur Systematischen Theologie*, 1:319–26. Göttingen: Vandenhoeck & Ruprecht, 1999.

———. *Jesus: God and Man*. Translated by Lewis L. Wilkins and Duane A. Priebe. 2nd ed. Philadelphia: Westminster, 1977.

———. "Kerygma and History." Translated by George H. Kehm. In *Basic Questions in Theology*, 1:81–95. Philadelphia: Fortress, 1983.

———. "Kerygma und Geschichte." In *Studien zur Theologie der alttestamentlichen Überlieferungen*, edited by Rolf Rentdorff and Klaus Koch, 129–40. Neukirchen: Neukirchener, 1961.

———. "Offenbarung und 'Offenbarungen' im Zeugnis der Geschichte." In *Beiträge zur Systematischen Theologie*, 1:212–37. Göttingen: Vandenhoeck & Ruprecht, 1999.

———. "On Historical and Theological Hermeneutic." Translated by George H. Kehm. In *Basic Questions in Theology*, 1:137–81. Philadelphia: Fortress, 1983.

———. "Redemptive Event and History." Translated by George H. Kehm. In *Basic Questions in Theology*, 1:15–80. Philadelphia: Fortress, 1983.

———. "The Resurrection of Jesus: History and Theology." *Dialog* 38 (1999) 20–25.

———. *Systematic Theology*. Vol. 3. Translated by Geoffrey W. Bromiley. Grand Rapids: Eerdmans, 1998.

———. "Über historische und theologische Hermeneutik." In *Grundfragen systematischer Theologie: Gesammelte Aufsätze*, 1:123–58. Göttingen: Vandenhoeck & Ruprecht, 1967.

———. "Was ist Wahrheit?" In *Vom Herrengeheimnis der Wahrheit: Festschrift für Heinrich Vogel*, edited by Kurt Scharf, 214–39. Berlin: Lettner, 1962.

———. "Die Weltgründende Funktion des Mythos und der christliche Offenbarungsglaube." In *Beiträge zur Systematischen Theologie*, 1:185–99. Göttingen: Vandenhoeck & Ruprecht, 1999.

———. "What Is Truth?" Translated by George H. Kehm. In *Basic Questions in Theology*, 2:1–27. Philadelphia: Fortress, 1971.

Perrin, Norman. *The Promise of Bultmann*. Promise of Theology. Philadelphia: Fortress, 1969.

Reimarus, Hermann Samuel. *Fragmente des Wolftenbüttelschen Ungenannten*. Edited by Gotthold Ephraim Lessing. 4th ed. Berlin: Eichhoff, 1835.

———. *Fragments*. Translated by Ralph Fraser. Edited by Charles Talbert. Lives of Jesus. Philadelphia: Fortress, 1970.

Ricoeur, Paul. "Biblical Hermeneutics." *Semeia* 4 (1975).

———. "Preface to Bultmann." Translated by Peter McCormick. In *The Conflict of Interpretations: Essays in Hermeneutics*, edited by Don Ihde, 381–401. Northwestern University Studies in Phenomenology and Existential Philosophy. Evanston, IL: Northwestern University Press, 1974.

———. "The Task of Hermeneutics." *PhilToday* 17 (1973) 112–28.

Saler, Robert C. *Theologia Crucis*. Cascade Companions. Eugene, OR: Cascade, 2016.

Schleiermacher, Friedrich. *The Christian Faith*. Edited by H. R. Mackintosh and J. S. Stewart. Edinburgh: T. & T. Clark, 1989.

———. *Der christliche Glaube (1830/31)*. Edited by Martin Redeker. Berlin: de Gruyter, 1999.

————. *Das Leben Jesu: Vorlesungen an der Universität zu Berlin im Jahr 1832.* Edited by K. A. Rütenik. Friedrich Schleiermachers sämmtliche Werke 6/1. Berlin: Reimer, 1864.

————. *The Life of Jesus.* Edited by Jack C. Verheyden. Translated by S. Maclean Gilmour. Lives of Jesus. Philadelphia: Fortress, 1975.

————. *On Religion: Speeches to Its Cultured Despisers.* Edited by Richard Crouter. Cambridge Texts in the History of Philosophy. Cambridge: Cambridge University Press, 1996.

————. *Über die Religion: Reden an die Gebildeten unter ihren Verächtern.* Stuttgart: Reclam, 1969.

Schmiechen, Peter. *Saving Power: Theories of Atonement and Forms of the Church.* Grand Rapids: Eerdmans, 2005.

Schweitzer, Albert. *The Quest of the Historical Jesus.* Edited by John Bowden. Translated by W. Montgomery et al. 1st complete ed. Minneapolis: Fortress, 2001.

————. *Von Reimarus zu Wrede: Eine Geschichte der Leben-Jesu-Forschung.* Tübingen: Mohr/Siebeck, 1906.

Segal, Robert A. *Myth: A Very Short Introduction.* New York: Oxford University Press, 2004.

Soden, Hans von. "Was ist Wahrheit?" In *Urchristentum und Geschichte: Gesammelte Aufsätze und Vorträge,* edited by Hans von Campenhausen, 1:1–24. Tübingen: Mohr/Siebeck, 1951.

Staats, Reinhart. "Der theologiegeschichtliche Hintergrund des Begriffes 'Tatsache.'" *ZThK* 70, no. 3 (1973) 316–45.

Strauss, David Friedrich. *Der alte und der neue Glaube: Ein Bekenntnis.* Leipzig: Hirzel, 1872.

————. "Hermann Samuel Reimarus and His Apology." Translated by Ralph Fraser. In *Fragments,* edited by Charles Talbert, 44–57. Lives of Jesus. Philadelphia: Fortress, 1970.

————. *Das Leben Jesu kritisch bearbeitet.* 2 vols. Tübingen: Osiander, 1835–1836.

————. *The Life of Jesus, Critically Examined.* Translated by George Eliot. Lives of Jesus. Philadelphia: Fortress, 1972.

————. *The Old Faith and the New.* Translated by G. A. Wells. Westminster College—Oxford Classics in the Study of Religion. Amherst, NY: Prometheus, 1997.

Stuhlmacher, Peter. *Historical Criticism and Theological Interpretation of Scripture: Toward a Hermeneutics of Consent.* Translated by Roy A. Harrisville. Eugene, OR: Wipf and Stock, 2003.

Tillich, Paul. *Dynamics of Faith.* Perennial Classics. New York: HarperOne, 2009.

————. "The Eternal Now." In *The Eternal Now,* 122–32. New York: Scribner's, 1963.

————. "The European Discussion of the Problem of the Demythologization of the New Testament." *FT* 2, no. 1 (1984) 39–48.

Tipler, Frank. *The Physics of Immortality: Modern Cosmology, God and the Resurrection of the Dead.* New York: Doubleday, 1994.

Tracy, David. *The Analogical Imagination: Christian Theology and the Culture of Pluralism.* New York: Crossroad, 1981.

————. *Plurality and Ambiguity: Hermeneutics, Religion, Hope.* Chicago: University of Chicago Press, 1987.

Troeltsch, Ernst. *Die Bedeutung der Geschichtlichkeit Jesu für den Glauben.* Tübingen: Mohr/Siebeck, 1911.

————. "Historical and Dogmatic Method in Theology." In *Religion in History*, translated by James Luther Adams and Walter F. Bense, 11–32. Fortress Texts in Modern Theology. Minneapolis: Fortress, 1991.

————. "Historiography." In *Encylcopaedia of Religion and Ethics*, edited by James Hastings, 6:716–23. Corrected ed. New York: Scribner, 1951.

————. *Der Historismus und seine Probleme*. Book 1, *Das logische Problem der Geschichtsphilosophie*. Gesammelte Schriften 3. Tübingen: Mohr/Siebeck, 1922.

————. "The Significance of the Historical Existence of Jesus for Faith." In *Writings on Theology and Religion*, translated and edited by Robert Morgan and Michael Pye, 182–207. Louisville: Westminster John Knox, 1990.

————. "Über historische und dogmatische Methode in der Theologie." In *Gesammelte Schriften*, 2:729–53. Aalen, Germany: Scientia, 1962.

Tyrrell, George. *Christianity at the Crossroads*. London: Longmans, Green, 1913.

Welker, Michael. *God the Revealed: Christology*. Translated by Douglas W. Stott. Grand Rapids: Eerdmans, 2013.

————. *God the Spirit*. Translated by John F. Hoffmeyer. Minneapolis: Fortress, 1994.

Index of Names

Index of Subjects

authenticity, 4, 47–48, 58, 61, 64, 67, 69–70, 84, 90, 104, 148

Bible, 2, 10, 12, 14, 16–22, 24, 25n49, 26–36, 41–46, 48–49, 51–52, 57–63, 66, 68, 70–71, 73–77, 79–80, 81–86, 88, 89–90, 91–92, 97–98, 101–3, 109–10, 112–13, 119–20, 123–28, 133–34, 135–37, 142–43

Christology: see Jesus Christ
Church, 1, 3, 11–12, 14, 15, 17, 24, 28, 34, 35–36, 50, 51, 64, 68, 71, 73–74 76, 88, 114, 121, 126, 130, 144, 147, 152, 153, 155
cross, 32, 58, 61–64, 68–71, 73, 76, 91, 128, 139–45, 147, 150, 153

demythologizing, 3–4, 41–49, 56–57, 59, 61, 63–65, 68, 69n106, 71n115, 72, 76–79, 81–88, 90n57, 92, 116, 122–24, 129, 131, 133–34, 136, 149, 150
disciples, 1, 19–22, 31–33, 76–78, 83, 88n53, 97, 111–13, 139, 141–44
Dogmatics: see Theology

Easter: see Resurrection
Enlightenment, 2, 18, 23, 23n44, 25, 57n67, 130–2, 150
eschatology, 21, 37, 44, 49, 51–52, 57–58, 62–64, 68–71, 76–77, 91, 98n4, 104, 109, 111, 114, 125–26, 132, 137–39, 143, 145, 148, 150

event, 2, 11–14, 18–20, 22, 27–30, 32, 37, 54–71, 72, 76–77, 79–81, 82n33, 83, 85n41, 90–91, 98–100, 104–14, 117–19, 121, 125n33, 127–28, 138–41, 143–44, 149, 150, 152, 154
existence, Existentialism, 3, 4, 42, 45, 47–48, 50, 55–58, 61, 64, 66–70, 72, 81, 82n33, 83–90, 92, 101–4, 109, 117–20, 124, 136–37, 148–49, 151

fact, 3n2, 15, 23, 27–29, 32, 34n75, 37, 53–54, 55n59, 59, 62, 66, 70, 73–74, 76–77, 79–80, 87, 90, 99–100, 105–7, 109, 112, 119, 122, 124, 130, 136, 140–41, 143
faith, x, 1, 4, 15–17, 20, 22, 25, 26, 28, 33–38, 42–45, 47, 48, 52, 56n62, 59–71, 74, 76–78, 81, 82n33, 83–84, 87–92, 102n19, 109, 111–12, 114, 116, 120–27, 131–32, 135, 137, 139, 141–46, 147, 149, 150–52, 154
freedom, 47, 52, 61, 69–70, 82n33, 140

God, 1, 4, 12, 20, 35, 42, 44–45, 46n24, 47n29, 48, 49, 51–52, 56n62, 57–59, 60n74, 61–87, 90–92, 97, 100–1, 103–4, 106–8, 121–29, 133, 136n77, 137–47, 150–53, 155
Gospel, 3n2, 4, 49, 69–70, 73, 85, 119, 123, 140, 144–45
grace, 52, 61, 64, 69–70, 73, 82n33, 87, 90, 154

Made in the USA
Middletown, DE
10 April 2023

28552135R00104